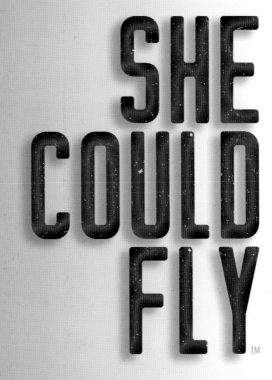

Volume One

BERGER BOOKS
AN IMPRINT OF
DARK HORSE COMICS

SHE COULD FLY

writer
Christopher Cantwell

artist
Martín Morazzo

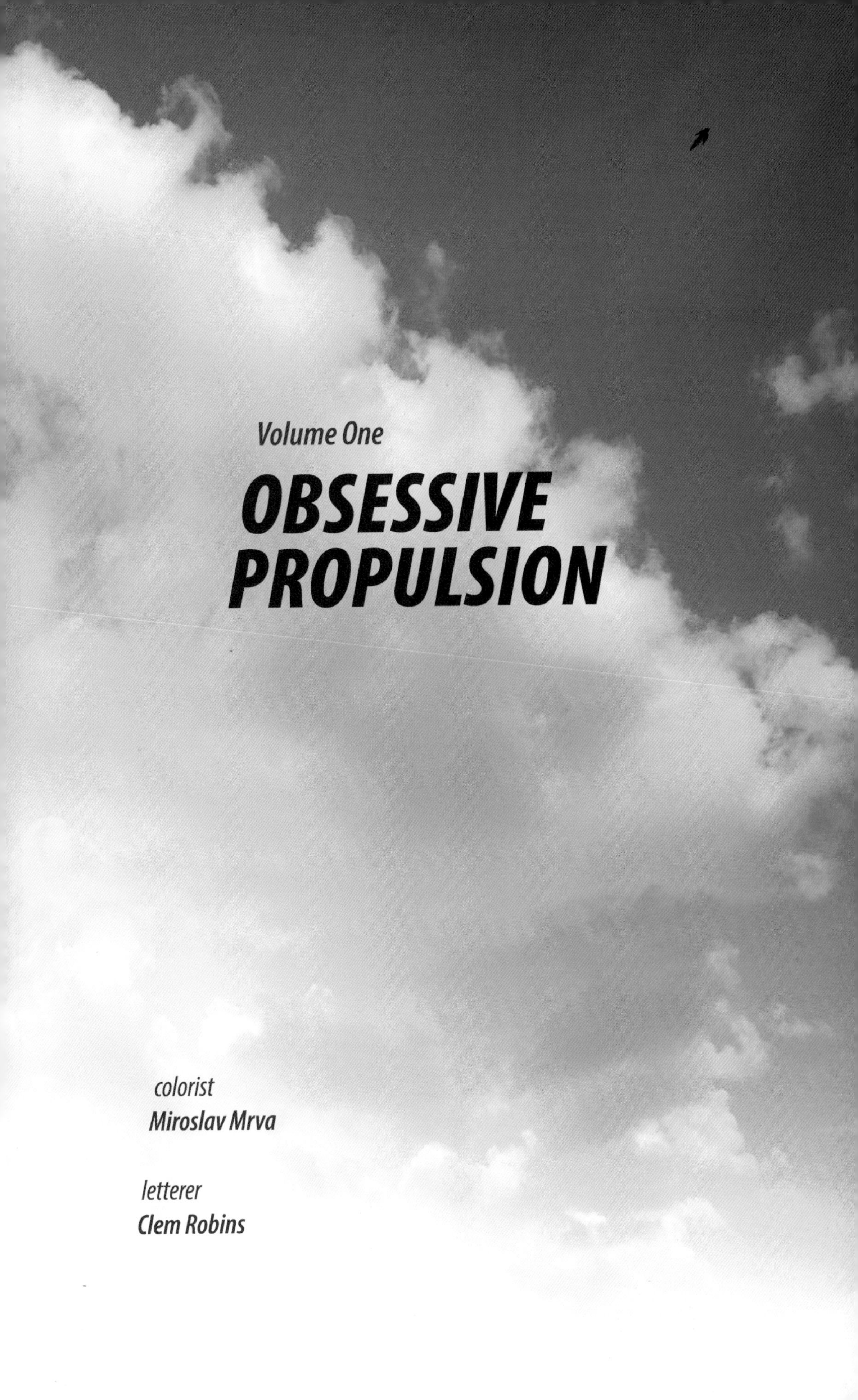

Volume One

OBSESSIVE PROPULSION

colorist
Miroslav Mrva

letterer
Clem Robins

Karen Berger
Editor

Richard Bruning
Logo/Book Designer

Adam Pruett
Digital Art Technician

Mike Richardson
Publisher

This volume collects issues #1–#4 of
SHE COULD FLY: Obsessive Propulsion.

Published by
Dark Horse Books
A division of
Dark Horse Comics LLC
10956 SE Main Street
Milwaukie, OR 97222

DarkHorse.com
ComicShopLocator.com

First Edition: March 2019
ISBN: 978-1-50670-949-9
Digital ISBN: 978-1-50670-961-1

Printed in Hong Kong
10 9 8 7 6 5 4 3 2 1

Library of Congress Cataloging-in-Publication Data
Names: Cantwell, Christopher, author. | Morazzo, Martín, artist. | Mrva,
  Miroslav, colourist. | Robins, Clem, 1955- letterer.
Title: She could fly / script, Christopher Cantwell ; art, Martin Morazzo ;
  colors, Miroslav Mrva ; lettering, Clem Robins.
Description: First hardcover edition. | Milwaukie, OR : Dark Horse Books,
  2019- | "This volume collects issues #1–#4 of She Could Fly."
Identifiers: LCCN 2018040393 (print) | LCCN 2018046525 (ebook) | ISBN
  9781506709611 (ebook) | ISBN 9781506709499 (v. 1 : alk. paper)
Subjects: LCSH: Graphic novels.
Classification: LCC PN6727.C367 (ebook) | LCC PN6727.C367 S54 2019 (print) |
  DDC 741.5/973--dc23
LC record available at https://lccn.loc.gov/2018040393

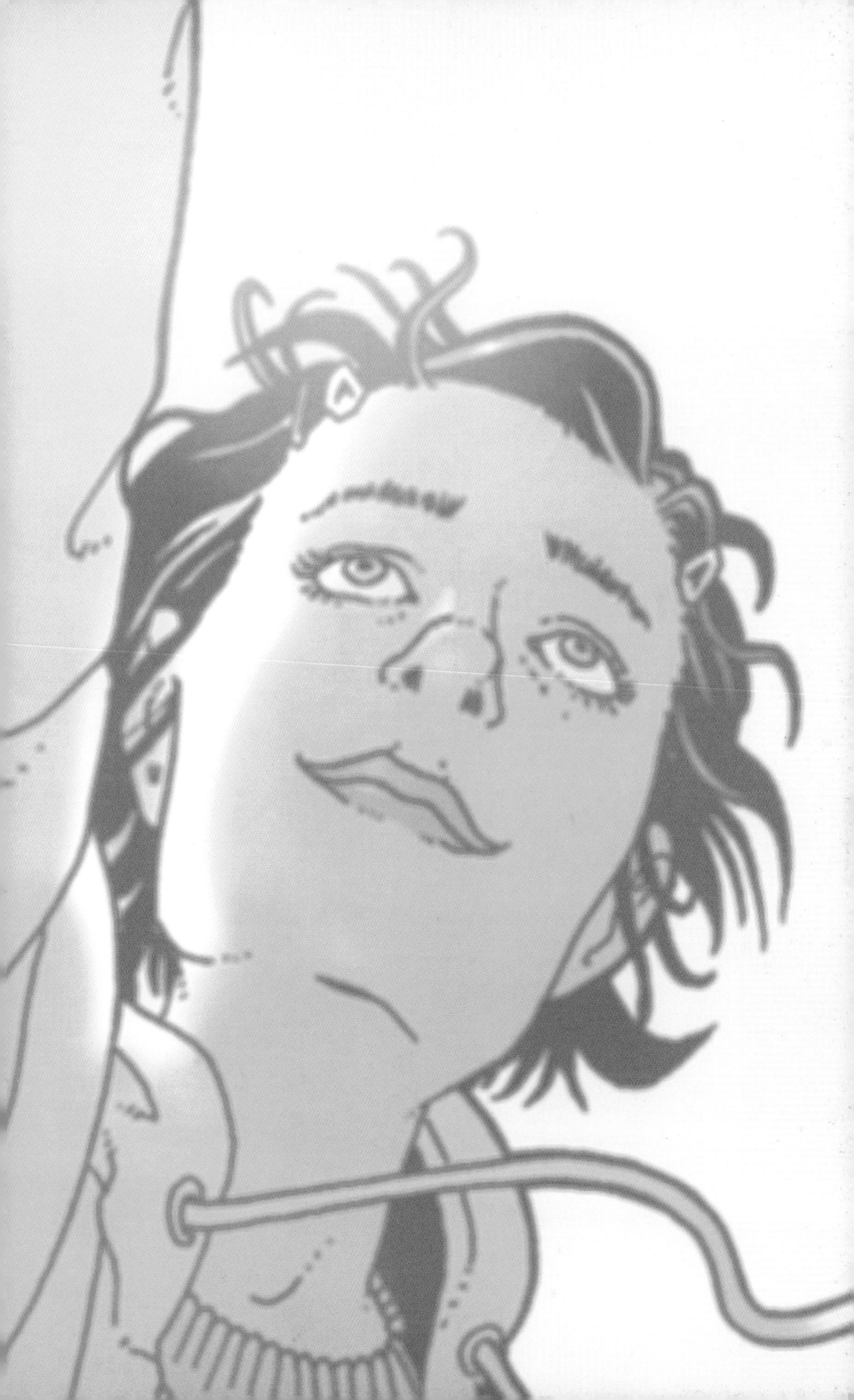

CHAPTER I
"Agony in eight fits"

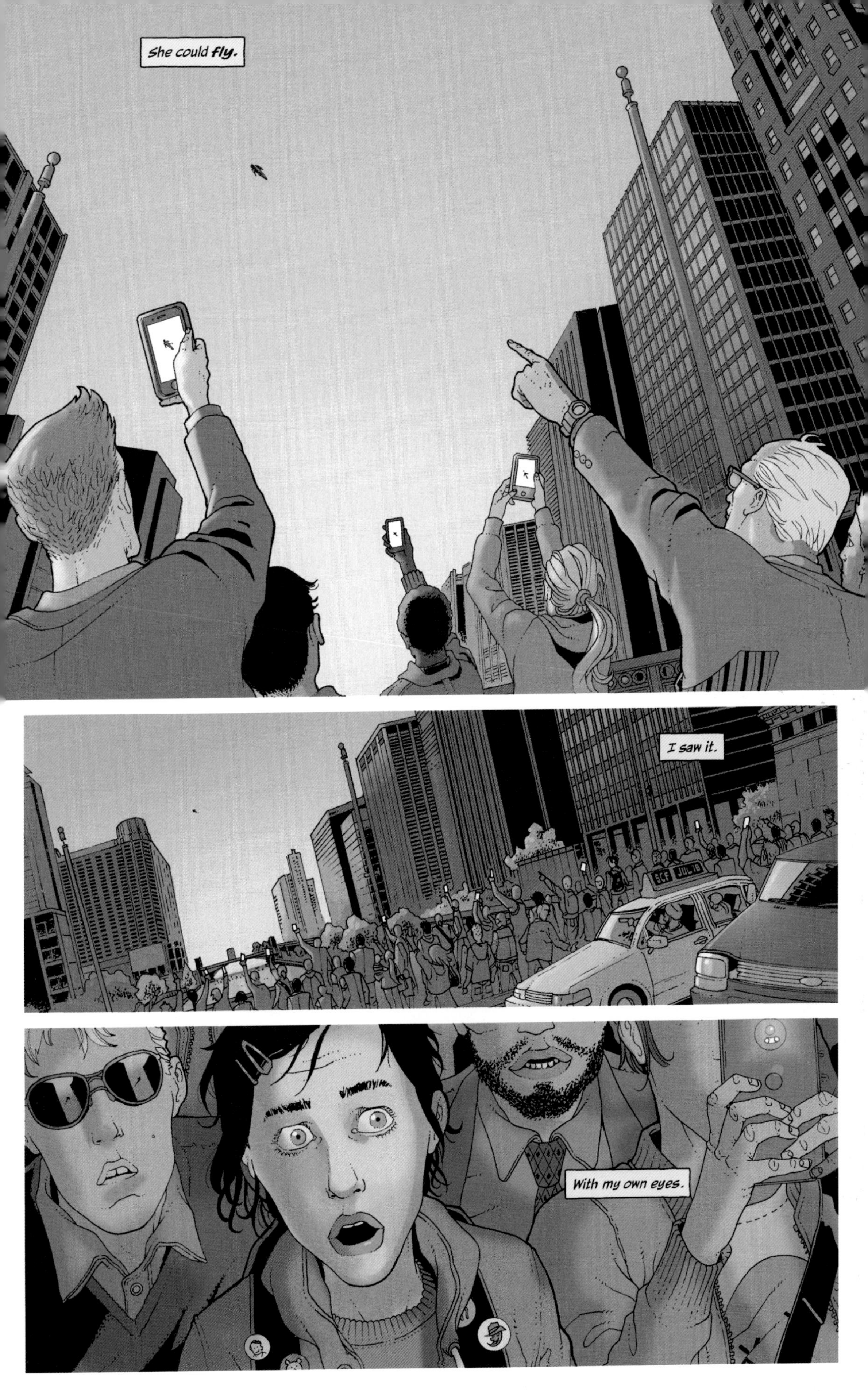
She could fly.
I saw it.
With my own eyes.

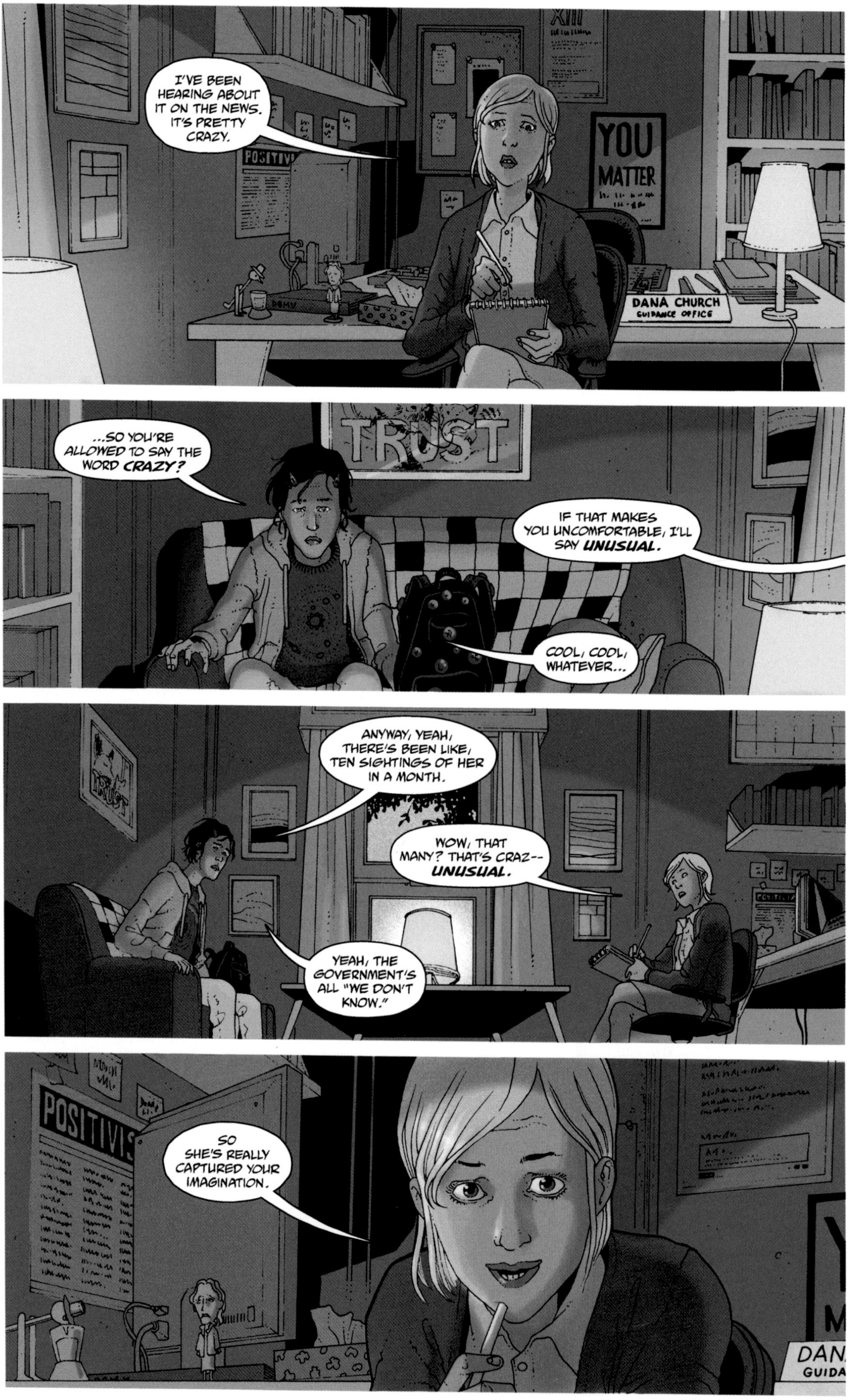
I'VE BEEN HEARING ABOUT IT ON THE NEWS. IT'S PRETTY CRAZY.
YOU MATTER
DANA CHURCH
GUIDANCE OFFICE
TRUST
...SO YOU'RE ALLOWED TO SAY THE WORD CRAZY?
IF THAT MAKES YOU UNCOMFORTABLE, I'LL SAY UNUSUAL.
COOL, COOL, WHATEVER...
ANYWAY, YEAH, THERE'S BEEN LIKE, TEN SIGHTINGS OF HER IN A MONTH.
WOW, THAT MANY? THAT'S CRAZ-- UNUSUAL.
YEAH, THE GOVERNMENT'S ALL "WE DON'T KNOW."
SO SHE'S REALLY CAPTURED YOUR IMAGINATION.

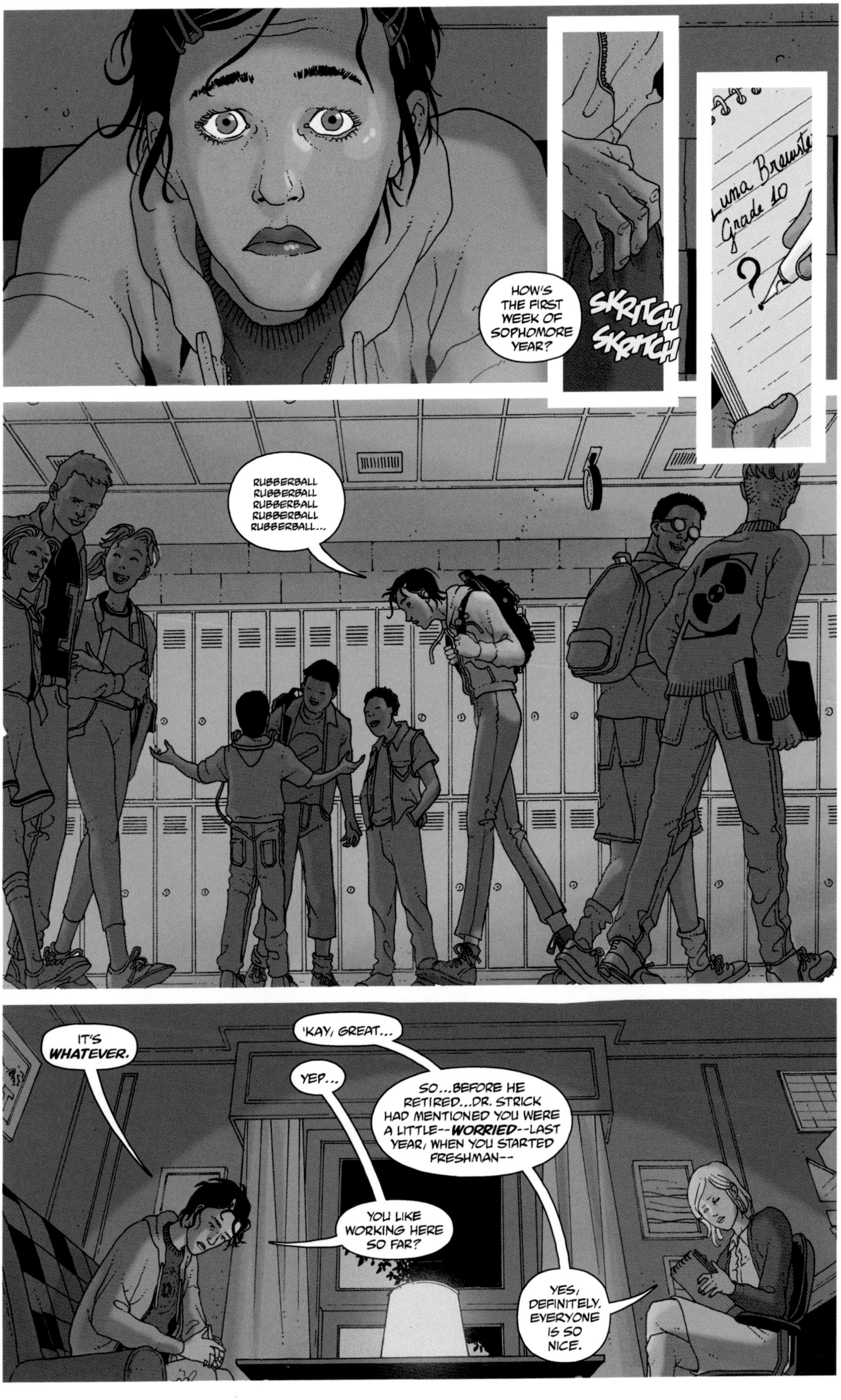
HOW'S THE FIRST WEEK OF SOPHOMORE YEAR?
SKRITCH
SKRITCH
Grade 10
?
RUBBERBALL RUBBERBALL RUBBERBALL RUBBERBALL RUBBERBALL...
IT'S **WHATEVER.**
'KAY, GREAT...
YEP...
SO...BEFORE HE RETIRED...DR. STRICK HAD MENTIONED YOU WERE A LITTLE--**WORRIED**--LAST YEAR, WHEN YOU STARTED FRESHMAN--
YOU LIKE WORKING HERE SO FAR?
YES, DEFINITELY. EVERYONE IS SO NICE.

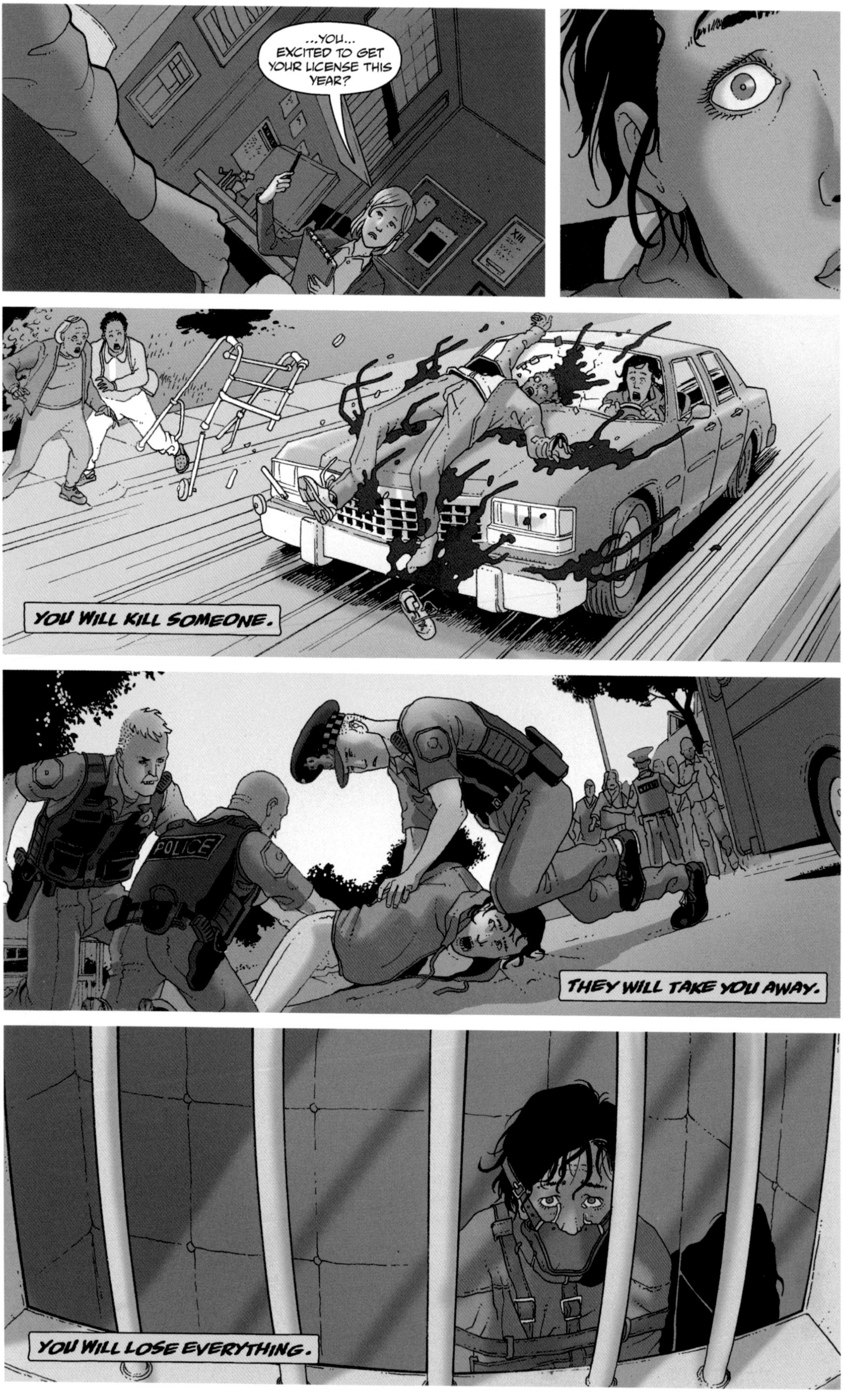
...YOU...
EXCITED TO GET
YOUR LICENSE THIS
YEAR?
YOU WILL KILL SOMEONE.
POLICE
THEY WILL TAKE YOU AWAY.
YOU WILL LOSE EVERYTHING.

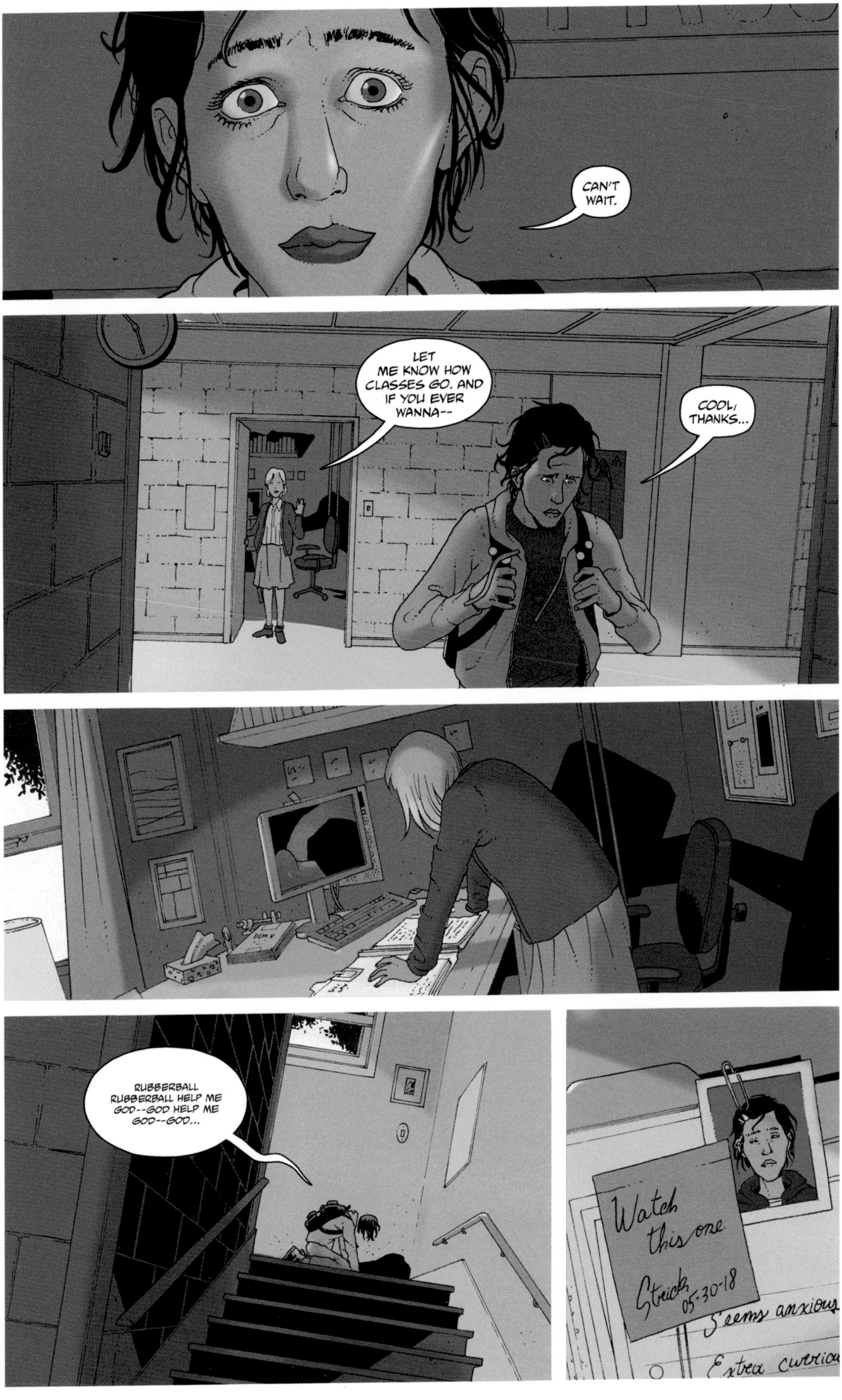
CAN'T WAIT.
LET ME KNOW HOW CLASSES GO. AND IF YOU EVER WANNA--
COOL, THANKS...
RUBBERBALL RUBBERBALL HELP ME GOD--GOD HELP ME GOD--GOD...
Watch this one. Strick 05-30-18
Seems anxious
Extra curious

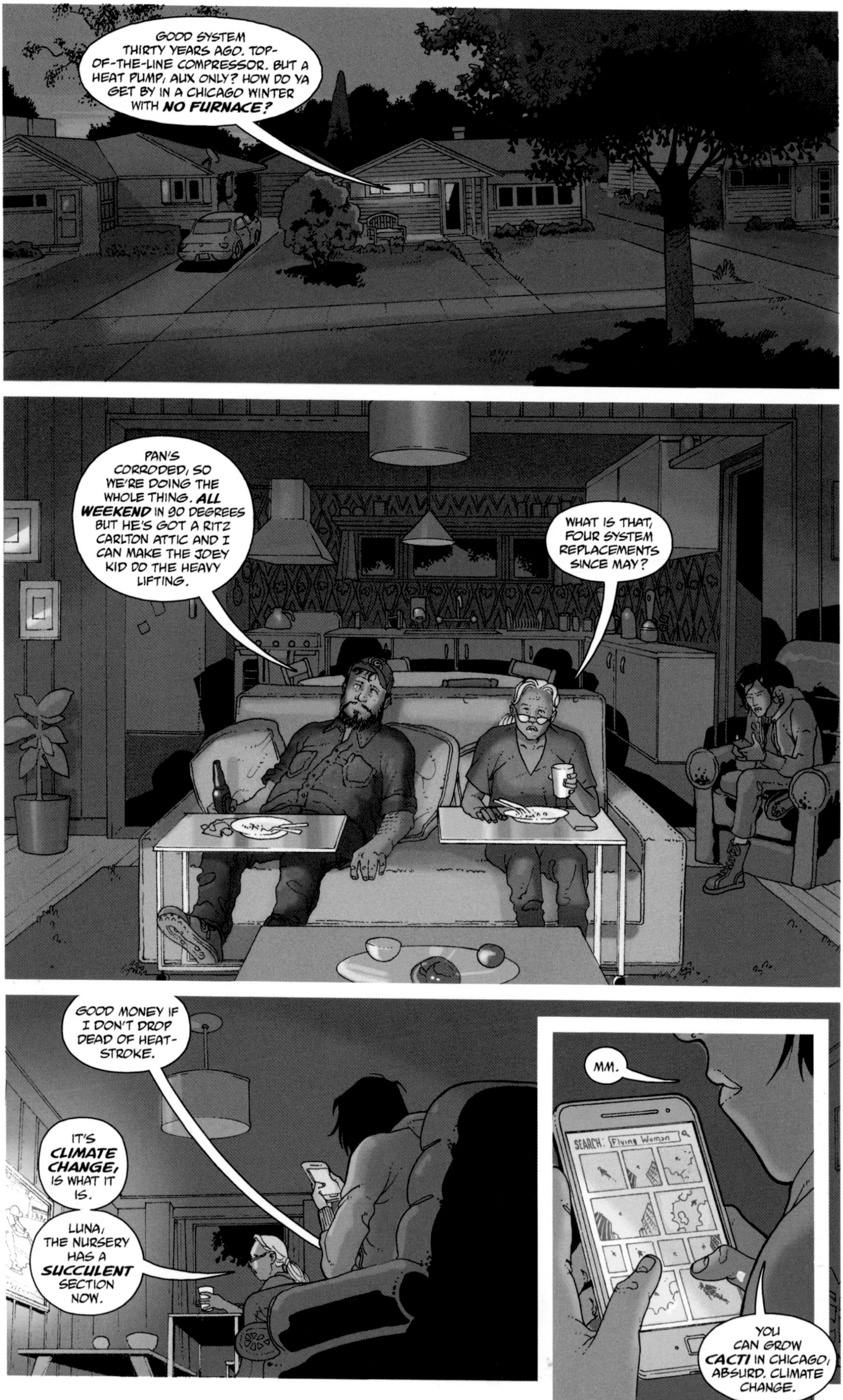
GOOD SYSTEM THIRTY YEARS AGO. TOP-OF-THE-LINE COMPRESSOR. BUT A HEAT PUMP, AUX ONLY? HOW DO YA GET BY IN A CHICAGO WINTER WITH **NO FURNACE?**
PAN'S CORRODED, SO WE'RE DOING THE WHOLE THING. **ALL WEEKEND** IN 90 DEGREES BUT HE'S GOT A RITZ CARLTON ATTIC AND I CAN MAKE THE JOEY KID DO THE HEAVY LIFTING.
WHAT IS THAT, FOUR SYSTEM REPLACEMENTS SINCE MAY?
GOOD MONEY IF I DON'T DROP DEAD OF HEAT-STROKE.
IT'S **CLIMATE CHANGE,** IS WHAT IT IS.
LUNA, THE NURSERY HAS A **SUCCULENT** SECTION NOW.
MM.
SEARCH: Flying Woman
YOU CAN GROW **CACTI** IN CHICAGO, ABSURD. CLIMATE CHANGE.

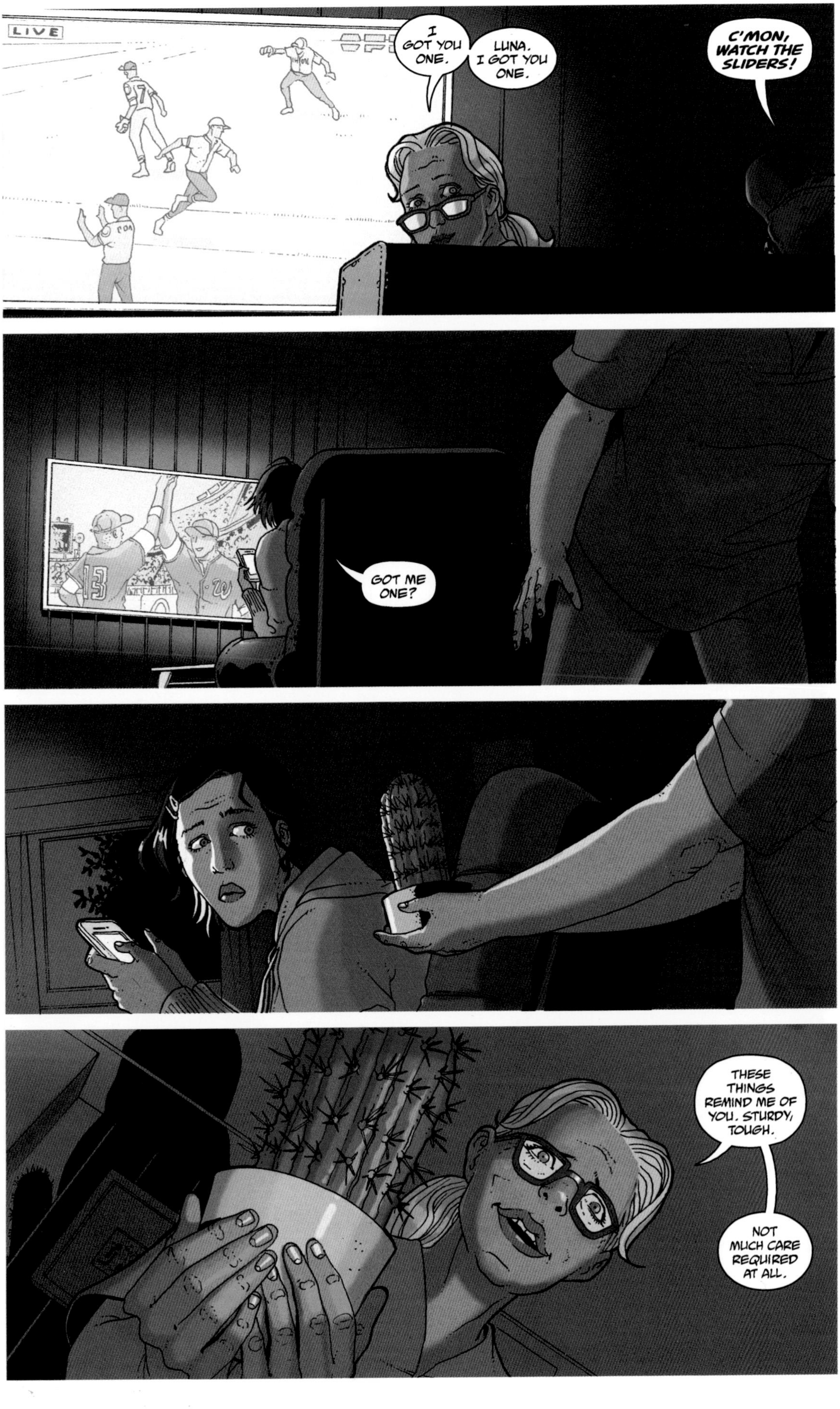
LIVE
I GOT YOU ONE.
LUNA. I GOT YOU ONE.
C'MON, WATCH THE SLIDERS!
GOT ME ONE?
THESE THINGS REMIND ME OF YOU. STURDY, TOUGH.
NOT MUCH CARE REQUIRED AT ALL.

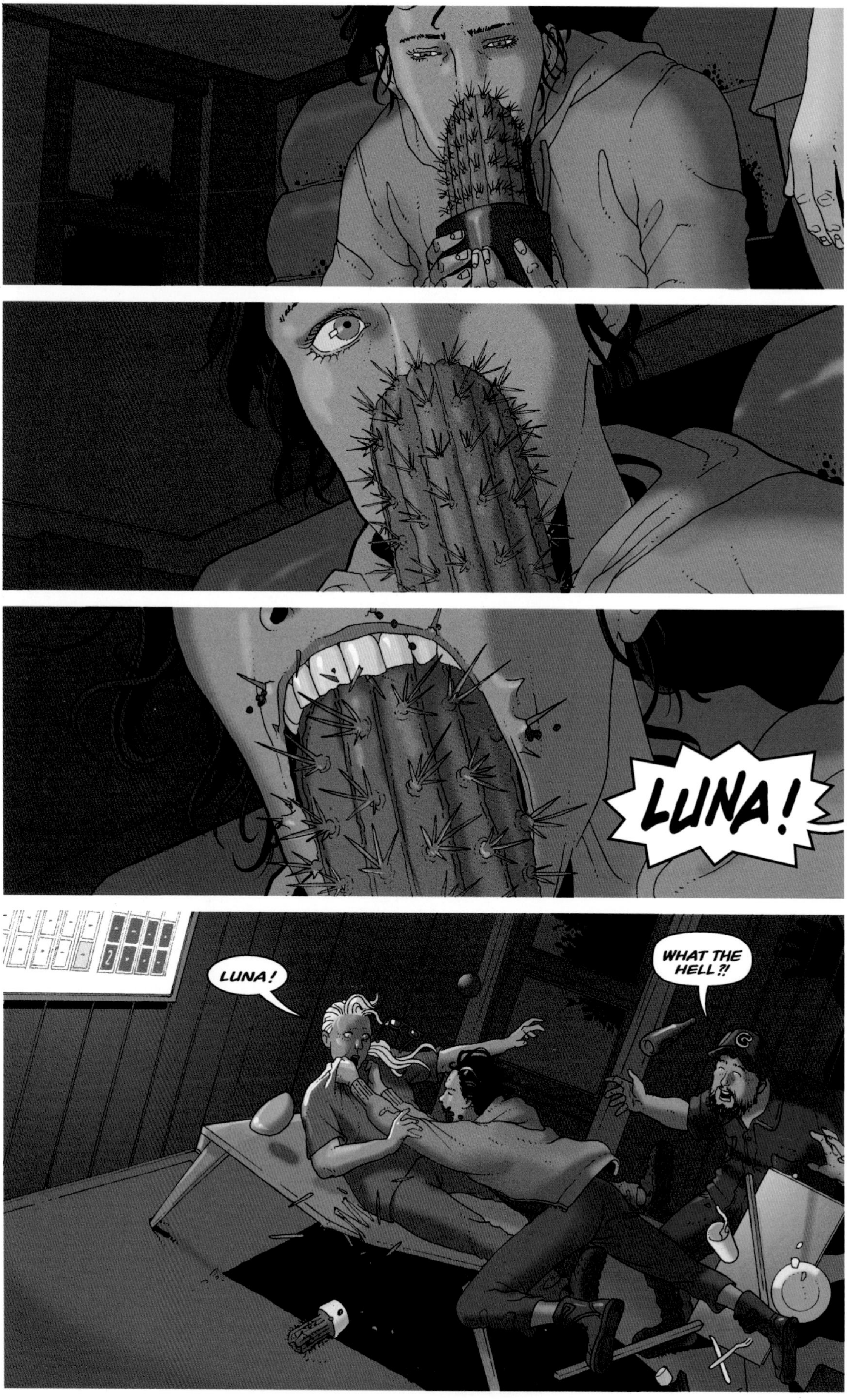
LUNA!
LUNA!
WHAT THE HELL?!

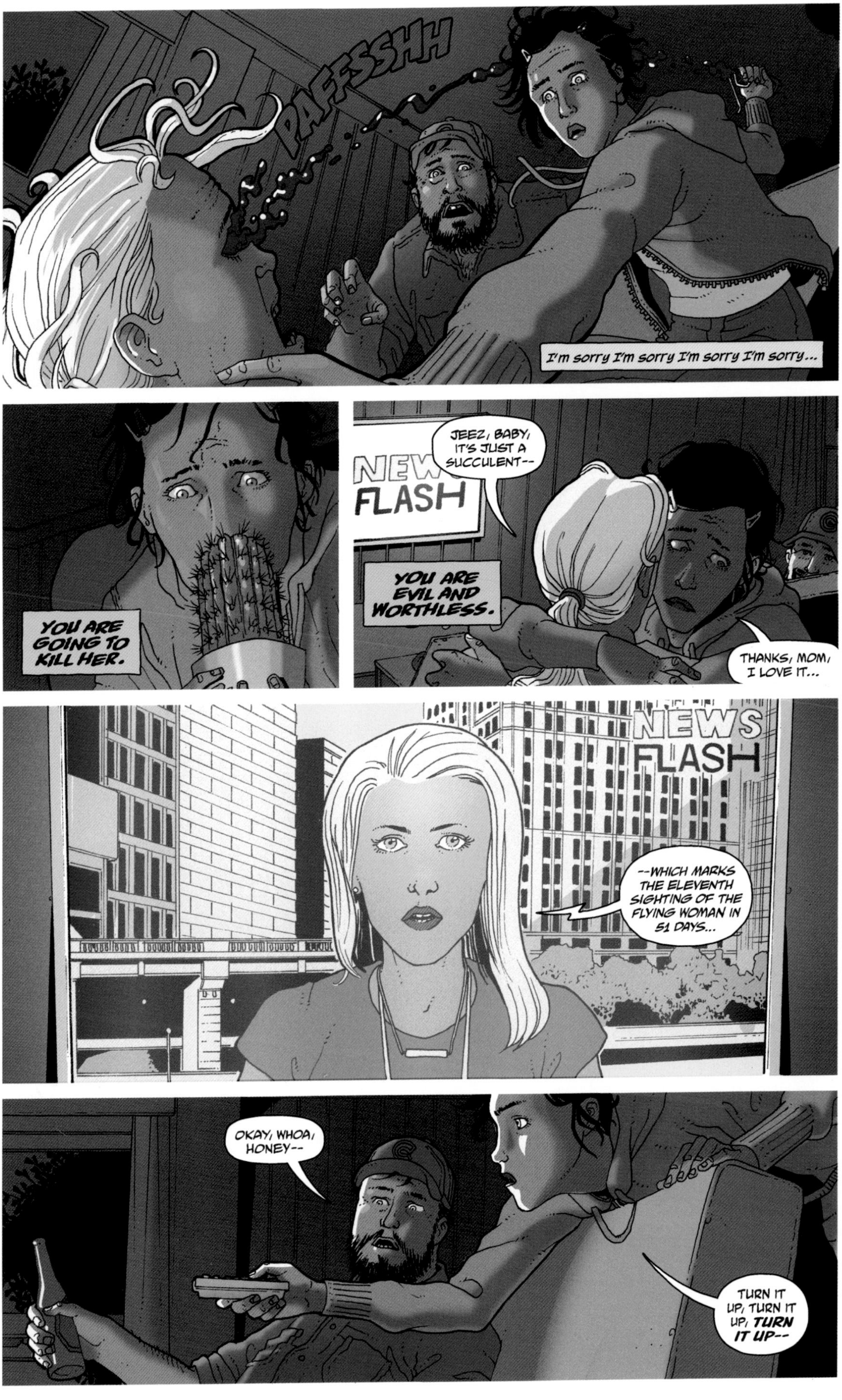
PAFFSSHH
I'm sorry I'm sorry I'm sorry I'm sorry...
YOU ARE GOING TO KILL HER.
NEWS FLASH
JEEZ, BABY, IT'S JUST A SUCCULENT--
YOU ARE EVIL AND WORTHLESS.
THANKS, MOM, I LOVE IT...
NEWS FLASH
--WHICH MARKS THE ELEVENTH SIGHTING OF THE FLYING WOMAN IN 51 DAYS...
OKAY, WHOA, HONEY--
TURN IT UP, TURN IT UP, ***TURN IT UP***--

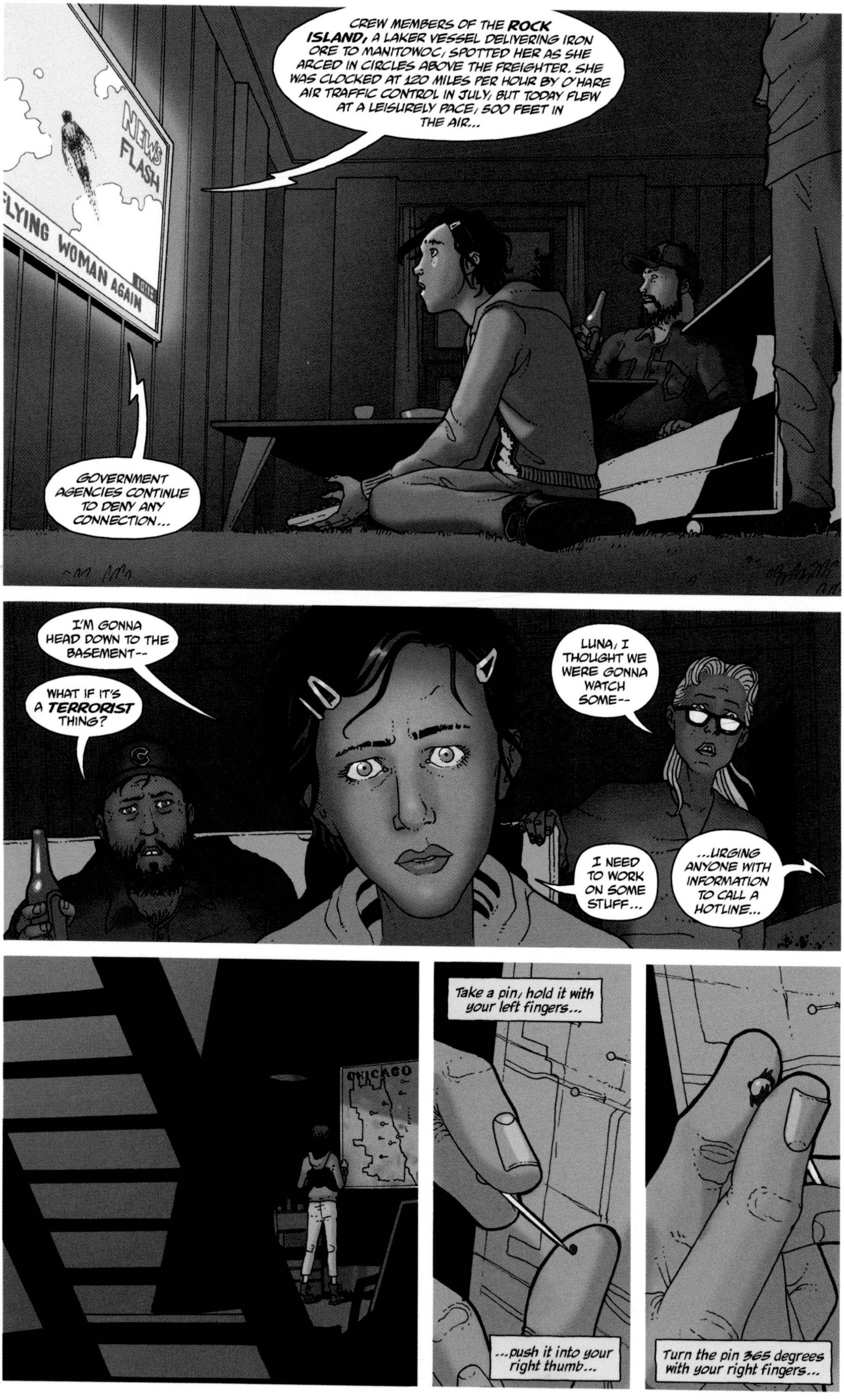
NEWS FLASH
FLYING WOMAN AGAIN
CREW MEMBERS OF THE **ROCK ISLAND,** A LAKER VESSEL DELIVERING IRON ORE TO MANITOWOC, SPOTTED HER AS SHE ARCED IN CIRCLES ABOVE THE FREIGHTER. SHE WAS CLOCKED AT 120 MILES PER HOUR BY O'HARE AIR TRAFFIC CONTROL IN JULY, BUT TODAY FLEW AT A LEISURELY PACE, 500 FEET IN THE AIR...
GOVERNMENT AGENCIES CONTINUE TO DENY ANY CONNECTION...
I'M GONNA HEAD DOWN TO THE BASEMENT--
WHAT IF IT'S A **TERRORIST** THING?
LUNA, I THOUGHT WE WERE GONNA WATCH SOME--
I NEED TO WORK ON SOME STUFF...
...URGING ANYONE WITH INFORMATION TO CALL A HOTLINE...
CHICAGO
Take a pin, hold it with your left fingers...
...push it into your right thumb...
Turn the pin 365 degrees with your right fingers...

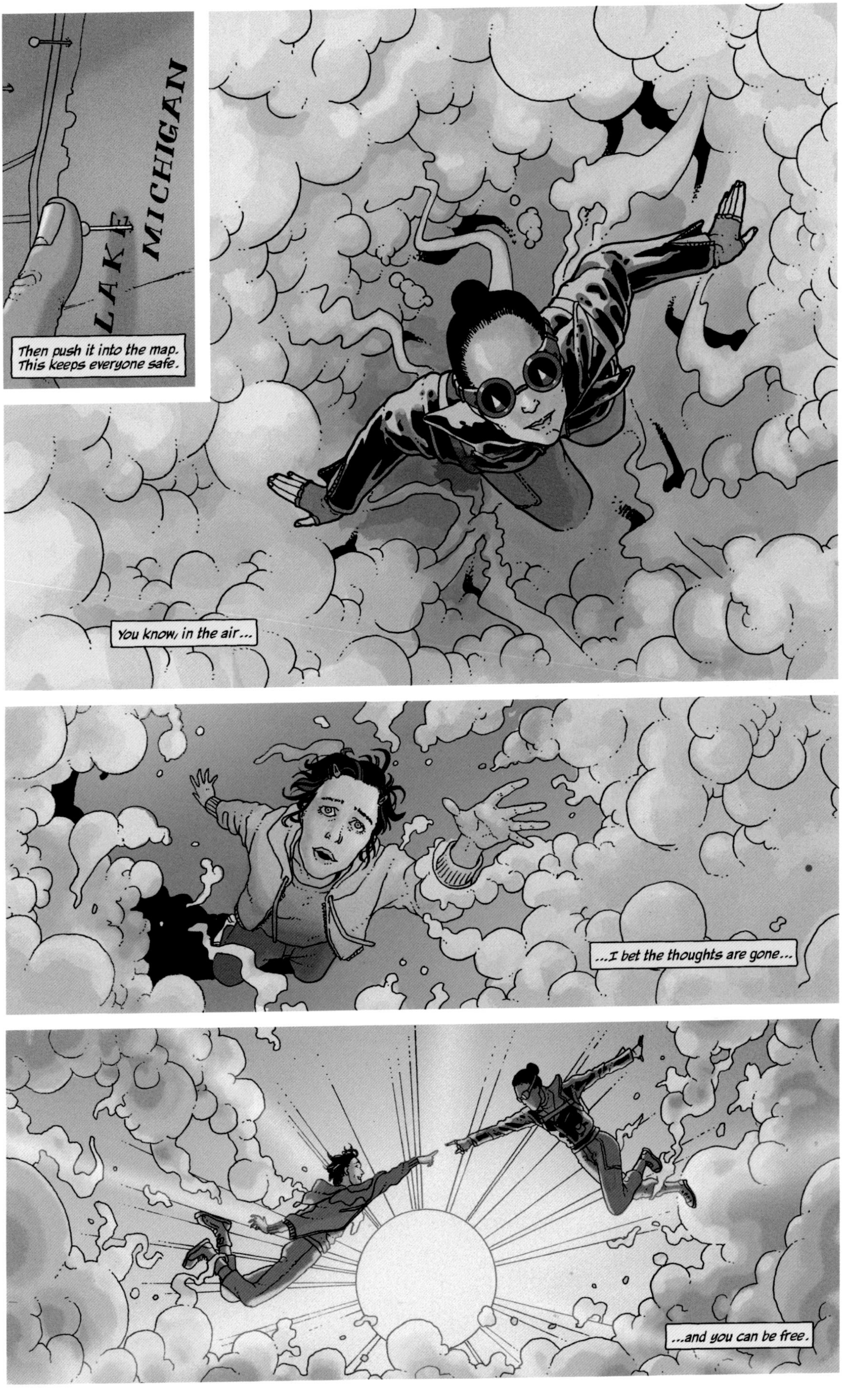
LAKE MICHIGAN
Then push it into the map. This keeps everyone safe.
You know, in the air...
...I bet the thoughts are gone...
...and you can be free.

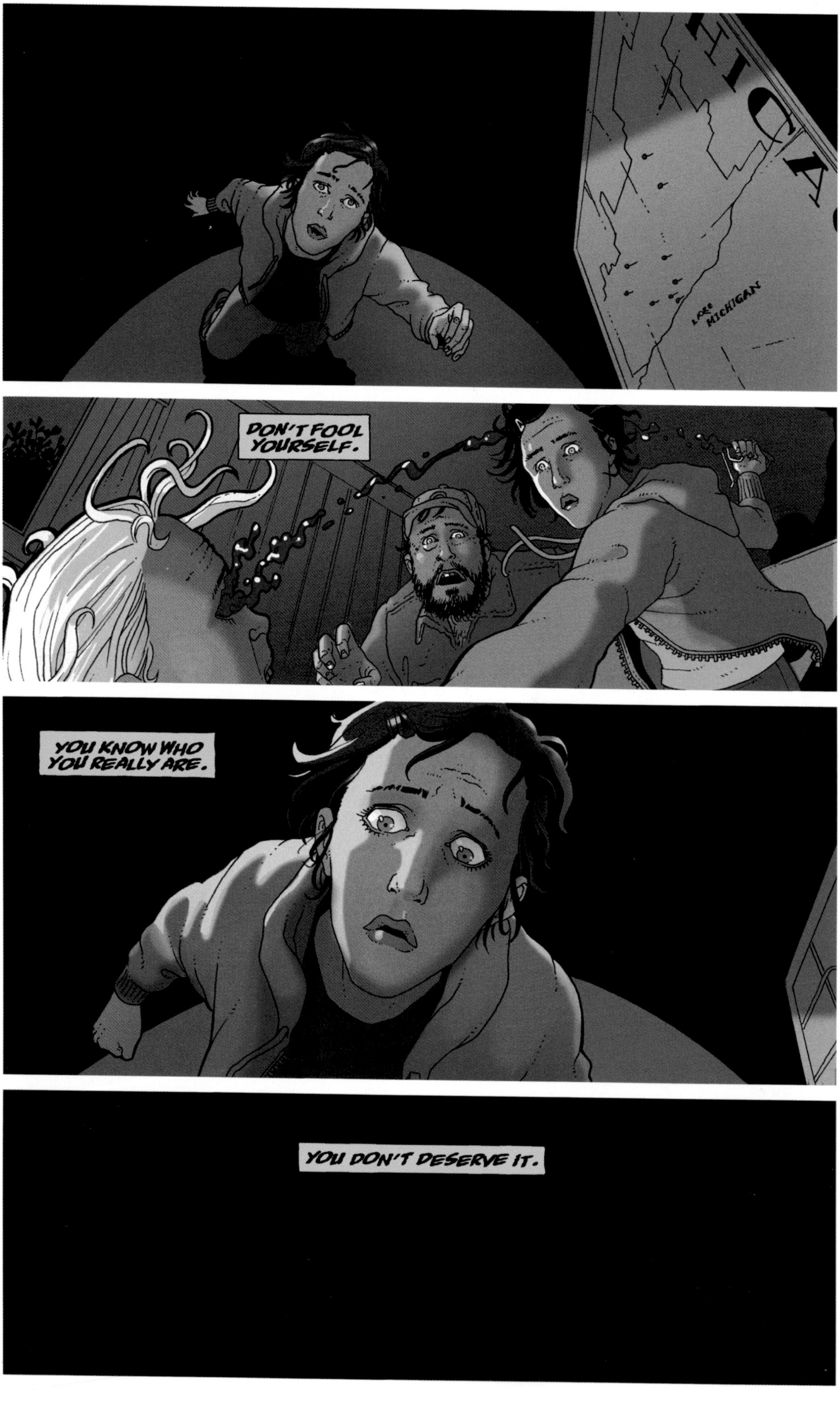

LAKE MICHIGAN
DON'T FOOL YOURSELF.
YOU KNOW WHO YOU REALLY ARE.
YOU DON'T DESERVE IT.

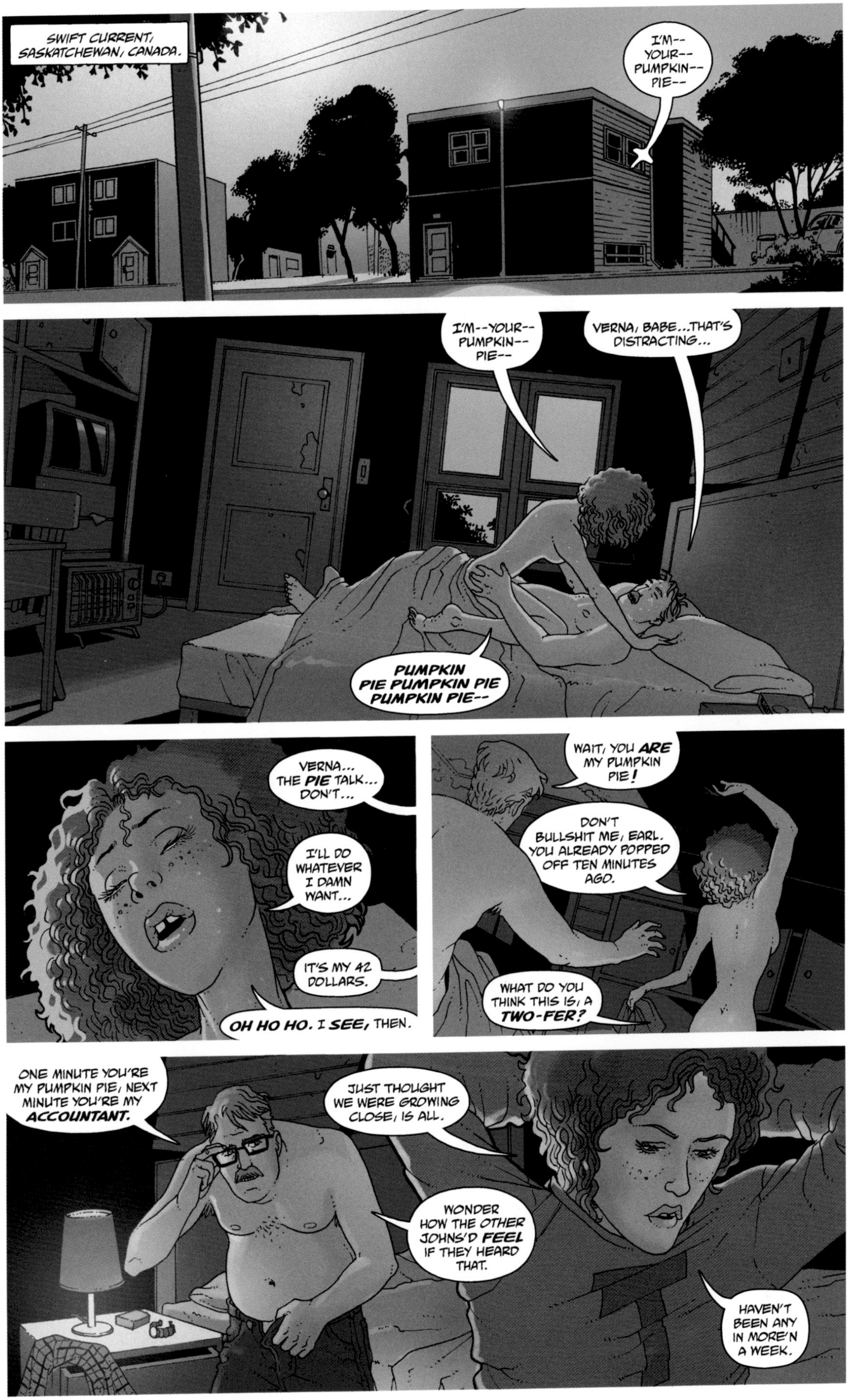
SWIFT CURRENT, SASKATCHEWAN, CANADA.
I'M-- YOUR-- PUMPKIN-- PIE--
I'M--YOUR-- PUMPKIN-- PIE--
VERNA, BABE...THAT'S DISTRACTING...
PUMPKIN PIE PUMPKIN PIE PUMPKIN PIE--
VERNA... THE PIE TALK... DON'T...
I'LL DO WHATEVER I DAMN WANT...
IT'S MY 42 DOLLARS.
OH HO HO. I SEE, THEN.
WAIT, YOU ARE MY PUMPKIN PIE!
DON'T BULLSHIT ME, EARL. YOU ALREADY POPPED OFF TEN MINUTES AGO.
WHAT DO YOU THINK THIS IS, A TWO-FER?
ONE MINUTE YOU'RE MY PUMPKIN PIE, NEXT MINUTE YOU'RE MY ACCOUNTANT.
JUST THOUGHT WE WERE GROWING CLOSE, IS ALL.
WONDER HOW THE OTHER JOHNS'D FEEL IF THEY HEARD THAT.
HAVEN'T BEEN ANY IN MORE'N A WEEK.

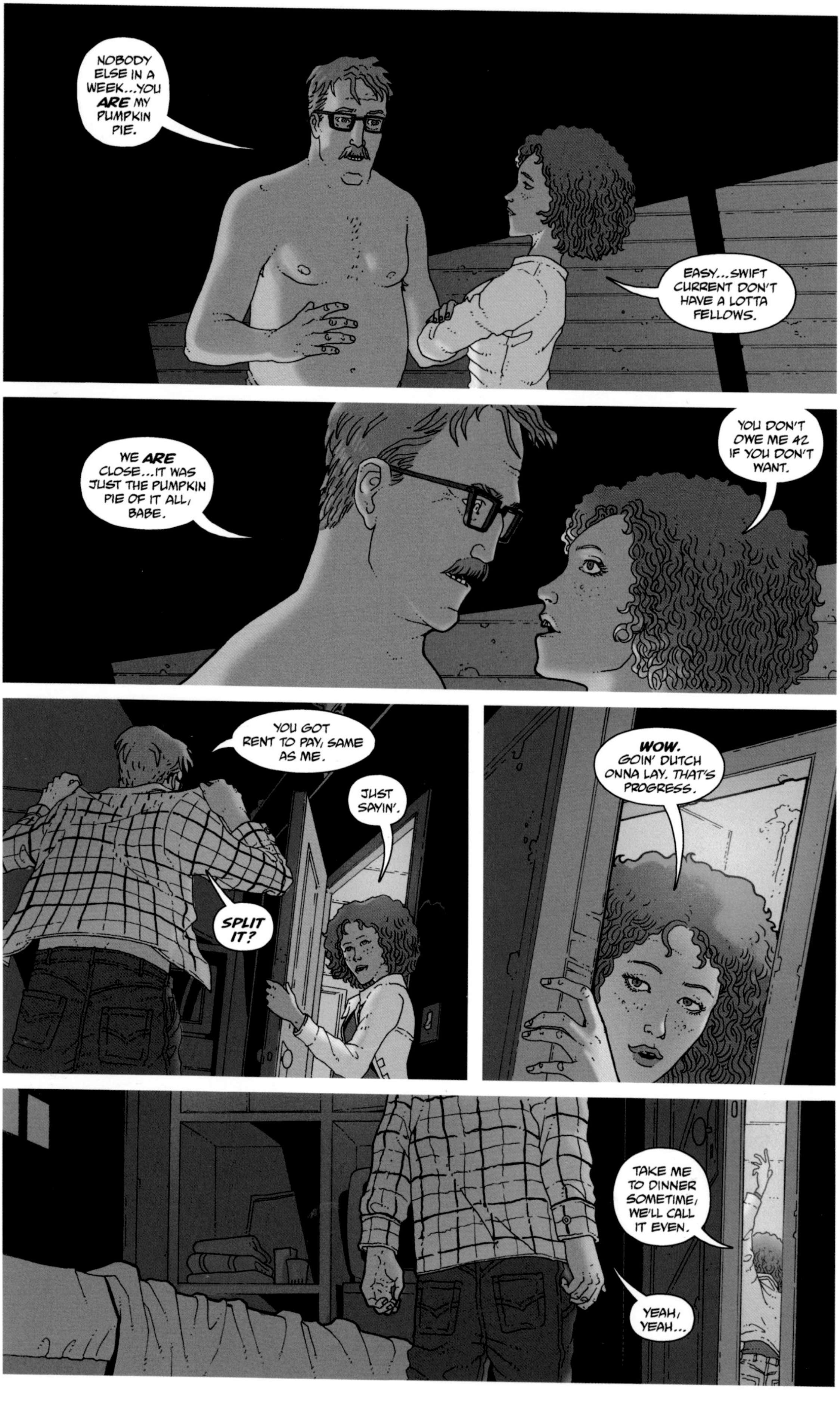
NOBODY ELSE IN A WEEK...YOU **ARE** MY PUMPKIN PIE.
EASY...SWIFT CURRENT DON'T HAVE A LOTTA FELLOWS.
WE **ARE** CLOSE...IT WAS JUST THE PUMPKIN PIE OF IT ALL, BABE.
YOU DON'T OWE ME 42 IF YOU DON'T WANT.
YOU GOT RENT TO PAY, SAME AS ME.
JUST SAYIN'.
SPLIT IT?
WOW. GOIN' DUTCH ONNA LAY. THAT'S PROGRESS.
TAKE ME TO DINNER SOMETIME, WE'LL CALL IT EVEN.
YEAH, YEAH...

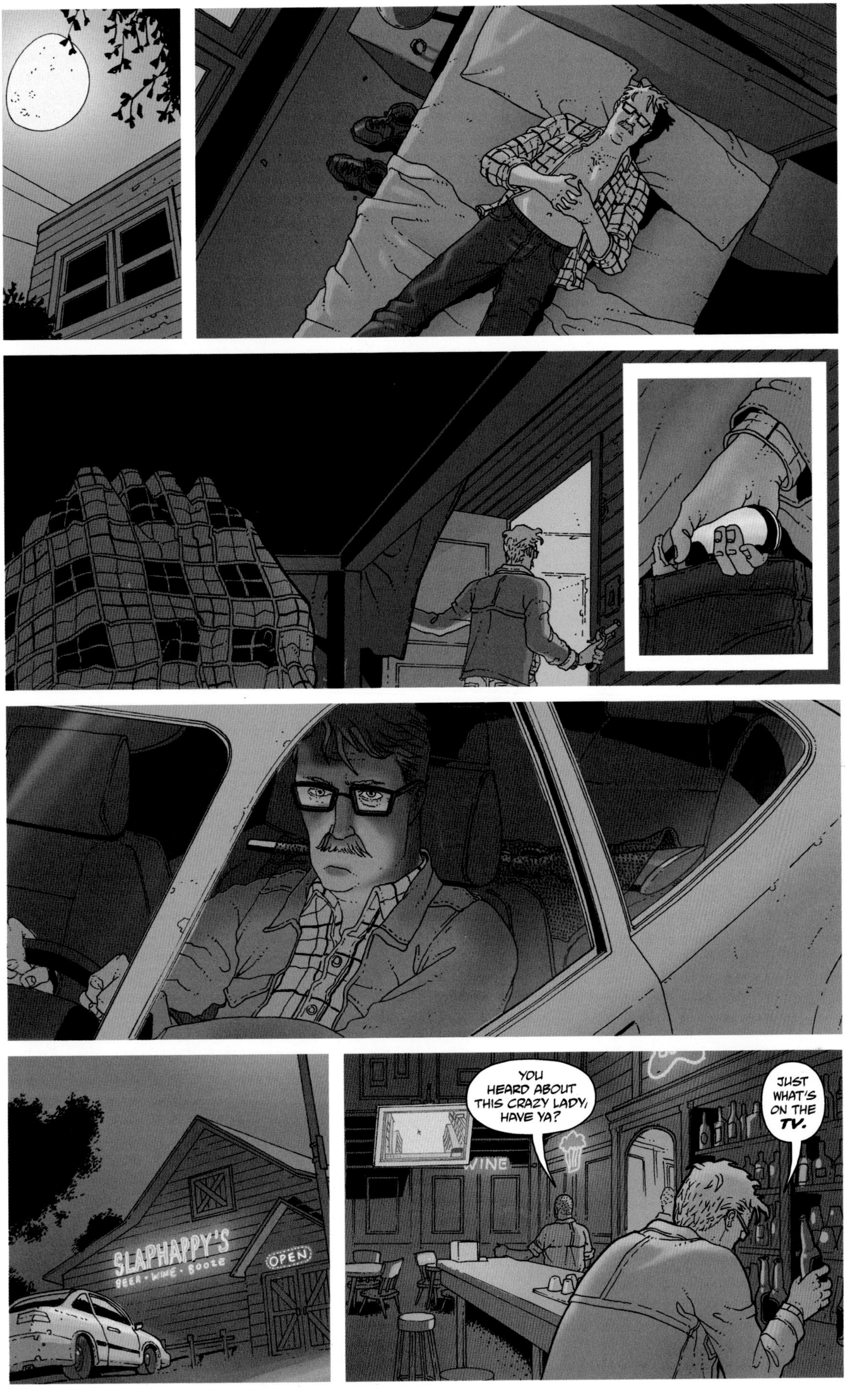
SLAPHAPPY'S
BEER · WINE · BOOZE
OPEN
WINE
YOU HEARD ABOUT THIS CRAZY LADY, HAVE YA?
JUST WHAT'S ON THE TV.

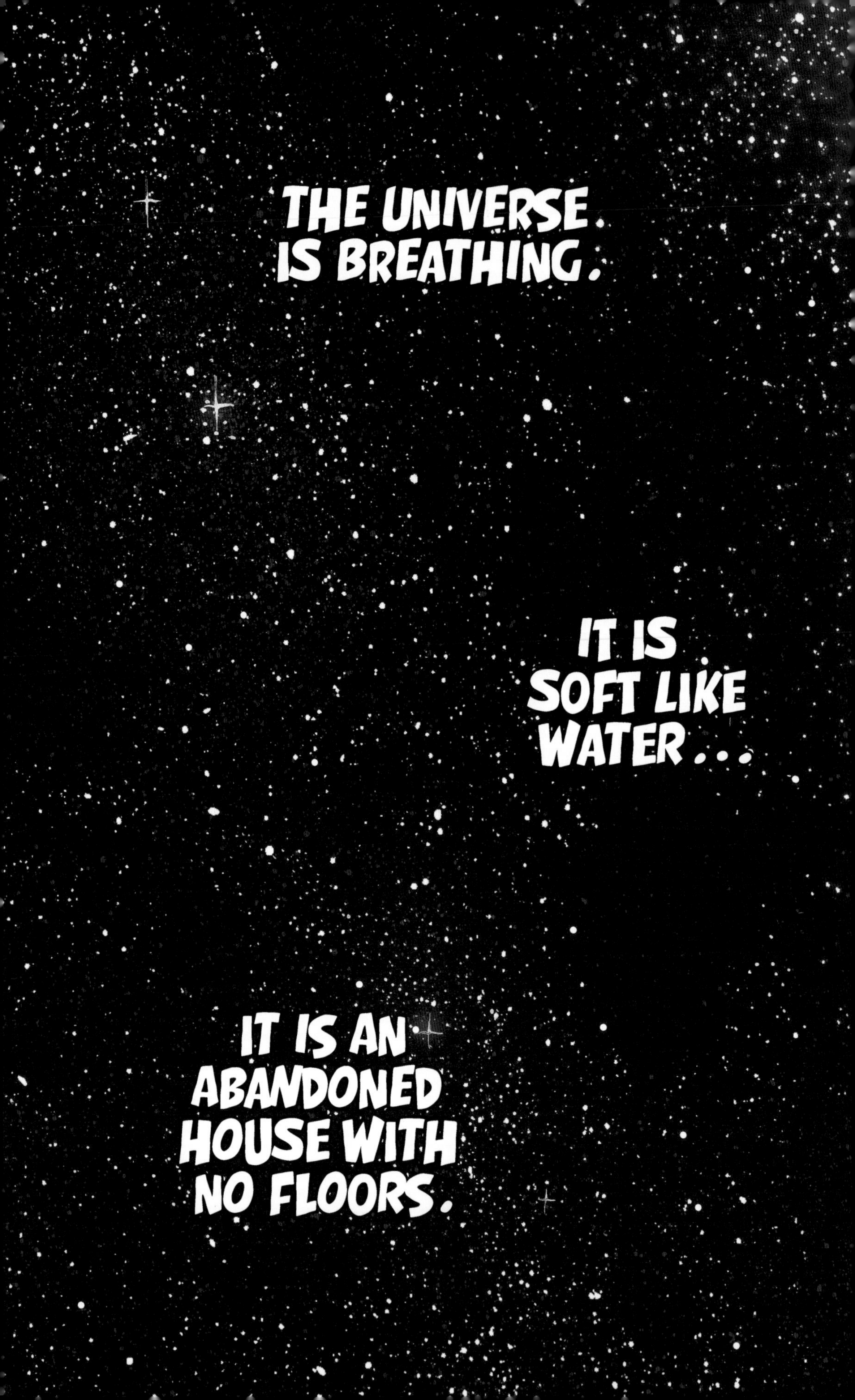
THE UNIVERSE IS BREATHING.
IT IS SOFT LIKE WATER...
IT IS AN ABANDONED HOUSE WITH NO FLOORS.

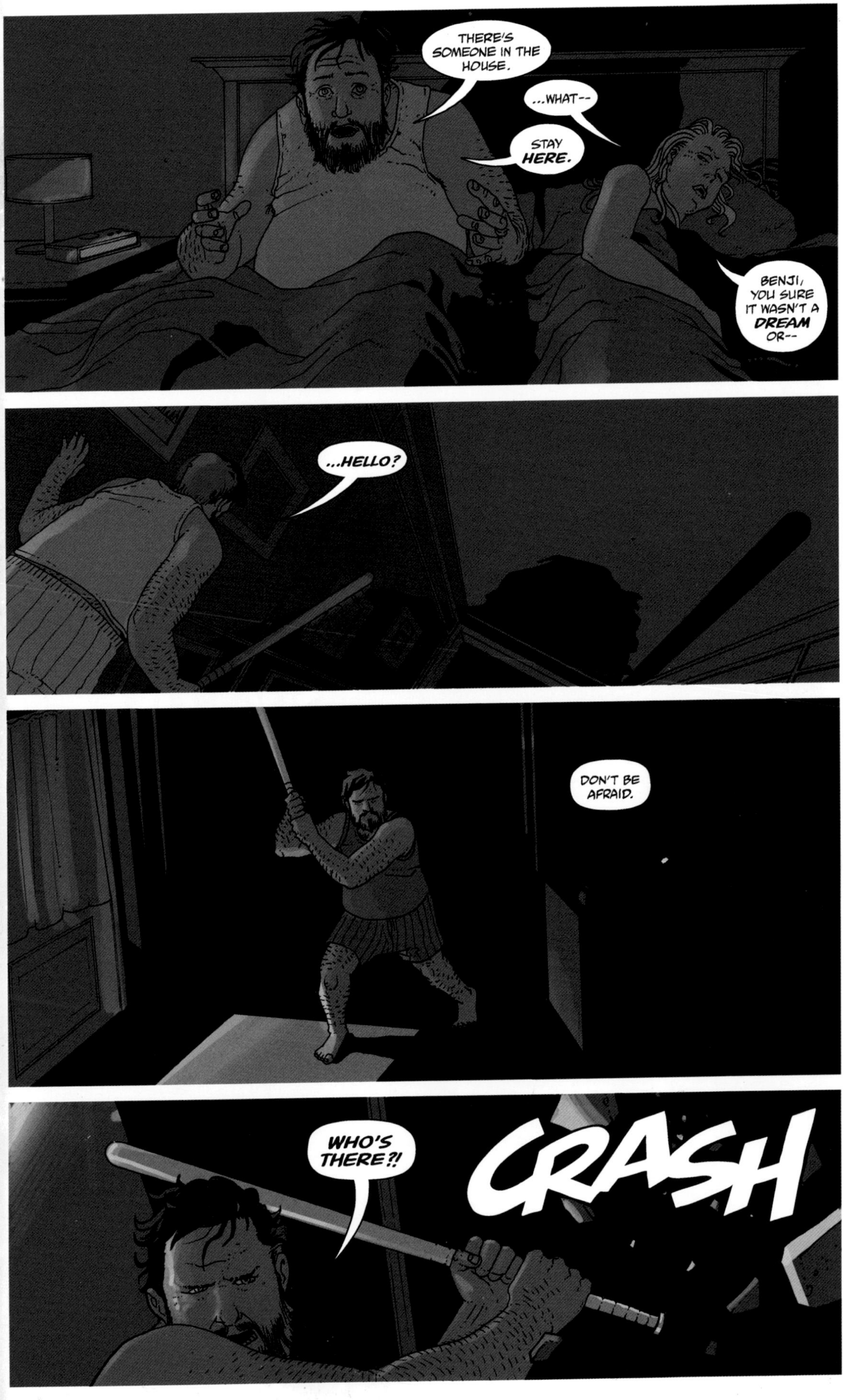
THERE'S SOMEONE IN THE HOUSE.
...WHAT--
STAY HERE.
BENJI, YOU SURE IT WASN'T A DREAM OR--
...HELLO?
DON'T BE AFRAID.
WHO'S THERE?!
CRASH

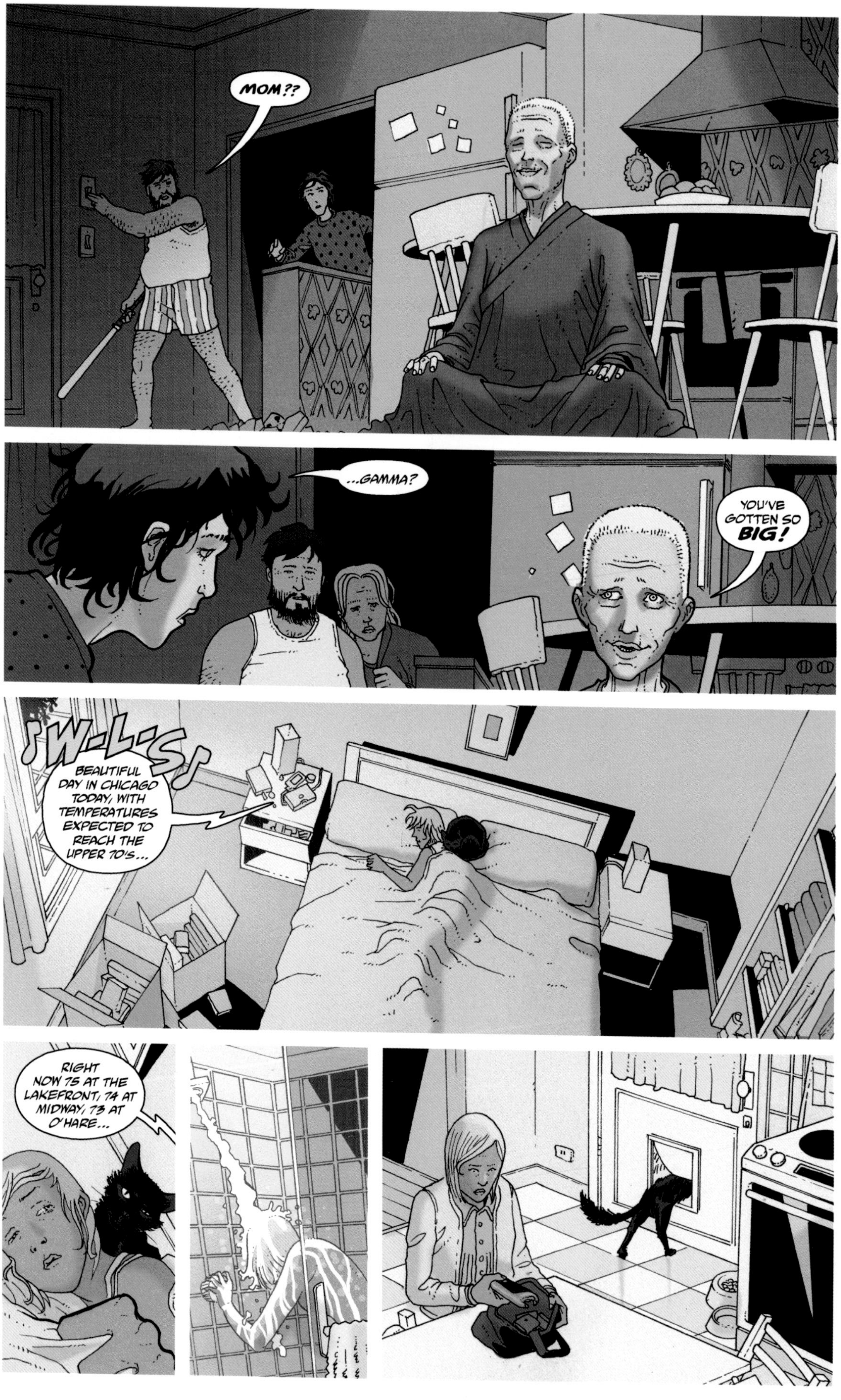

MOM??
...GAMMA?
YOU'VE GOTTEN SO BIG!
W-L-S
BEAUTIFUL DAY IN CHICAGO TODAY, WITH TEMPERATURES EXPECTED TO REACH THE UPPER 70'S...
RIGHT NOW 75 AT THE LAKEFRONT, 74 AT MIDWAY, 73 AT O'HARE...

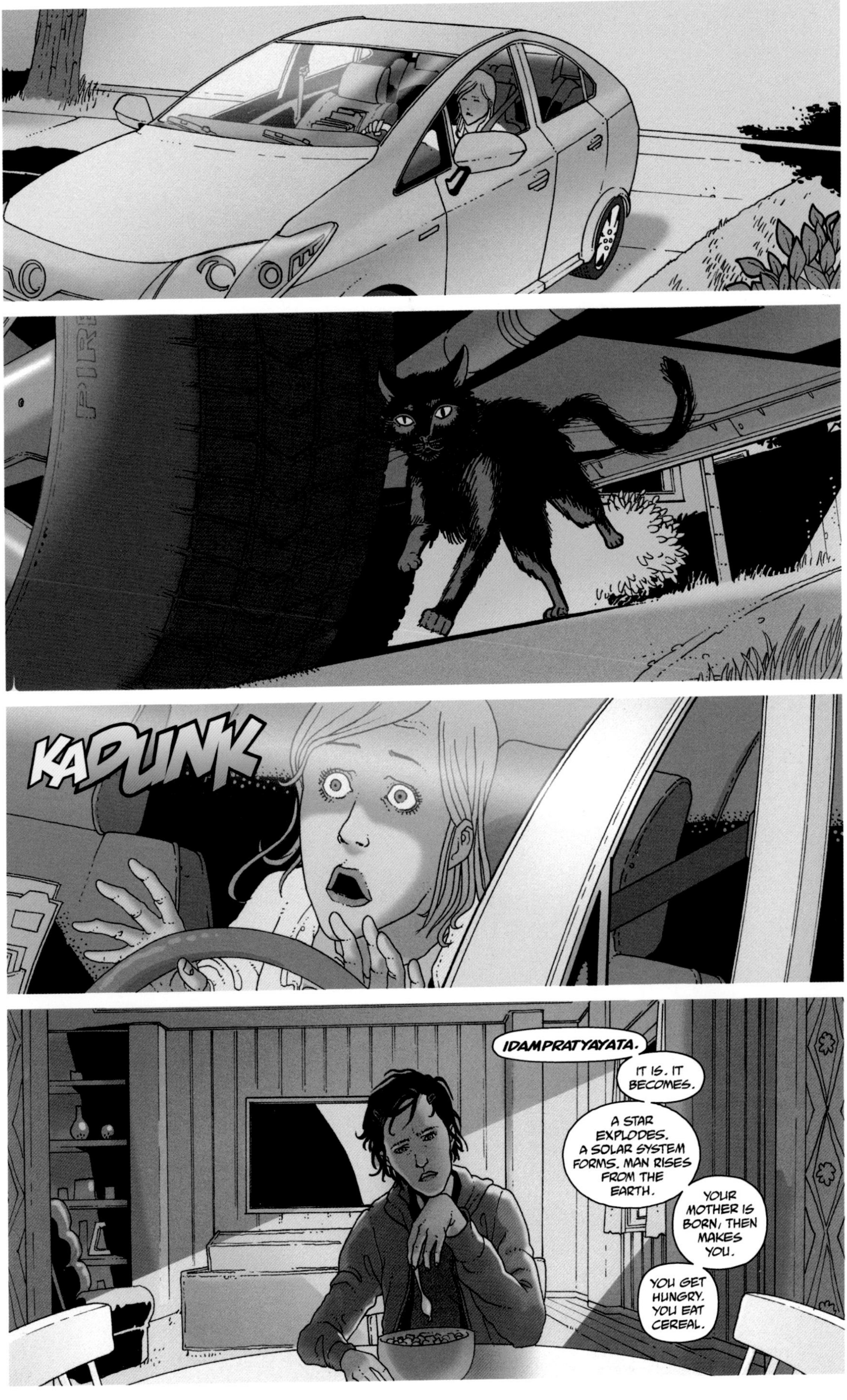
KADUNK
IDAMPRATYAYATA.
IT IS. IT BECOMES.
A STAR EXPLODES. A SOLAR SYSTEM FORMS. MAN RISES FROM THE EARTH.
YOUR MOTHER IS BORN, THEN MAKES YOU.
YOU GET HUNGRY. YOU EAT CEREAL.

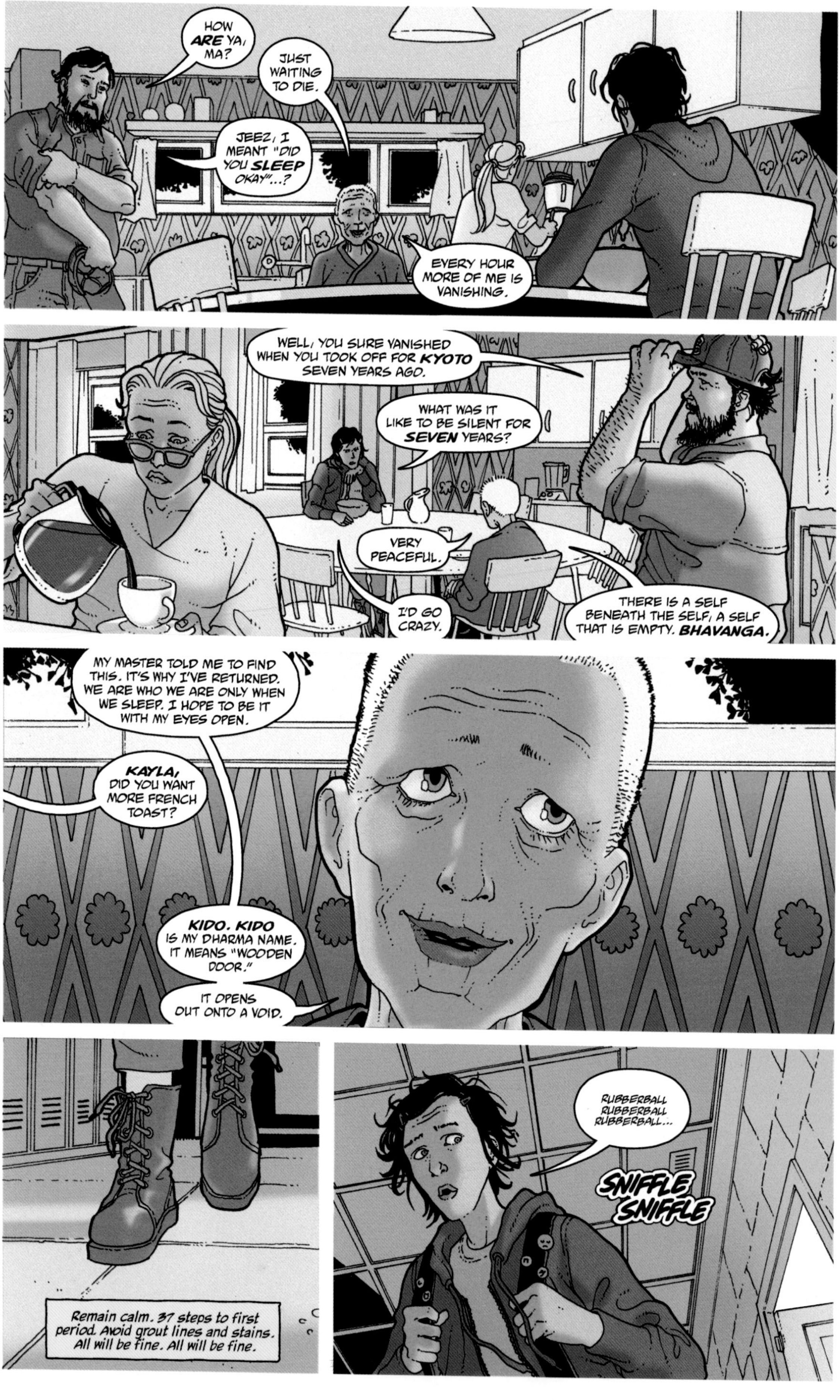
HOW ARE YA, MA?
JUST WAITING TO DIE.
JEEZ, I MEANT "DID YOU SLEEP OKAY"...?
EVERY HOUR MORE OF ME IS VANISHING.
WELL, YOU SURE VANISHED WHEN YOU TOOK OFF FOR KYOTO SEVEN YEARS AGO.
WHAT WAS IT LIKE TO BE SILENT FOR SEVEN YEARS?
VERY PEACEFUL.
I'D GO CRAZY.
THERE IS A SELF BENEATH THE SELF, A SELF THAT IS EMPTY. BHAVANGA.
MY MASTER TOLD ME TO FIND THIS. IT'S WHY I'VE RETURNED. WE ARE WHO WE ARE ONLY WHEN WE SLEEP. I HOPE TO BE IT WITH MY EYES OPEN.
KAYLA, DID YOU WANT MORE FRENCH TOAST?
KIDO. KIDO IS MY DHARMA NAME. IT MEANS "WOODEN DOOR."
IT OPENS OUT ONTO A VOID.
Remain calm. 37 steps to first period. Avoid grout lines and stains. All will be fine. All will be fine.
RUBBERBALL RUBBERBALL RUBBERBALL...
SNIFFLE SNIFFLE

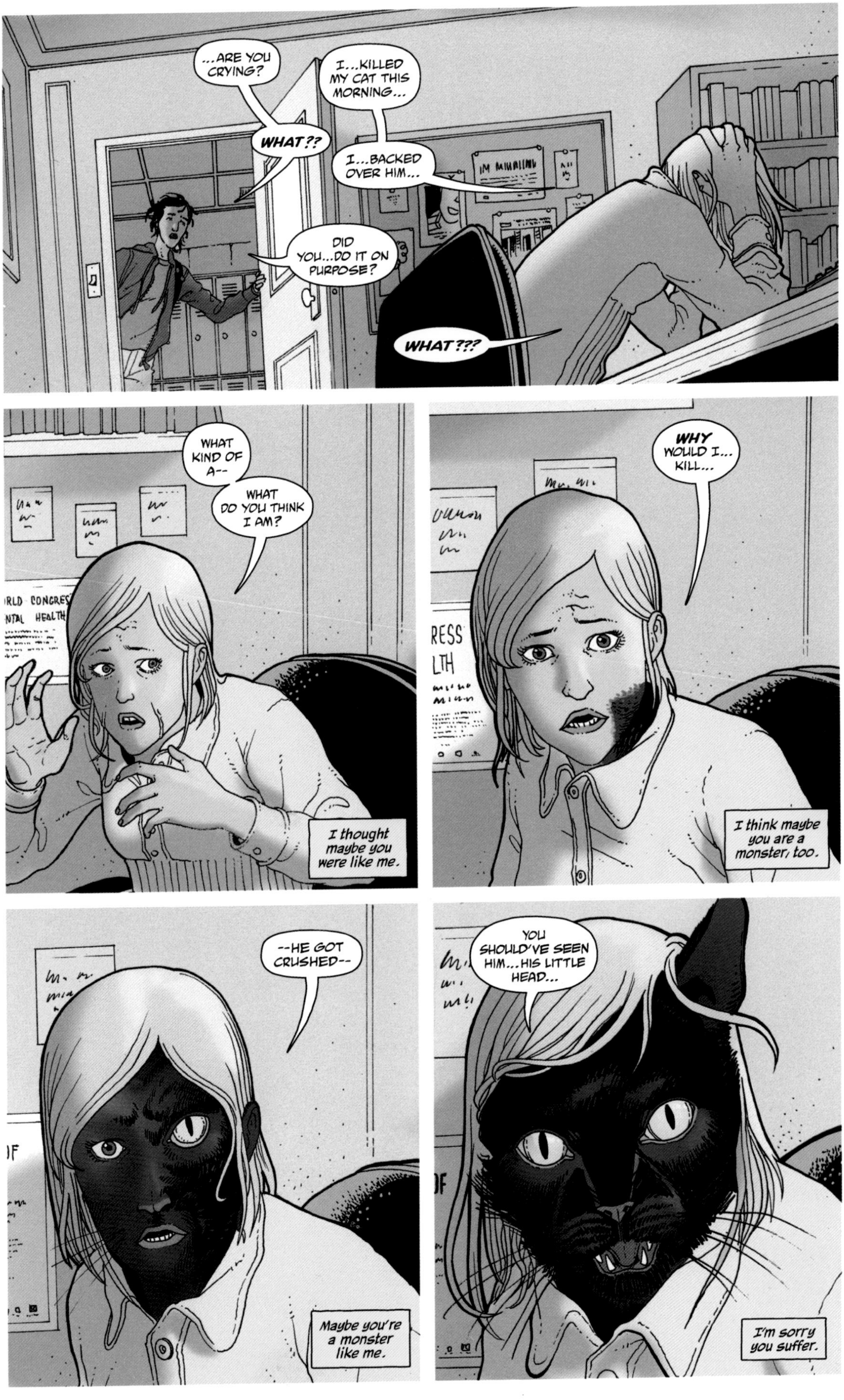
...ARE YOU CRYING?
I...KILLED MY CAT THIS MORNING...
WHAT??
I...BACKED OVER HIM...
DID YOU...DO IT ON PURPOSE?
WHAT???
WHAT KIND OF A--
WHAT DO YOU THINK I AM?
I thought maybe you were like me.
WHY WOULD I... KILL...
I think maybe you are a monster, too.
--HE GOT CRUSHED--
Maybe you're a monster like me.
YOU SHOULD'VE SEEN HIM...HIS LITTLE HEAD...
I'm sorry you suffer.

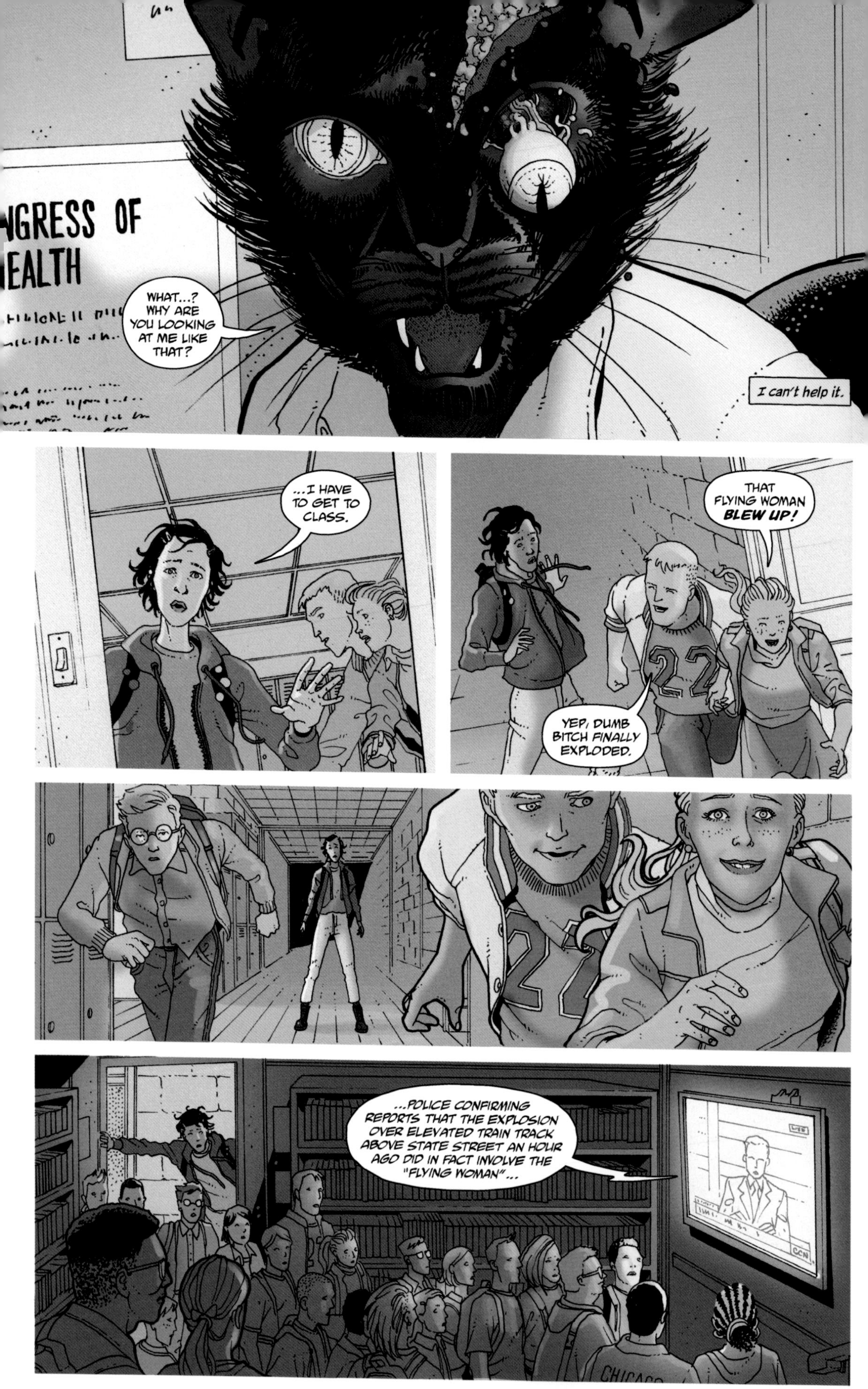

NGRESS OF
EALTH
WHAT...? WHY ARE YOU LOOKING AT ME LIKE THAT?
I can't help it.
...I HAVE TO GET TO CLASS.
THAT FLYING WOMAN **BLEW UP!**
YEP, DUMB BITCH FINALLY EXPLODED.
...POLICE CONFIRMING REPORTS THAT THE EXPLOSION OVER ELEVATED TRAIN TRACK ABOVE STATE STREET AN HOUR AGO DID IN FACT INVOLVE THE "FLYING WOMAN"...
GCN

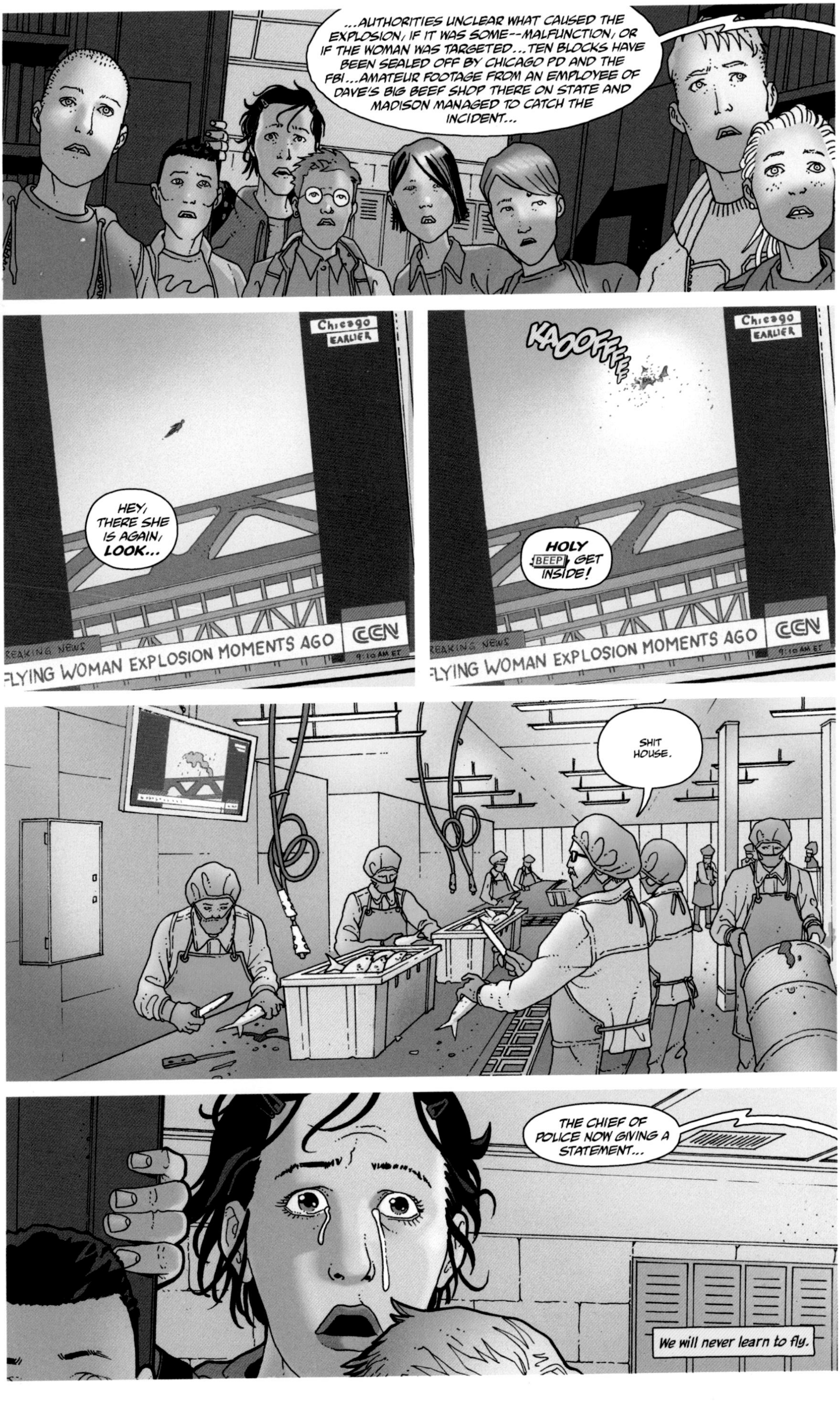
...AUTHORITIES UNCLEAR WHAT CAUSED THE EXPLOSION, IF IT WAS SOME--MALFUNCTION, OR IF THE WOMAN WAS TARGETED...TEN BLOCKS HAVE BEEN SEALED OFF BY CHICAGO PD AND THE FBI...AMATEUR FOOTAGE FROM AN EMPLOYEE OF DAVE'S BIG BEEF SHOP THERE ON STATE AND MADISON MANAGED TO CATCH THE INCIDENT...
Chicago
EARLIER
HEY, THERE SHE IS AGAIN, LOOK...
CCN
FLYING WOMAN EXPLOSION MOMENTS AGO
9:10 AM ET
Chicago
EARLIER
KAOOFFFF
HOLY BEEP GET INSIDE!
CCN
FLYING WOMAN EXPLOSION MOMENTS AGO
9:10 AM ET
SHIT HOUSE.
THE CHIEF OF POLICE NOW GIVING A STATEMENT...
We will never learn to fly.

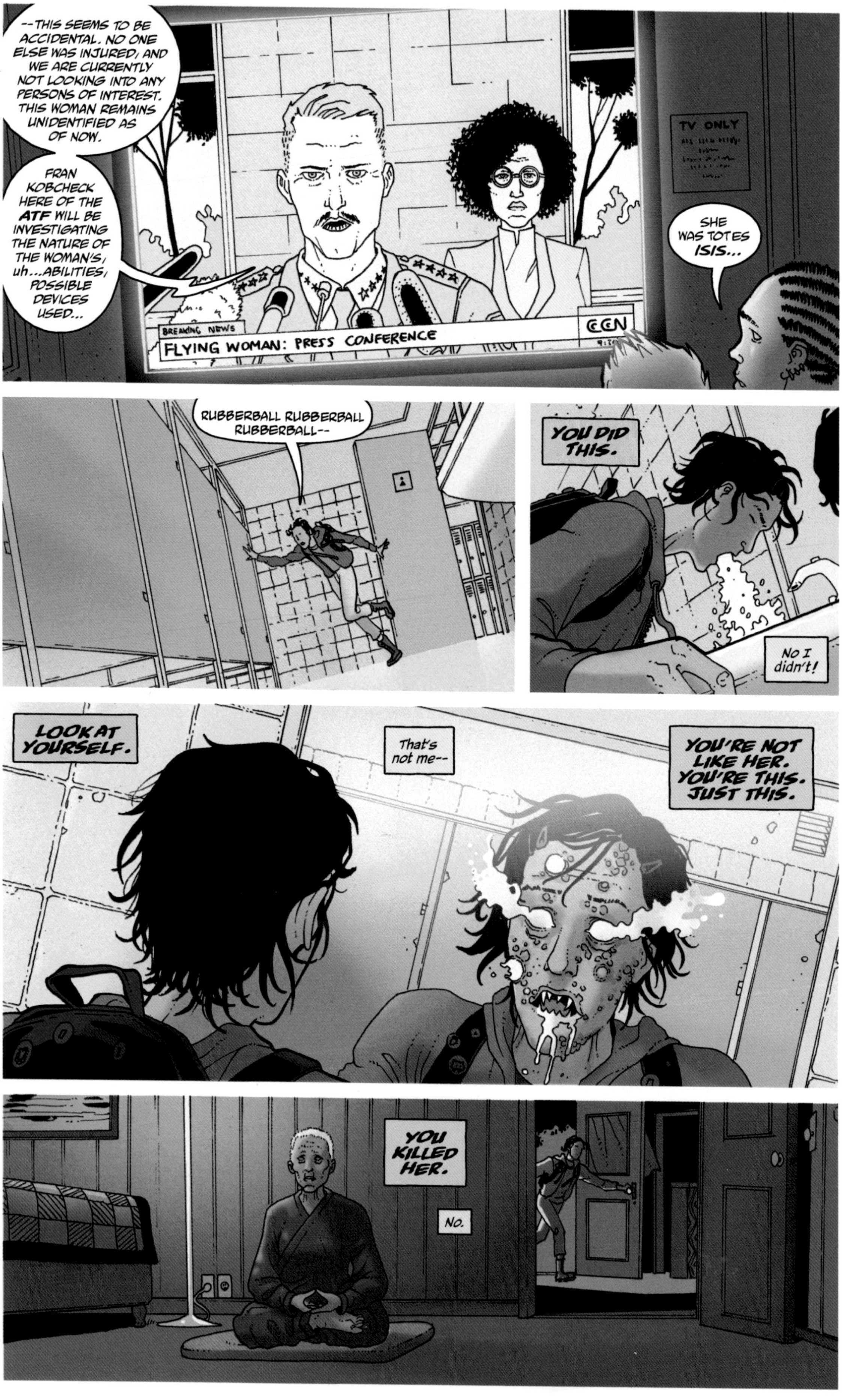
--THIS SEEMS TO BE ACCIDENTAL. NO ONE ELSE WAS INJURED, AND WE ARE CURRENTLY NOT LOOKING INTO ANY PERSONS OF INTEREST. THIS WOMAN REMAINS UNIDENTIFIED AS OF NOW.
FRAN KOBCHECK HERE OF THE ATF WILL BE INVESTIGATING THE NATURE OF THE WOMAN'S, uh...ABILITIES, POSSIBLE DEVICES USED...
TV ONLY
BREAKING NEWS
FLYING WOMAN: PRESS CONFERENCE
CCN
SHE WAS TOTES ISIS...
RUBBERBALL RUBBERBALL RUBBERBALL--
YOU DID THIS.
No I didn't!
LOOK AT YOURSELF.
That's not me--
YOU'RE NOT LIKE HER. YOU'RE THIS. JUST THIS.
YOU KILLED HER.
No.

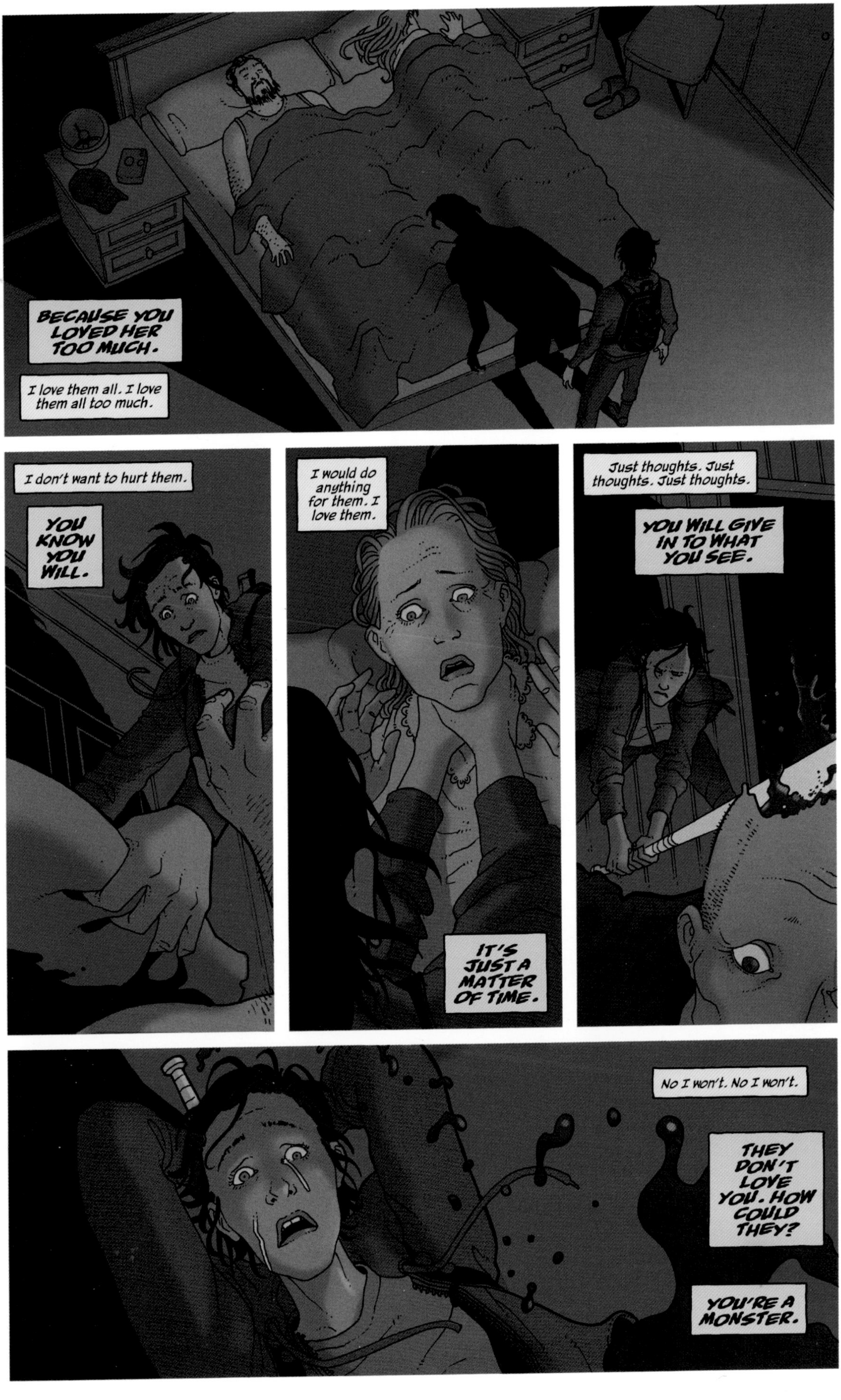

BECAUSE YOU LOVED HER TOO MUCH.
I love them all. I love them all too much.
I don't want to hurt them.
YOU KNOW YOU WILL.
I would do anything for them. I love them.
IT'S JUST A MATTER OF TIME.
Just thoughts. Just thoughts. Just thoughts.
YOU WILL GIVE IN TO WHAT YOU SEE.
No I won't. No I won't.
THEY DON'T LOVE YOU. HOW COULD THEY?
YOU'RE A MONSTER.

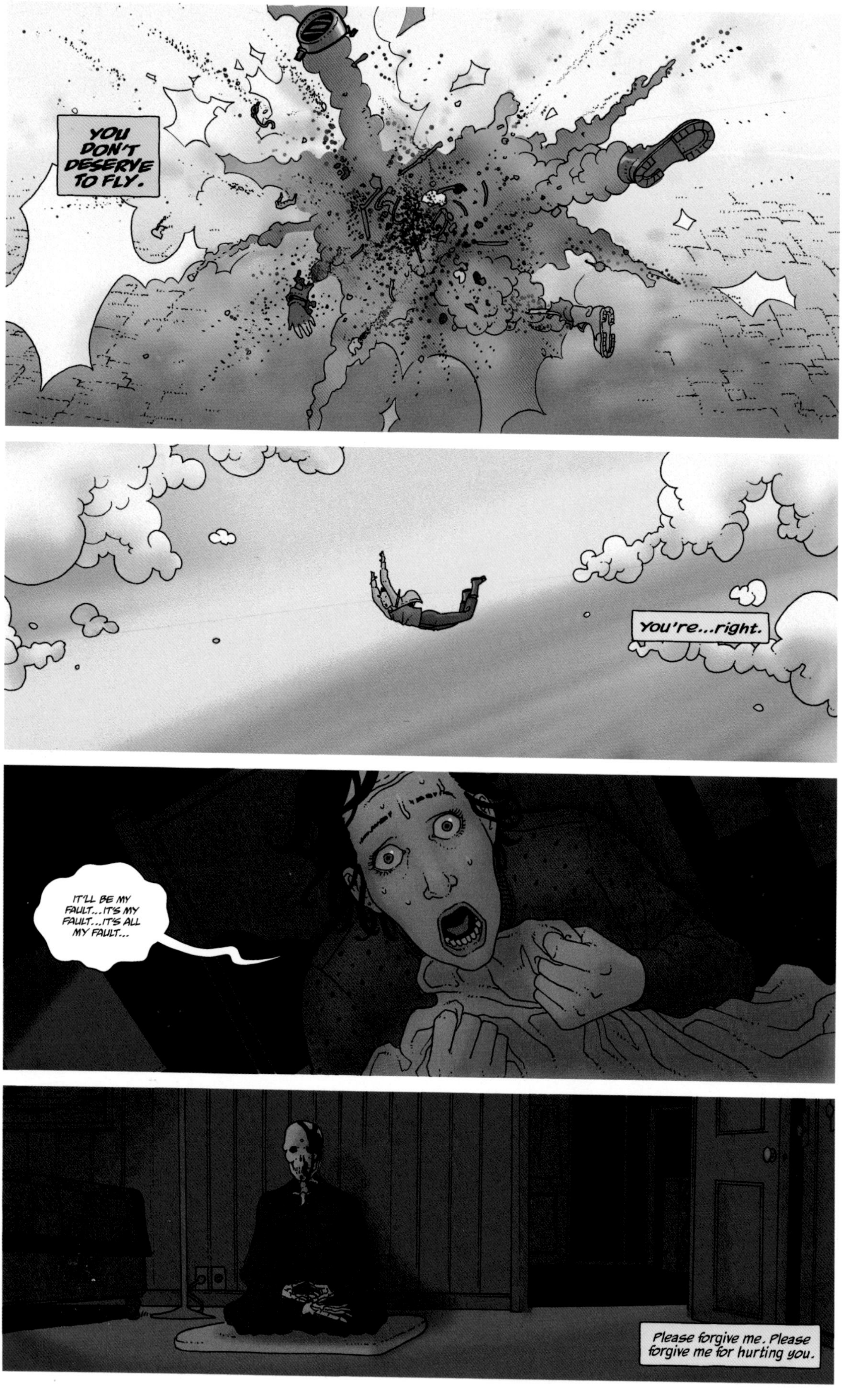
YOU DON'T DESERVE TO FLY.
You're...right.
IT'LL BE MY FAULT...IT'S MY FAULT...IT'S ALL MY FAULT...
Please forgive me. Please forgive me for hurting you.

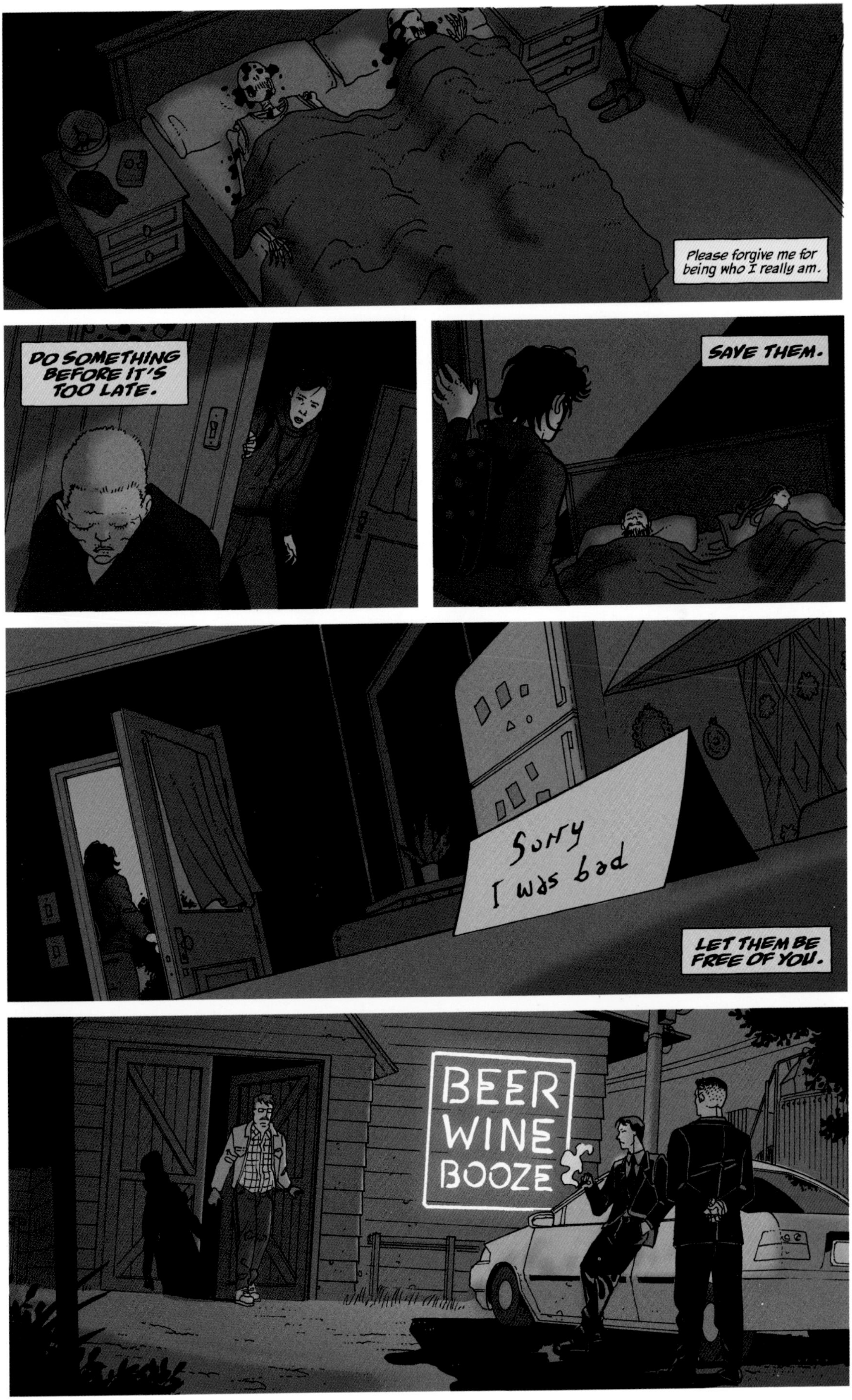
Please forgive me for being who I really am.
DO SOMETHING BEFORE IT'S TOO LATE.
SAVE THEM.
Sorry I was bad
LET THEM BE FREE OF YOU.
BEER
WINE
BOOZE

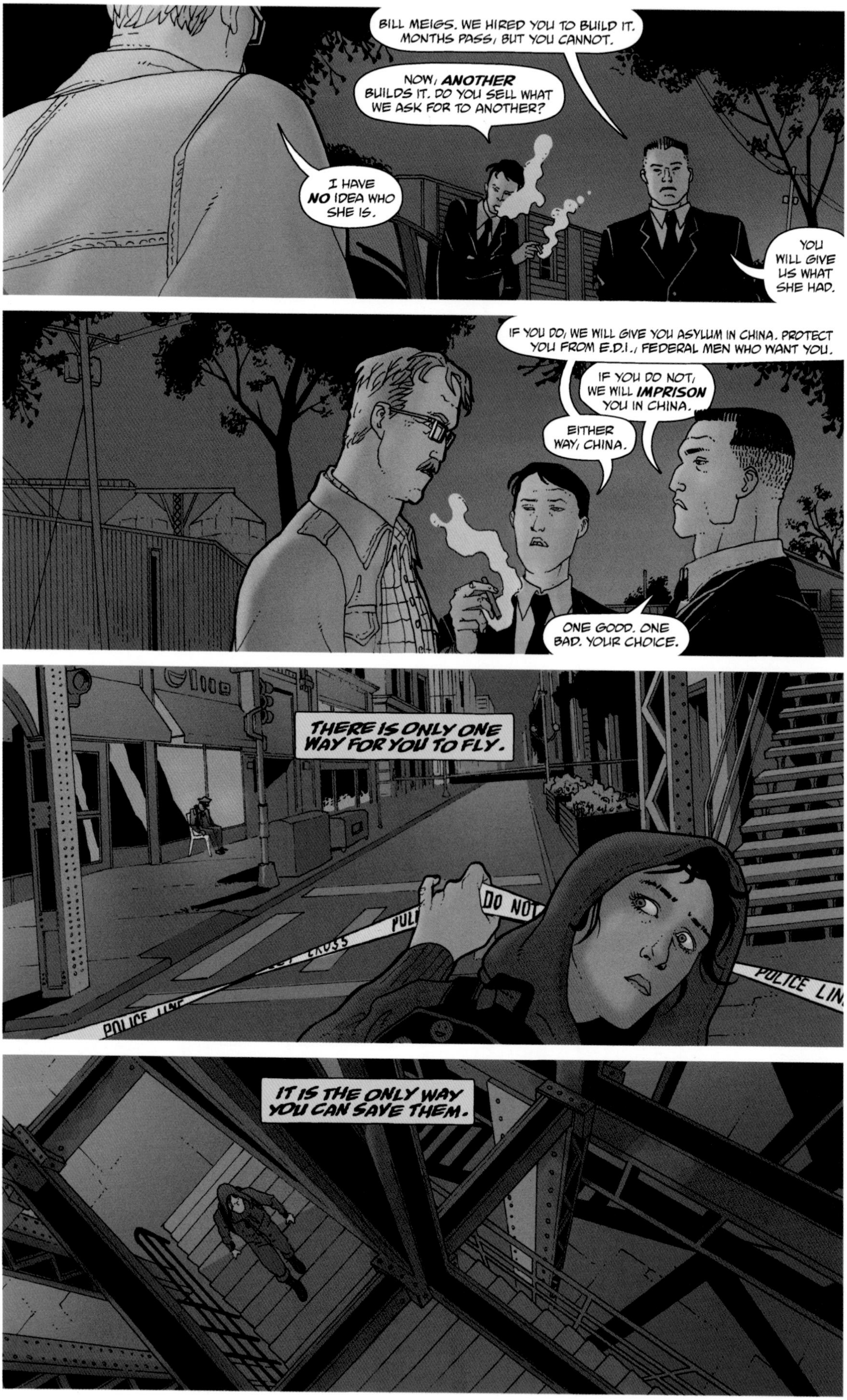
BILL MEIGS. WE HIRED YOU TO BUILD IT. MONTHS PASS, BUT YOU CANNOT.
NOW, **ANOTHER** BUILDS IT. DO YOU SELL WHAT WE ASK FOR TO ANOTHER?
I HAVE **NO** IDEA WHO SHE IS.
YOU WILL GIVE US WHAT SHE HAD.
IF YOU DO, WE WILL GIVE YOU ASYLUM IN CHINA. PROTECT YOU FROM E.D.I., FEDERAL MEN WHO WANT YOU.
IF YOU DO NOT, WE WILL **IMPRISON** YOU IN CHINA.
EITHER WAY, CHINA.
ONE GOOD. ONE BAD. YOUR CHOICE.
THERE IS ONLY ONE WAY FOR YOU TO FLY.
DO NOT
POLICE LINE
IT IS THE ONLY WAY YOU CAN SAVE THEM.

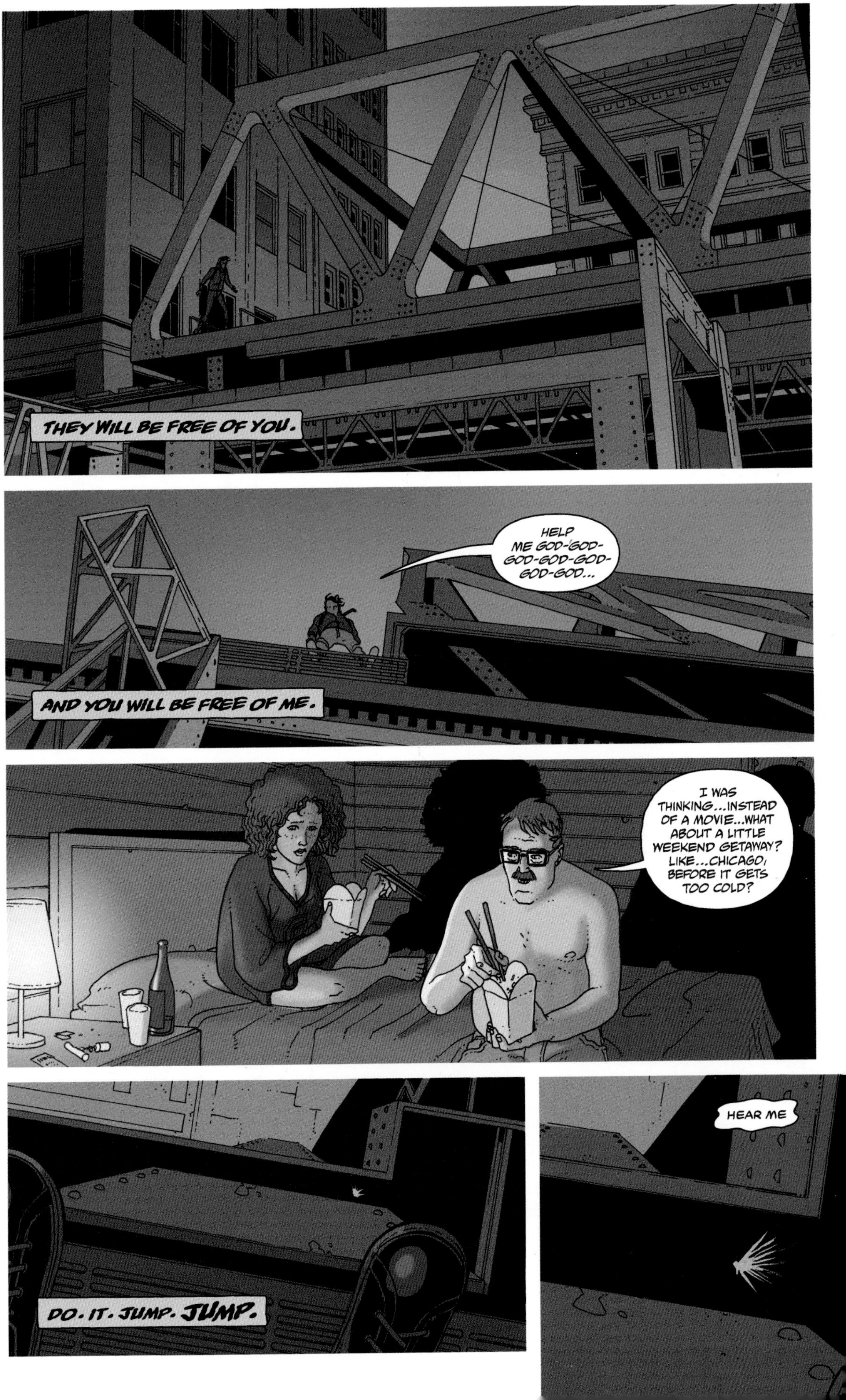
THEY WILL BE FREE OF YOU.
HELP ME GOD-GOD-GOD-GOD-GOD-GOD-GOD...
AND YOU WILL BE FREE OF ME.
I WAS THINKING...INSTEAD OF A MOVIE...WHAT ABOUT A LITTLE WEEKEND GETAWAY? LIKE...CHICAGO, BEFORE IT GETS TOO COLD?
DO. IT. JUMP. JUMP.
HEAR ME

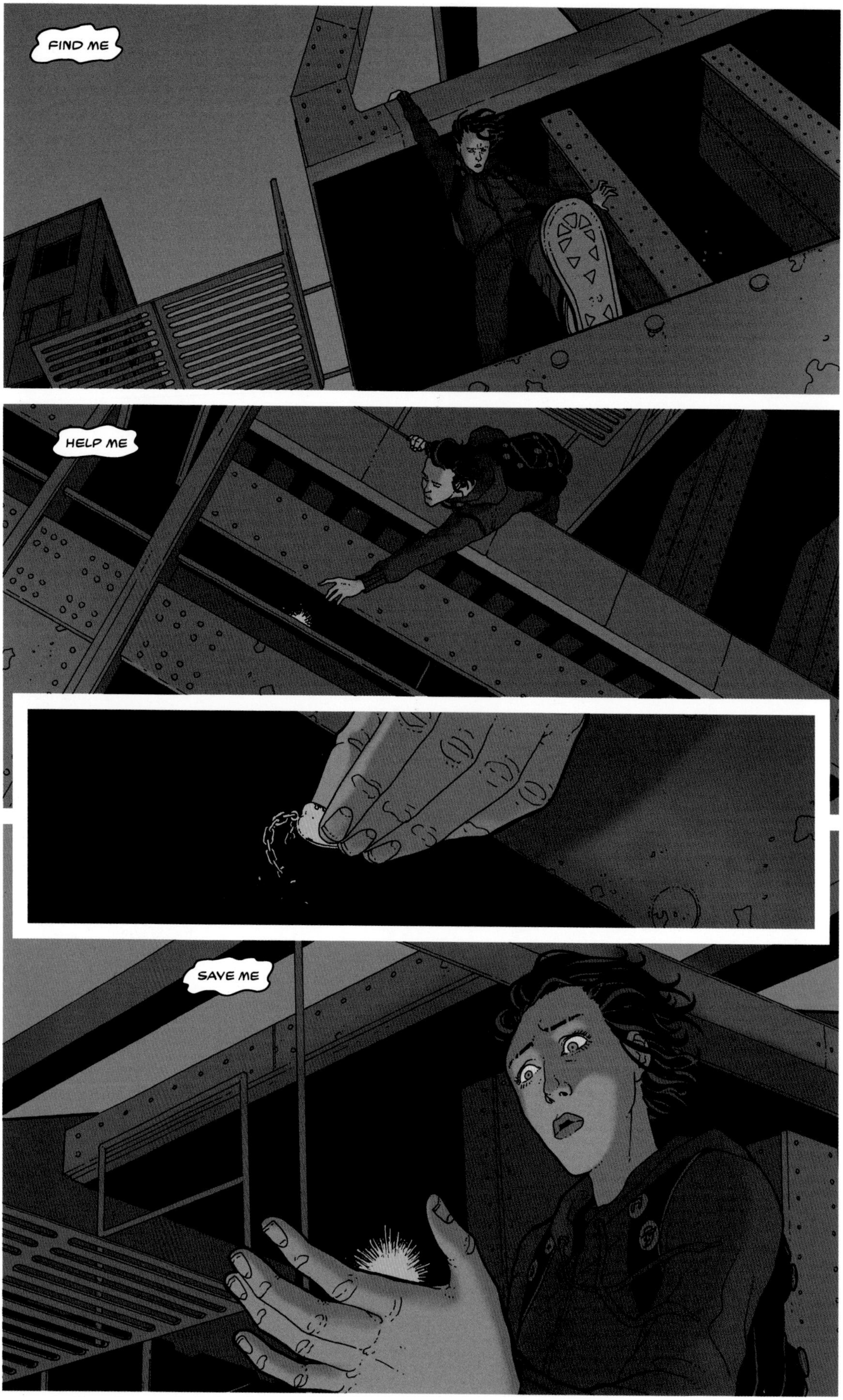
FIND ME
HELP ME
SAVE ME

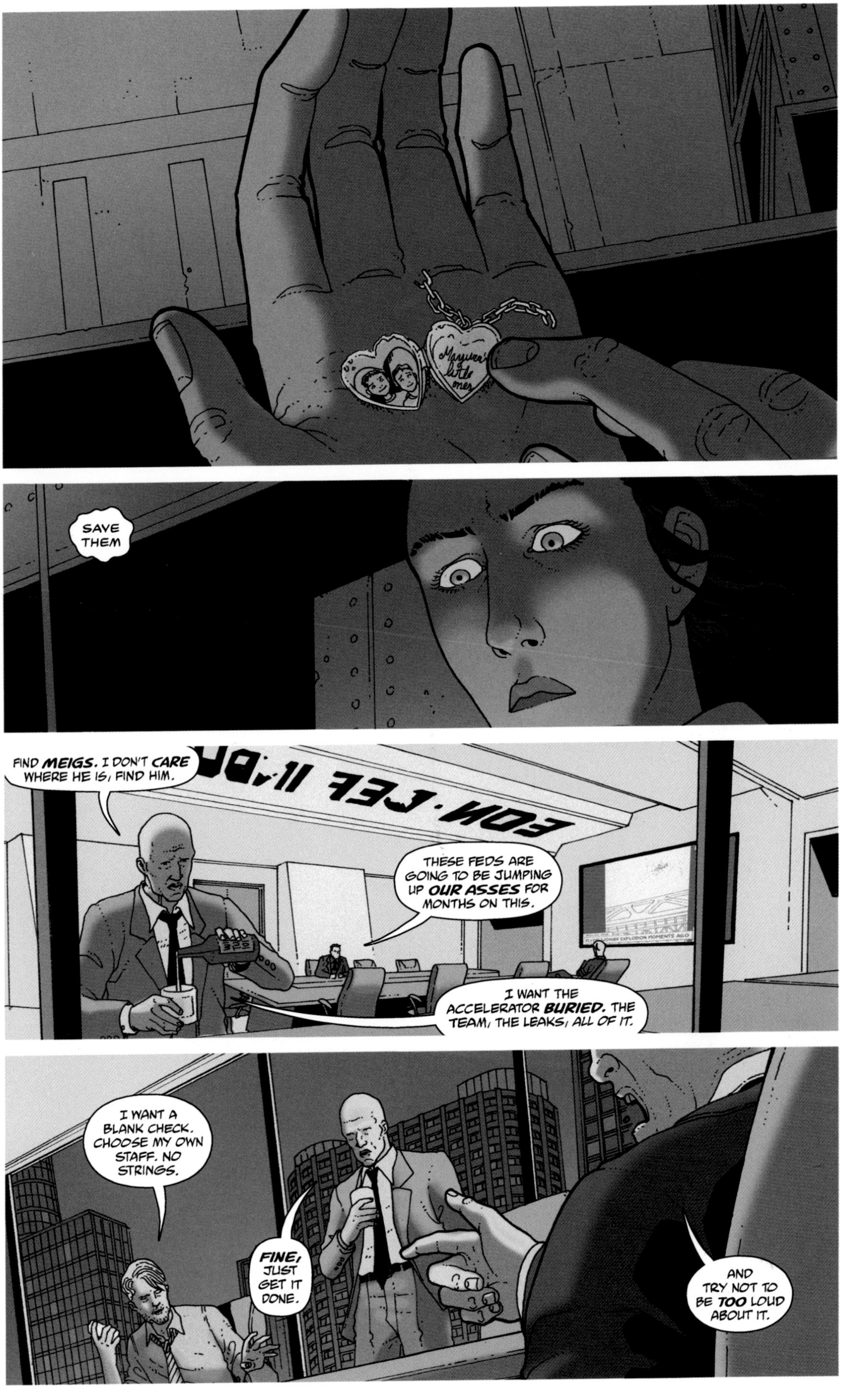
SAVE THEM
FIND **MEIGS.** I DON'T **CARE** WHERE HE IS, FIND HIM.
THESE FEDS ARE GOING TO BE JUMPING UP **OUR ASSES** FOR MONTHS ON THIS.
I WANT THE ACCELERATOR **BURIED.** THE TEAM, THE LEAKS, ALL OF IT.
I WANT A BLANK CHECK. CHOOSE MY OWN STAFF. NO STRINGS.
FINE, JUST GET IT DONE.
AND TRY NOT TO BE **TOO** LOUD ABOUT IT.

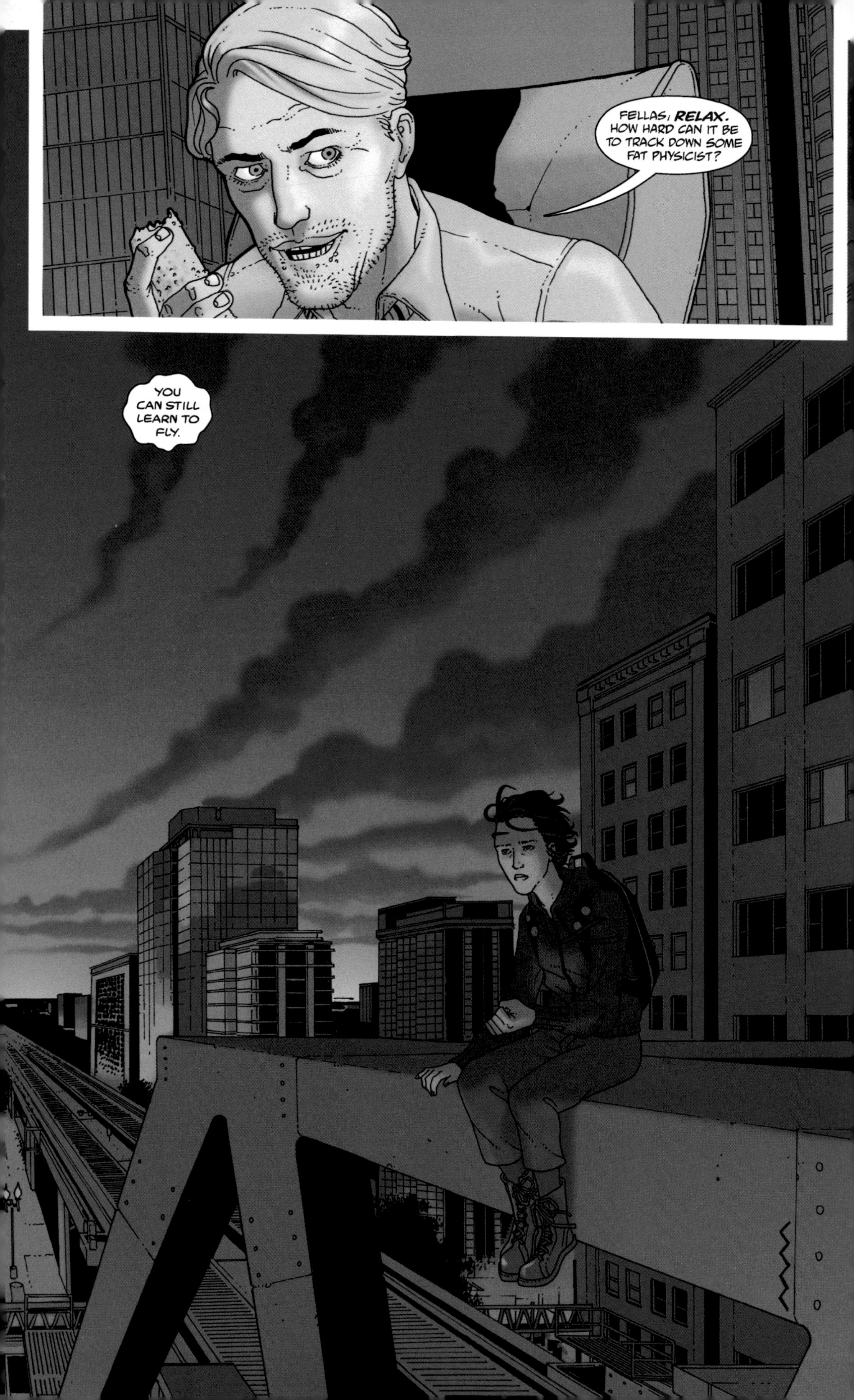
FELLAS, **RELAX.** HOW HARD CAN IT BE TO TRACK DOWN SOME FAT PHYSICIST?
YOU CAN STILL LEARN TO FLY.

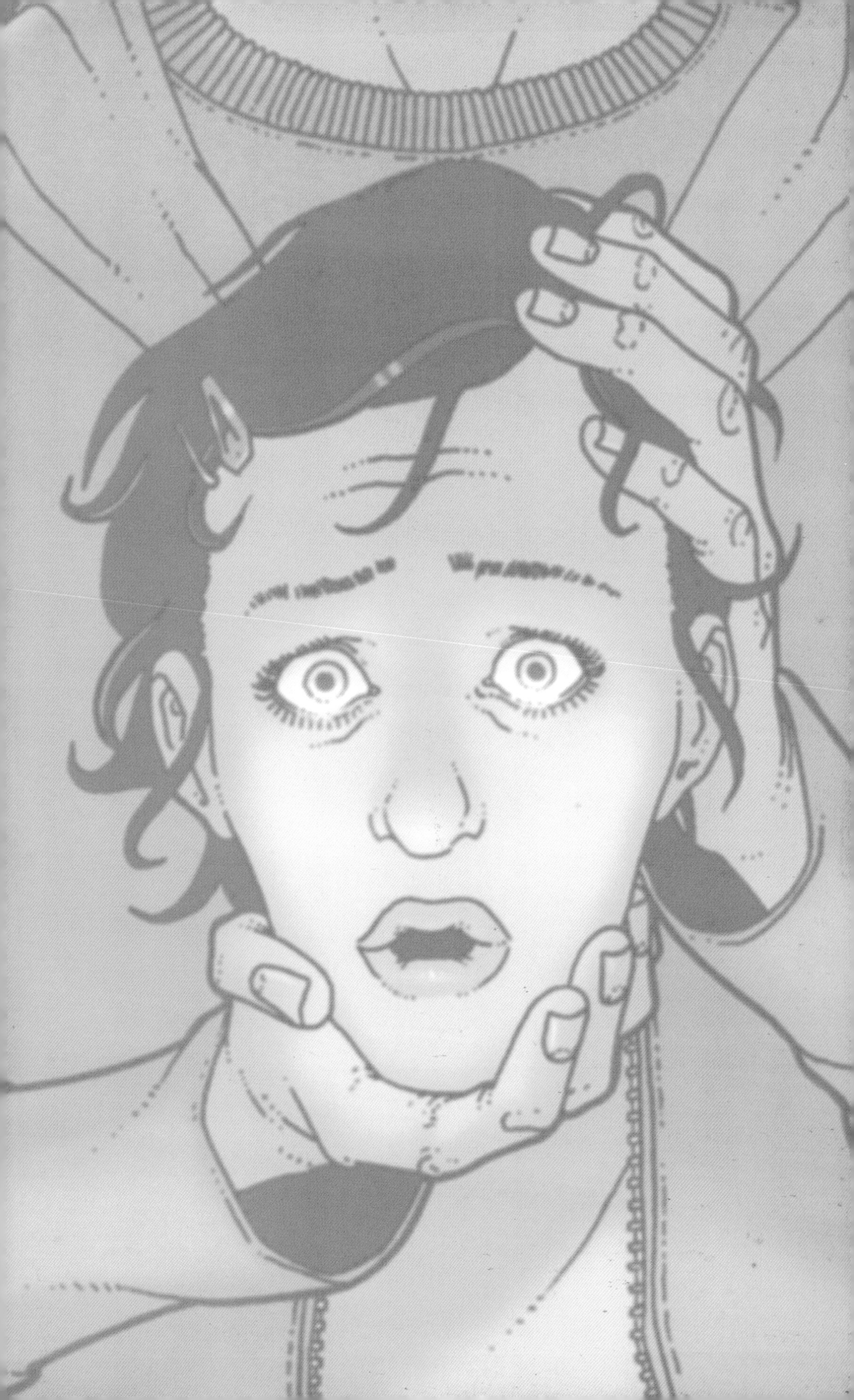

CHAPTER II

"Beware the Bandersnatch"

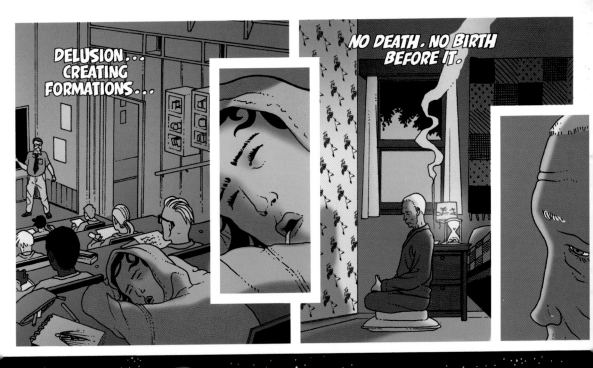

DELUSION...
CREATING
FORMATIONS...

NO DEATH. NO BIRTH
BEFORE IT.

THINGS MAKING
CONSCIOUSNESS...
THEN MIND, BODY...

NO BECOMING
ANYTHING.
NO CLINGING TO
ANYTHING.

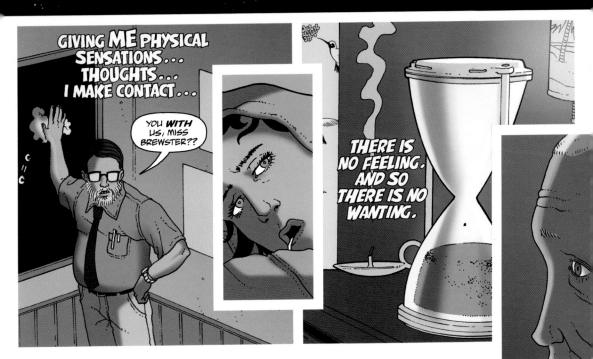

GIVING **ME** PHYSICAL
SENSATIONS...
THOUGHTS...
I MAKE CONTACT...

YOU **WITH**
US, MISS
BREWSTER??

THERE IS
NO FEELING.
AND SO
THERE IS NO
WANTING.

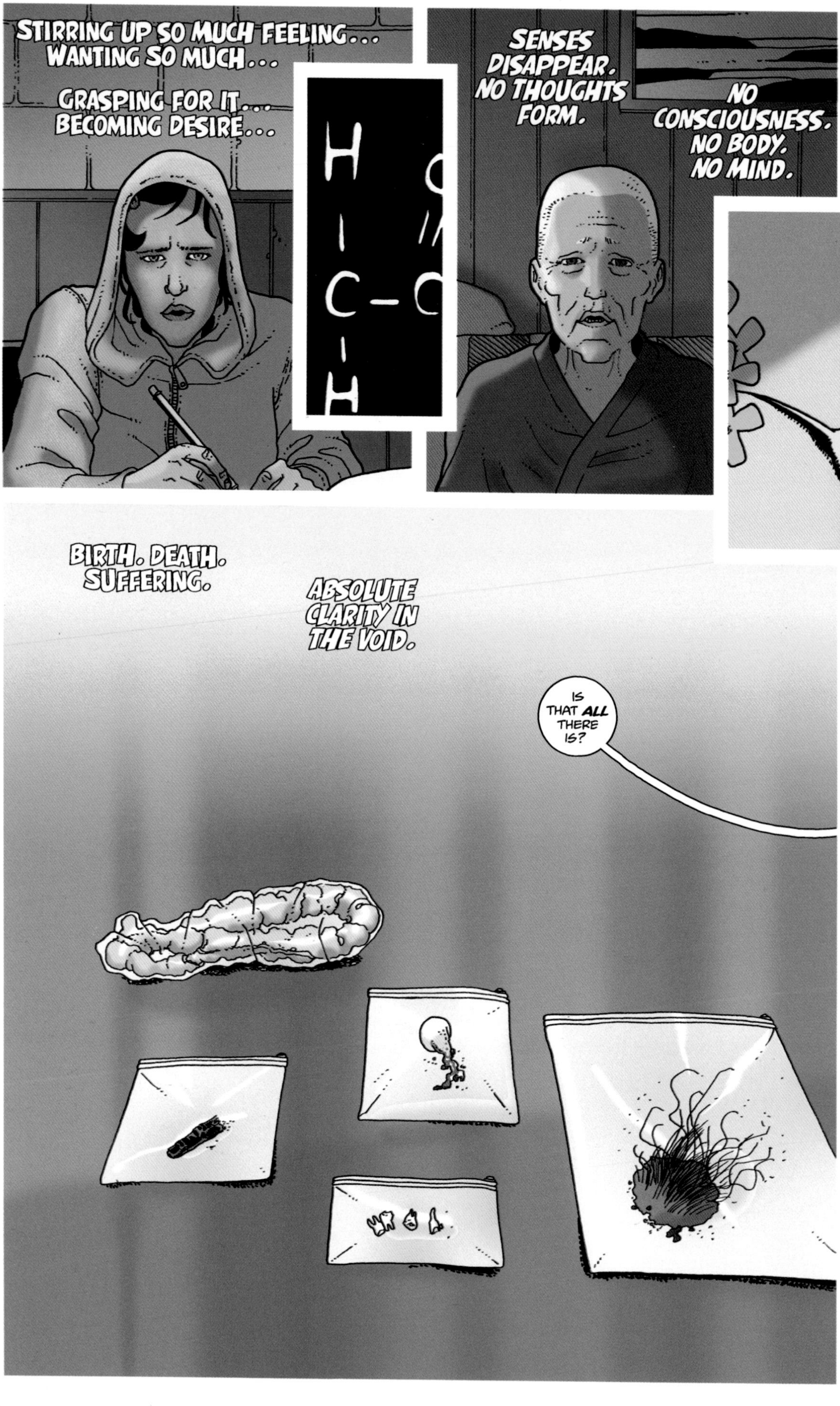
STIRRING UP SO MUCH FEELING... WANTING SO MUCH...
GRASPING FOR IT... BECOMING DESIRE...
SENSES DISAPPEAR. NO THOUGHTS FORM.
NO CONSCIOUSNESS. NO BODY. NO MIND.
BIRTH. DEATH. SUFFERING.
ABSOLUTE CLARITY IN THE VOID.
IS THAT **ALL** THERE IS?

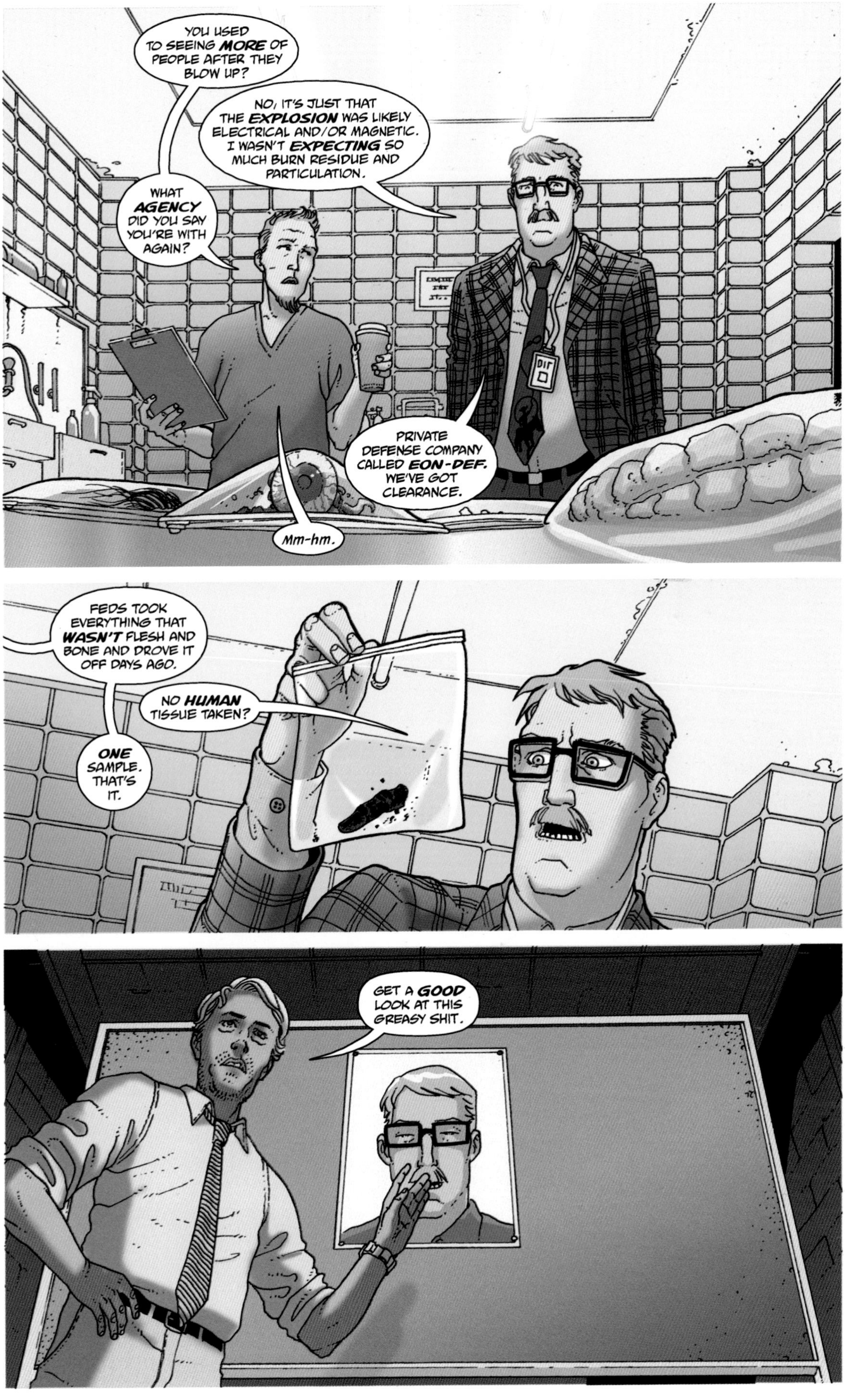

YOU USED TO SEEING MORE OF PEOPLE AFTER THEY BLOW UP?
NO, IT'S JUST THAT THE EXPLOSION WAS LIKELY ELECTRICAL AND/OR MAGNETIC. I WASN'T EXPECTING SO MUCH BURN RESIDUE AND PARTICULATION.
WHAT AGENCY DID YOU SAY YOU'RE WITH AGAIN?
PRIVATE DEFENSE COMPANY CALLED EON-DEF. WE'VE GOT CLEARANCE.
Mm-hm.
FEDS TOOK EVERYTHING THAT WASN'T FLESH AND BONE AND DROVE IT OFF DAYS AGO.
NO HUMAN TISSUE TAKEN?
ONE SAMPLE. THAT'S IT.
GET A GOOD LOOK AT THIS GREASY SHIT.

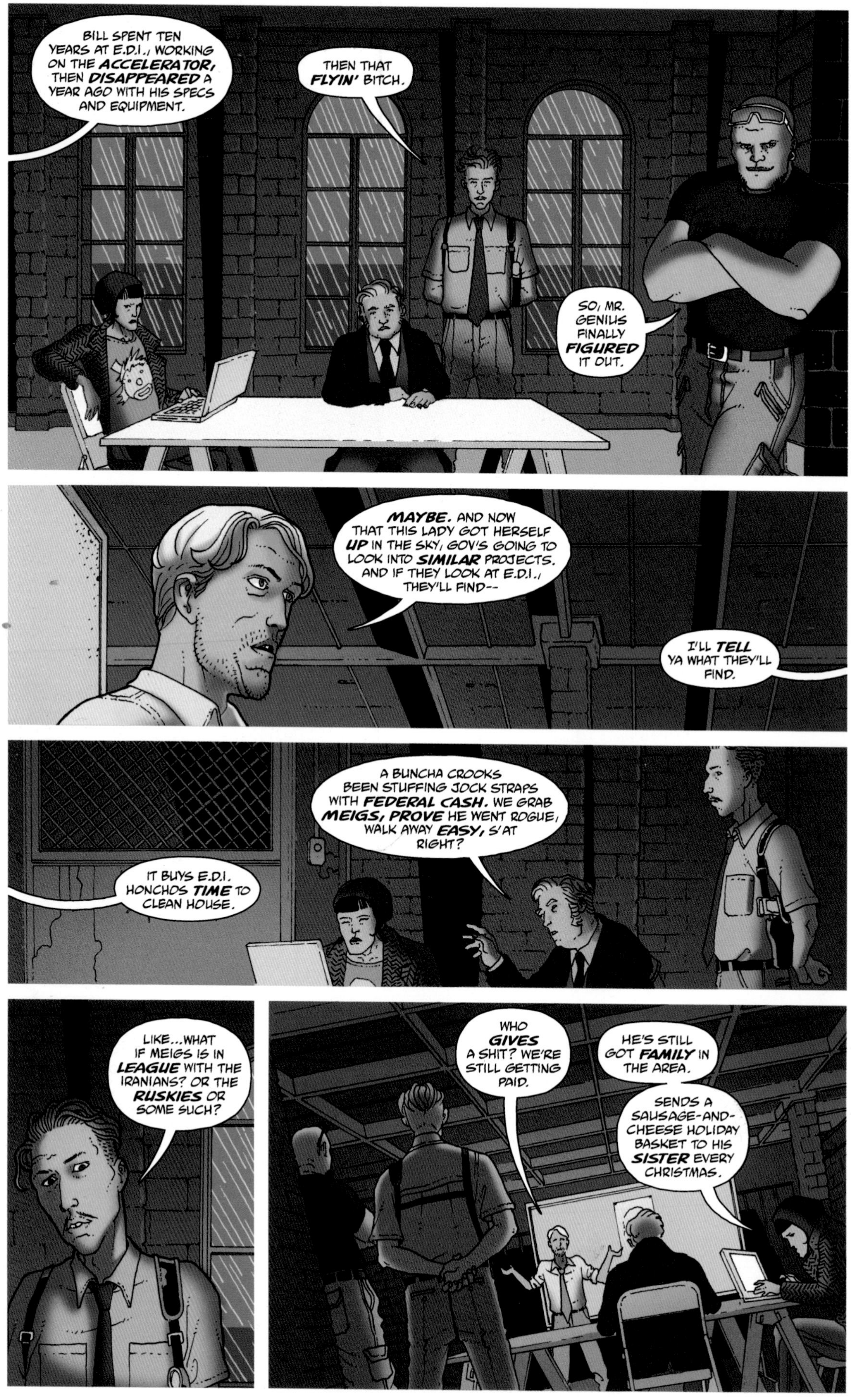
BILL SPENT TEN YEARS AT E.D.I., WORKING ON THE ACCELERATOR, THEN DISAPPEARED A YEAR AGO WITH HIS SPECS AND EQUIPMENT.
THEN THAT FLYIN' BITCH.
SO, MR. GENIUS FINALLY FIGURED IT OUT.
MAYBE. AND NOW THAT THIS LADY GOT HERSELF UP IN THE SKY, GOV'S GOING TO LOOK INTO SIMILAR PROJECTS. AND IF THEY LOOK AT E.D.I., THEY'LL FIND--
I'LL TELL YA WHAT THEY'LL FIND.
IT BUYS E.D.I. HONCHOS TIME TO CLEAN HOUSE.
A BUNCHA CROOKS BEEN STUFFING JOCK STRAPS WITH FEDERAL CASH. WE GRAB MEIGS, PROVE HE WENT ROGUE, WALK AWAY EASY, S'AT RIGHT?
LIKE...WHAT IF MEIGS IS IN LEAGUE WITH THE IRANIANS? OR THE RUSKIES OR SOME SUCH?
WHO GIVES A SHIT? WE'RE STILL GETTING PAID.
HE'S STILL GOT FAMILY IN THE AREA.
SENDS A SAUSAGE-AND-CHEESE HOLIDAY BASKET TO HIS SISTER EVERY CHRISTMAS.

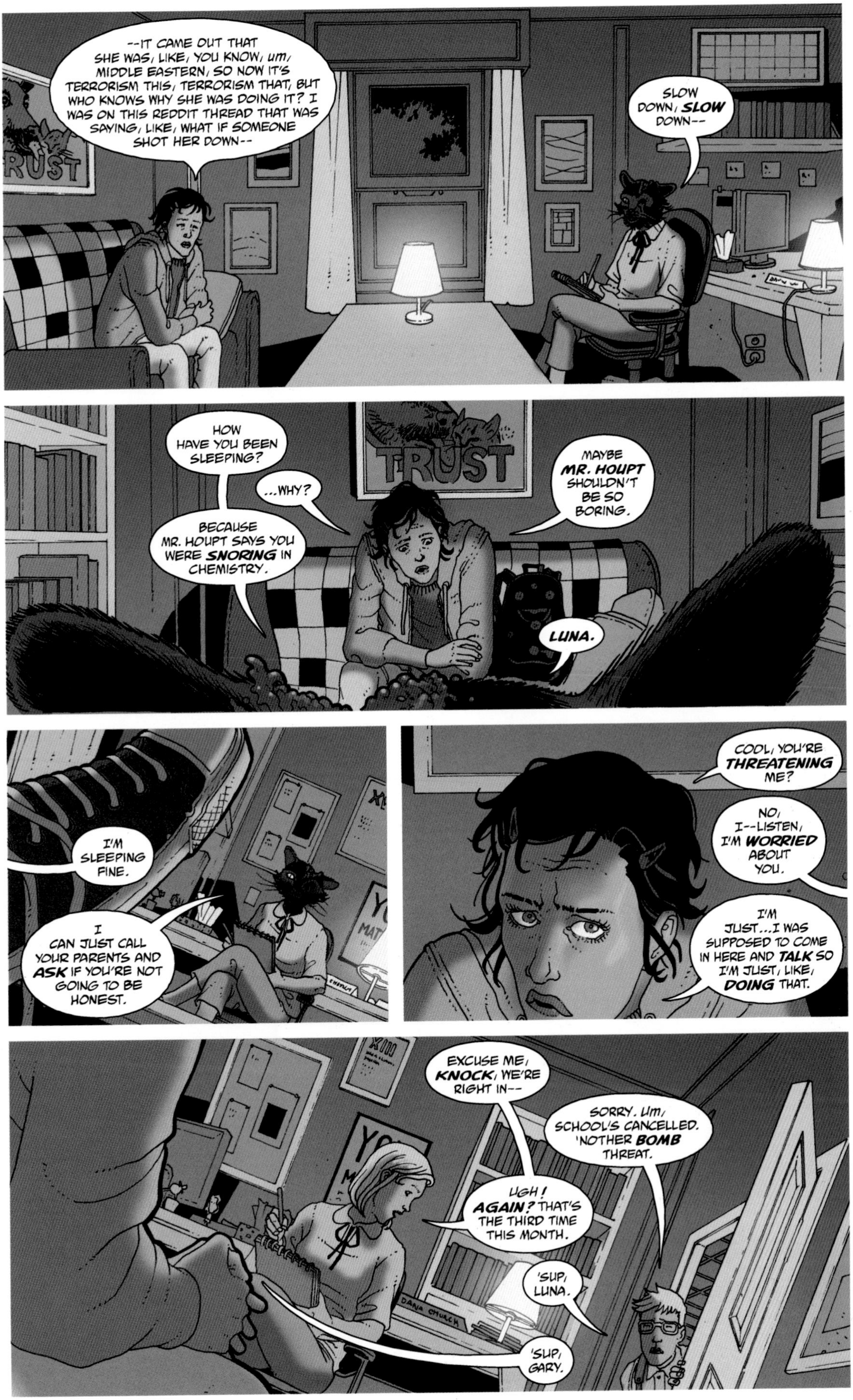
--IT CAME OUT THAT SHE WAS, LIKE, YOU KNOW, um, MIDDLE EASTERN, SO NOW IT'S TERRORISM THIS, TERRORISM THAT, BUT WHO KNOWS WHY SHE WAS DOING IT? I WAS ON THIS REDDIT THREAD THAT WAS SAYING, LIKE, WHAT IF SOMEONE SHOT HER DOWN--
SLOW DOWN, SLOW DOWN--
TRUST
HOW HAVE YOU BEEN SLEEPING?
...WHY?
BECAUSE MR. HOUPT SAYS YOU WERE SNORING IN CHEMISTRY.
MAYBE MR. HOUPT SHOULDN'T BE SO BORING.
LUNA.
I'M SLEEPING FINE.
I CAN JUST CALL YOUR PARENTS AND ASK IF YOU'RE NOT GOING TO BE HONEST.
COOL, YOU'RE THREATENING ME?
NO, I--LISTEN, I'M WORRIED ABOUT YOU.
I'M JUST...I WAS SUPPOSED TO COME IN HERE AND TALK SO I'M JUST, LIKE, DOING THAT.
EXCUSE ME, KNOCK, WE'RE RIGHT IN--
SORRY. um, SCHOOL'S CANCELLED. 'NOTHER BOMB THREAT.
UGH! AGAIN? THAT'S THE THIRD TIME THIS MONTH.
'SUP, LUNA.
'SUP, GARY.
DANA CHURCH

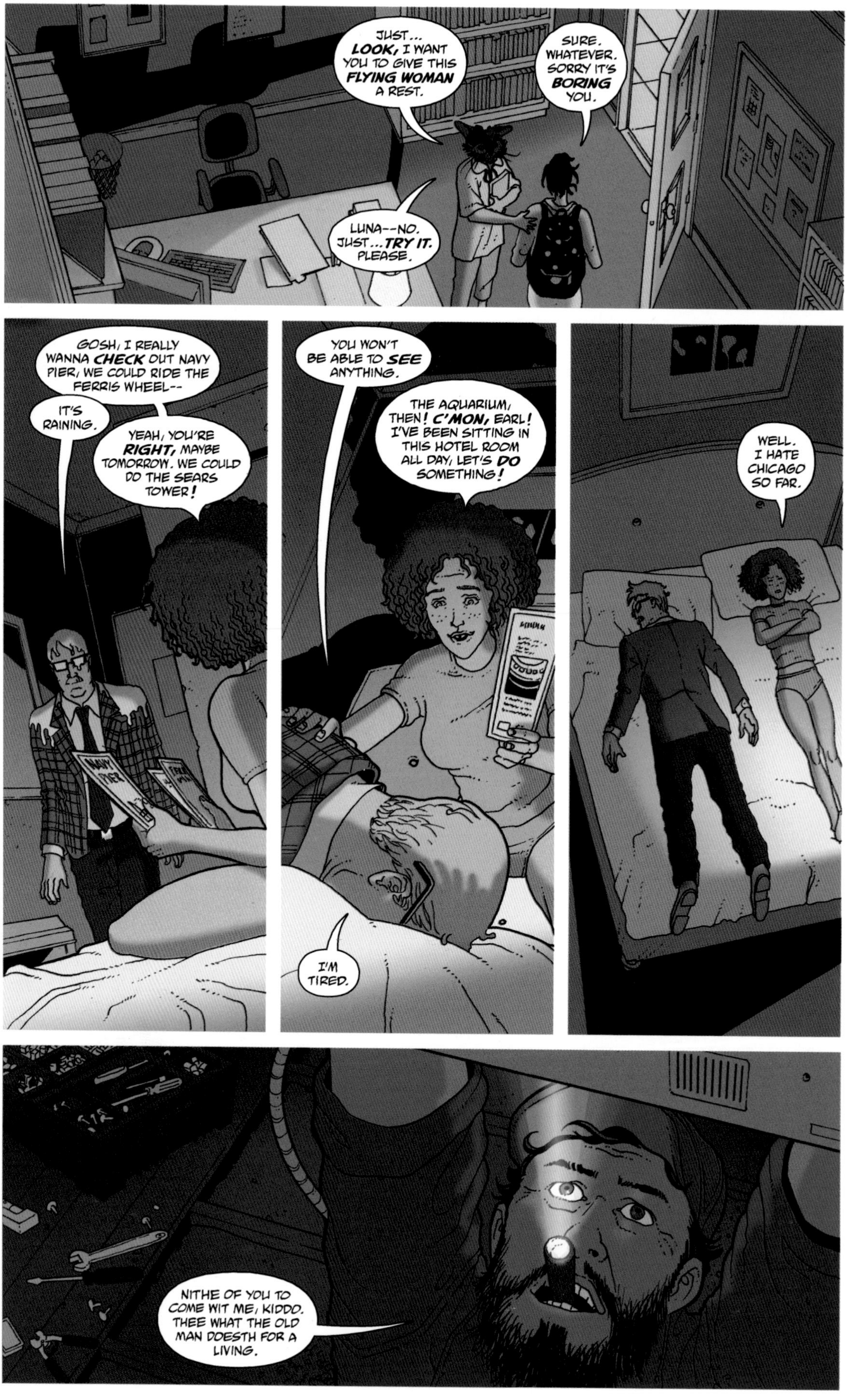
JUST... LOOK, I WANT YOU TO GIVE THIS FLYING WOMAN A REST.
SURE. WHATEVER. SORRY IT'S BORING YOU.
LUNA--NO. JUST...TRY IT. PLEASE.
GOSH, I REALLY WANNA CHECK OUT NAVY PIER, WE COULD RIDE THE FERRIS WHEEL--
IT'S RAINING.
YEAH, YOU'RE RIGHT, MAYBE TOMORROW. WE COULD DO THE SEARS TOWER!
YOU WON'T BE ABLE TO SEE ANYTHING.
THE AQUARIUM, THEN! C'MON, EARL! I'VE BEEN SITTING IN THIS HOTEL ROOM ALL DAY, LET'S DO SOMETHING!
I'M TIRED.
WELL. I HATE CHICAGO SO FAR.
NITHE OF YOU TO COME WIT ME, KIDDO. THEE WHAT THE OLD MAN DOESTH FOR A LIVING.

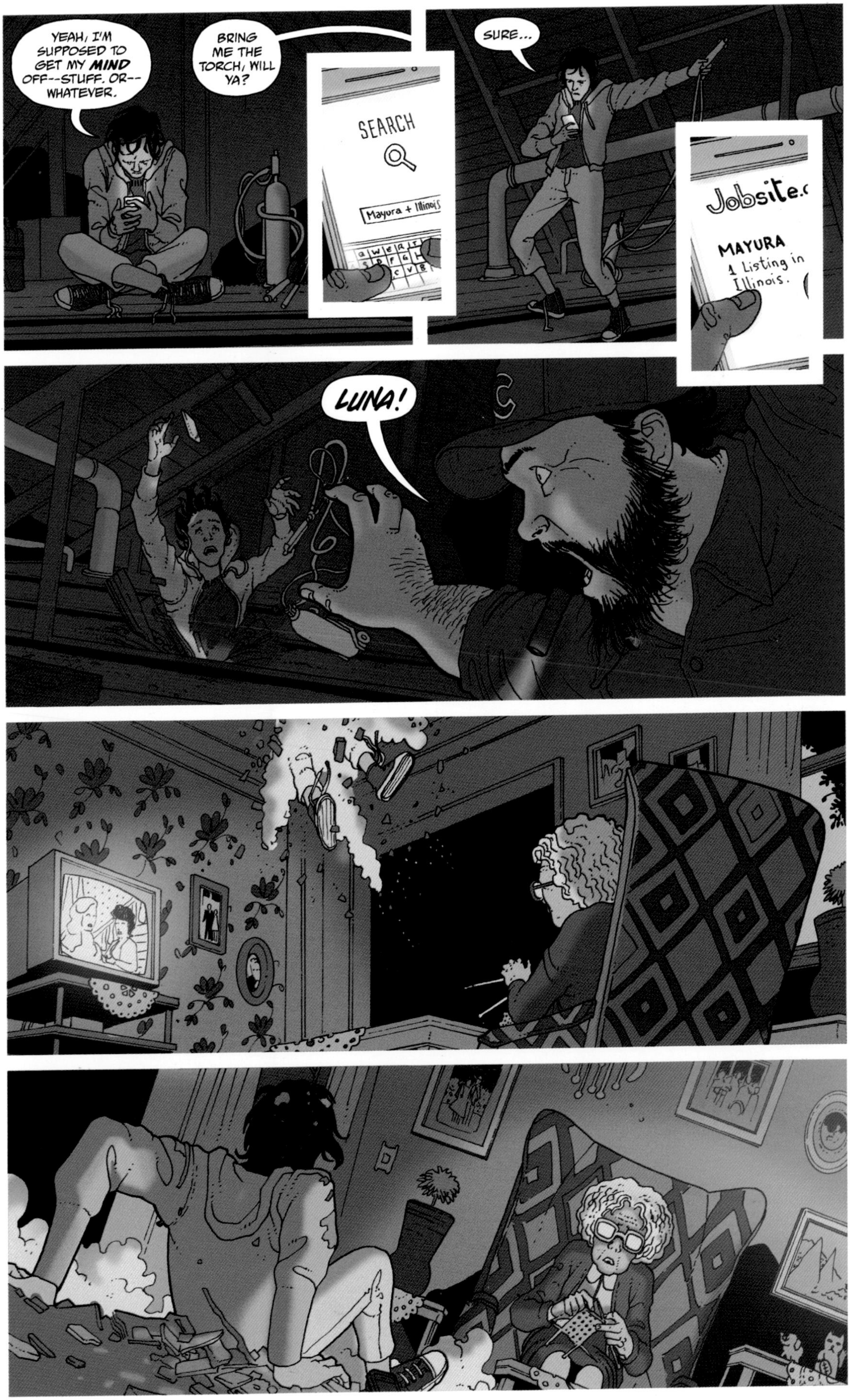
YEAH, I'M SUPPOSED TO GET MY MIND OFF--STUFF. OR--WHATEVER.
BRING ME THE TORCH, WILL YA?
SEARCH
Mayura + Illinois
SURE...
Jobsite.
MAYURA
1 Listing in Illinois.
LUNA!

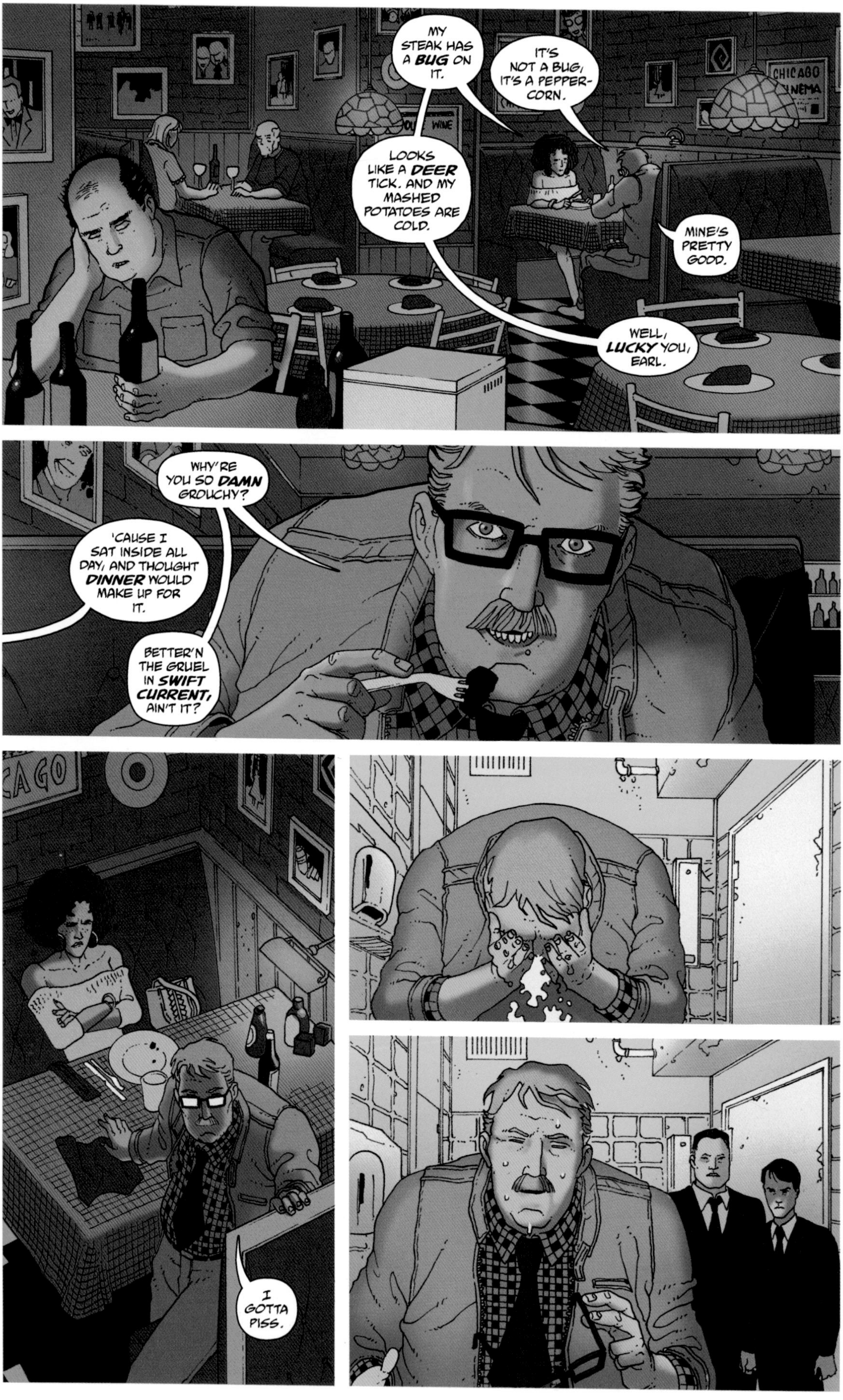

MY STEAK HAS A **BUG** ON IT.
IT'S NOT A BUG, IT'S A PEPPER-CORN.
LOOKS LIKE A **DEER** TICK. AND MY MASHED POTATOES ARE COLD.
MINE'S PRETTY GOOD.
WELL, **LUCKY** YOU, EARL.
WHY'RE YOU SO **DAMN** GROUCHY?
'CAUSE I SAT INSIDE ALL DAY, AND THOUGHT **DINNER** WOULD MAKE UP FOR IT.
BETTER'N THE GRUEL IN **SWIFT CURRENT,** AIN'T IT?
I GOTTA PISS.

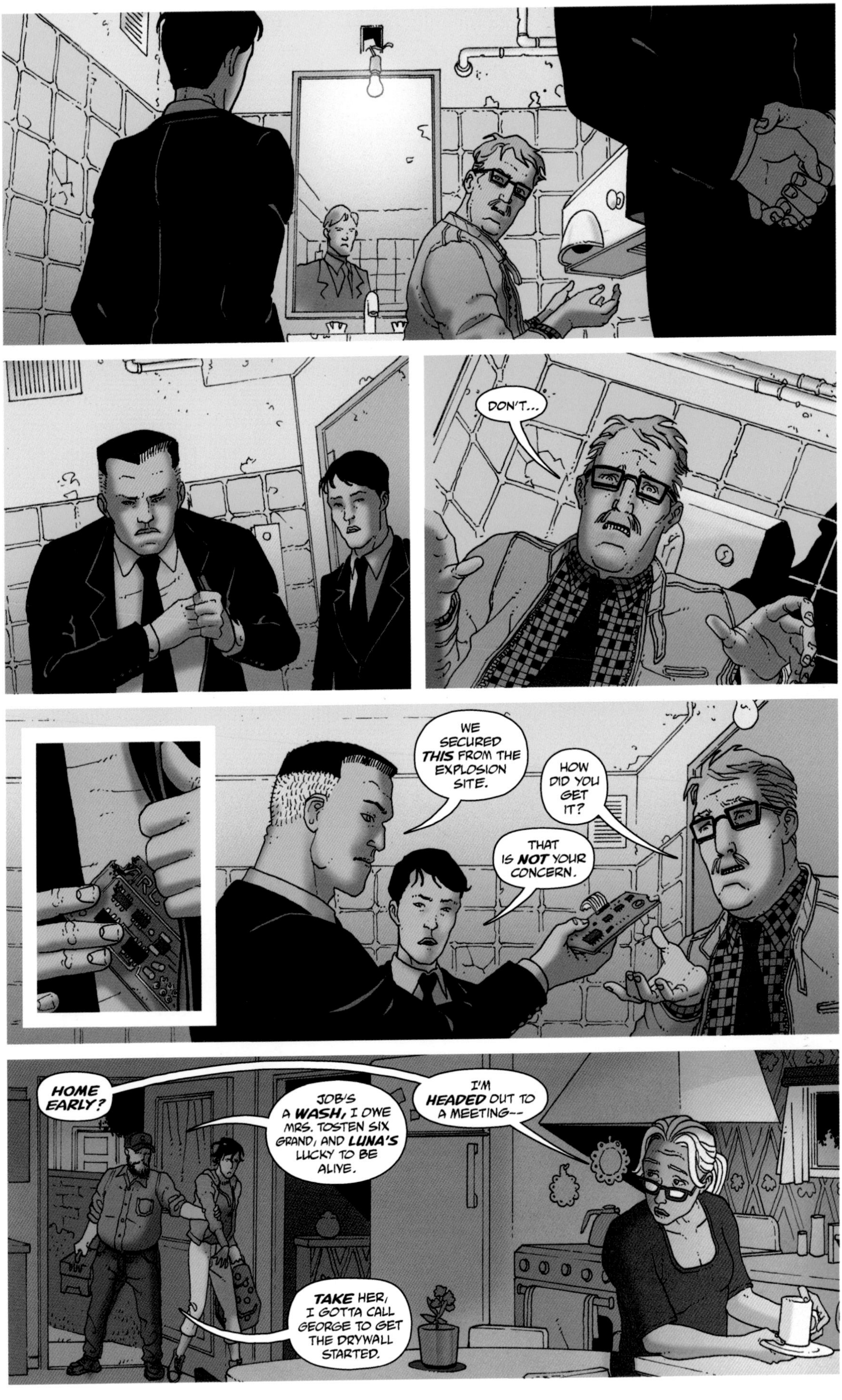
DON'T...
WE SECURED THIS FROM THE EXPLOSION SITE.
HOW DID YOU GET IT?
THAT IS NOT YOUR CONCERN.
HOME EARLY?
I'M HEADED OUT TO A MEETING--
JOB'S A WASH, I OWE MRS. TOSTEN SIX GRAND, AND LUNA'S LUCKY TO BE ALIVE.
TAKE HER, I GOTTA CALL GEORGE TO GET THE DRYWALL STARTED.

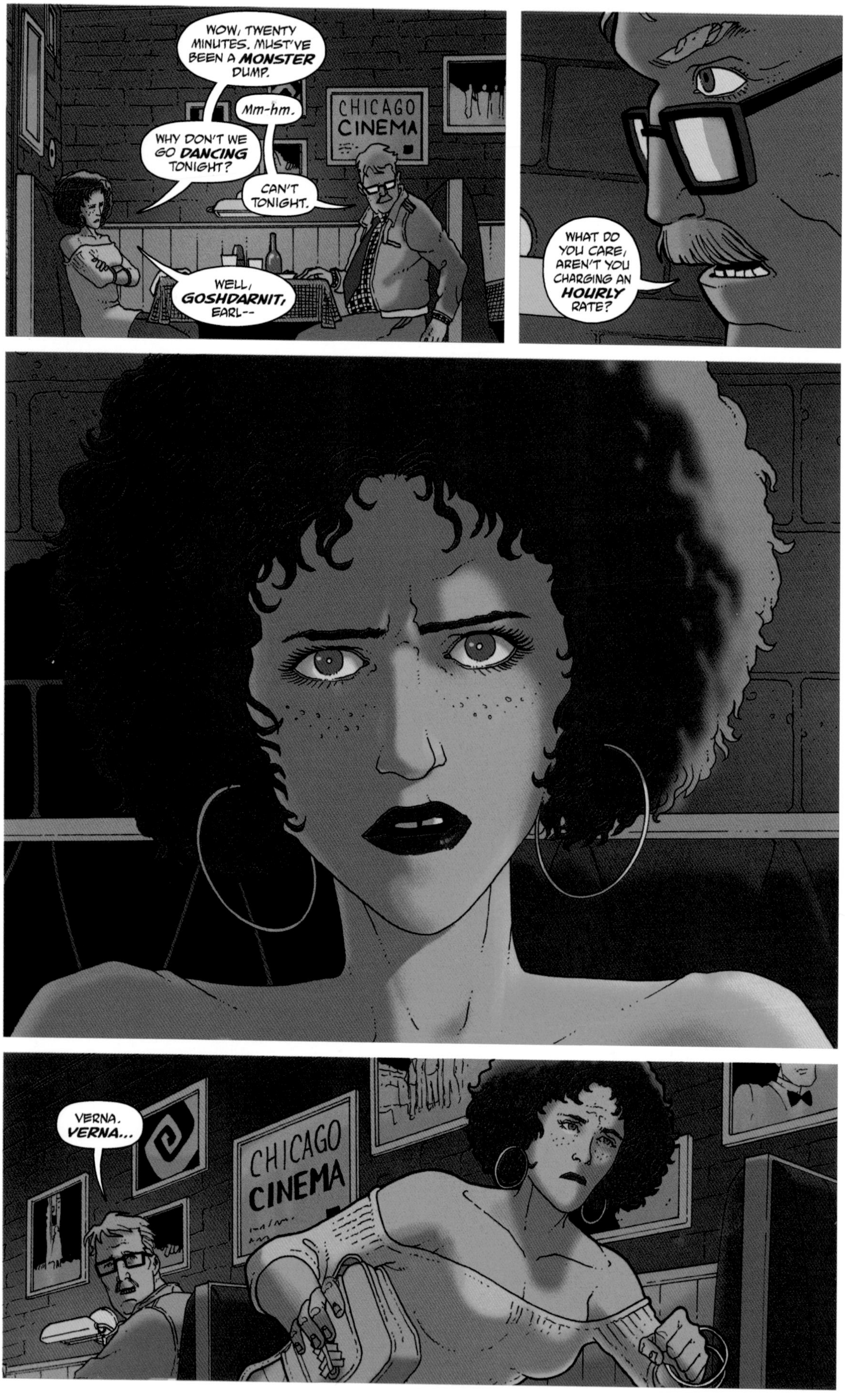
WOW, TWENTY MINUTES. MUST'VE BEEN A **MONSTER** DUMP.
Mm-hm.
WHY DON'T WE GO **DANCING** TONIGHT?
CAN'T TONIGHT.
WELL, **GOSHDARNIT,** EARL--
CHICAGO CINEMA
WHAT DO YOU CARE, AREN'T YOU CHARGING AN **HOURLY** RATE?
VERNA. **VERNA...**
CHICAGO CINEMA

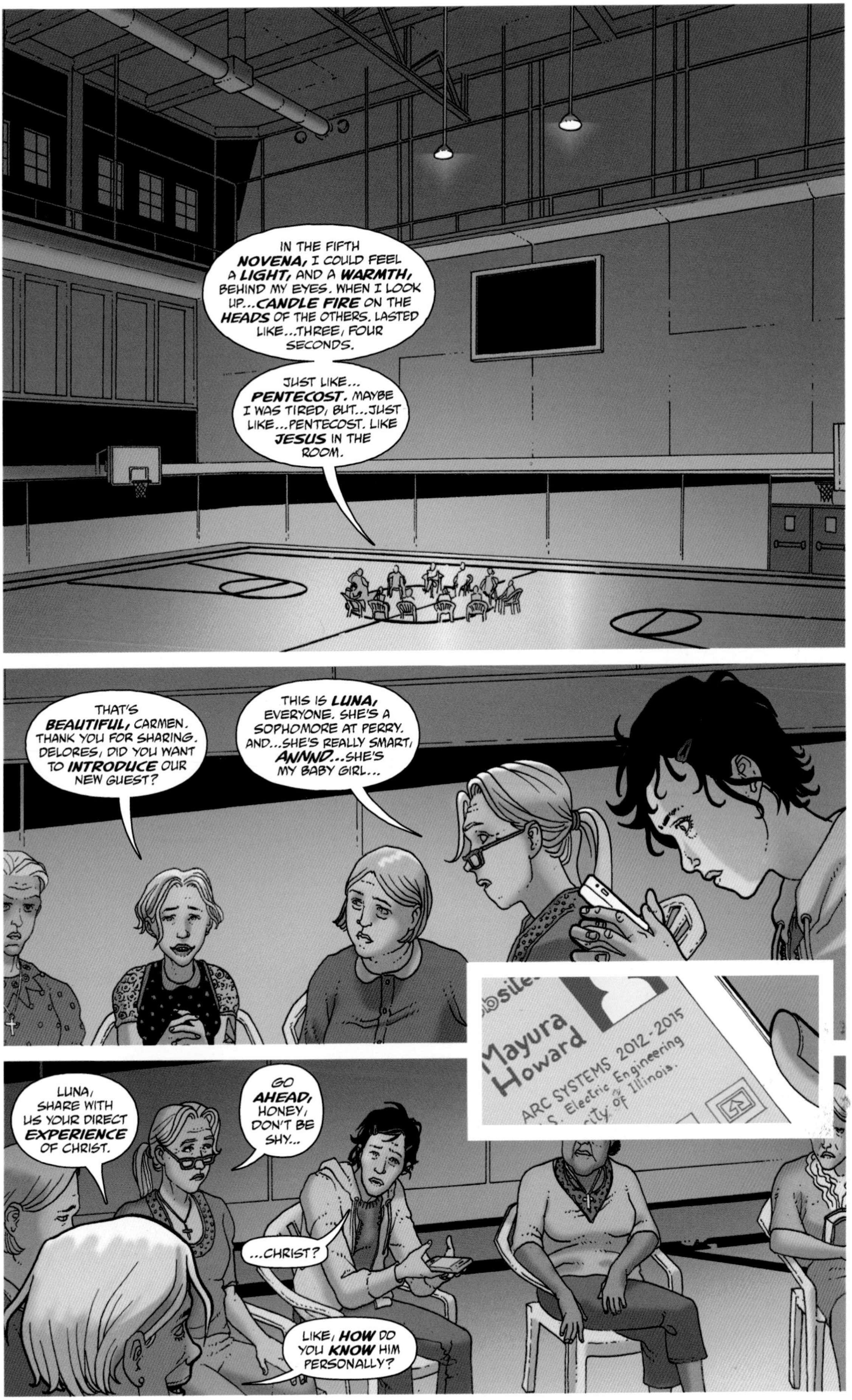
IN THE FIFTH NOVENA, I COULD FEEL A LIGHT, AND A WARMTH, BEHIND MY EYES. WHEN I LOOK UP...CANDLE FIRE ON THE HEADS OF THE OTHERS. LASTED LIKE...THREE, FOUR SECONDS.
JUST LIKE... PENTECOST. MAYBE I WAS TIRED, BUT...JUST LIKE...PENTECOST. LIKE JESUS IN THE ROOM.
THAT'S BEAUTIFUL, CARMEN. THANK YOU FOR SHARING. DELORES, DID YOU WANT TO INTRODUCE OUR NEW GUEST?
THIS IS LUNA, EVERYONE. SHE'S A SOPHOMORE AT PERRY. AND...SHE'S REALLY SMART, ANNND...SHE'S MY BABY GIRL...
Mayura Howard
ARC SYSTEMS 2012 - 2015
Electric Engineering
LUNA, SHARE WITH US YOUR DIRECT EXPERIENCE OF CHRIST.
GO AHEAD, HONEY, DON'T BE SHY...
...CHRIST?
LIKE, HOW DO YOU KNOW HIM PERSONALLY?

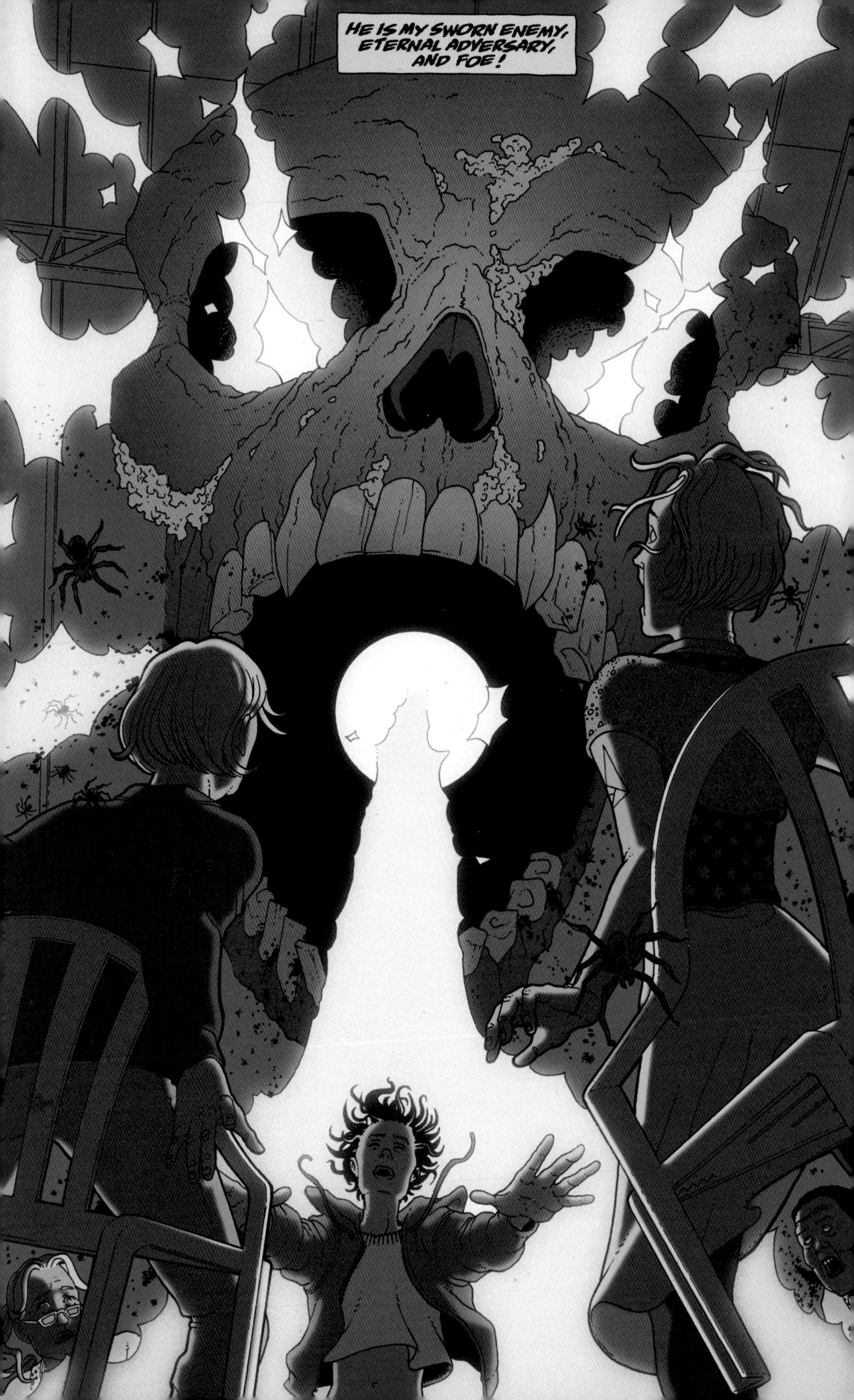
HE IS MY SWORN ENEMY, ETERNAL ADVERSARY, AND FOE!

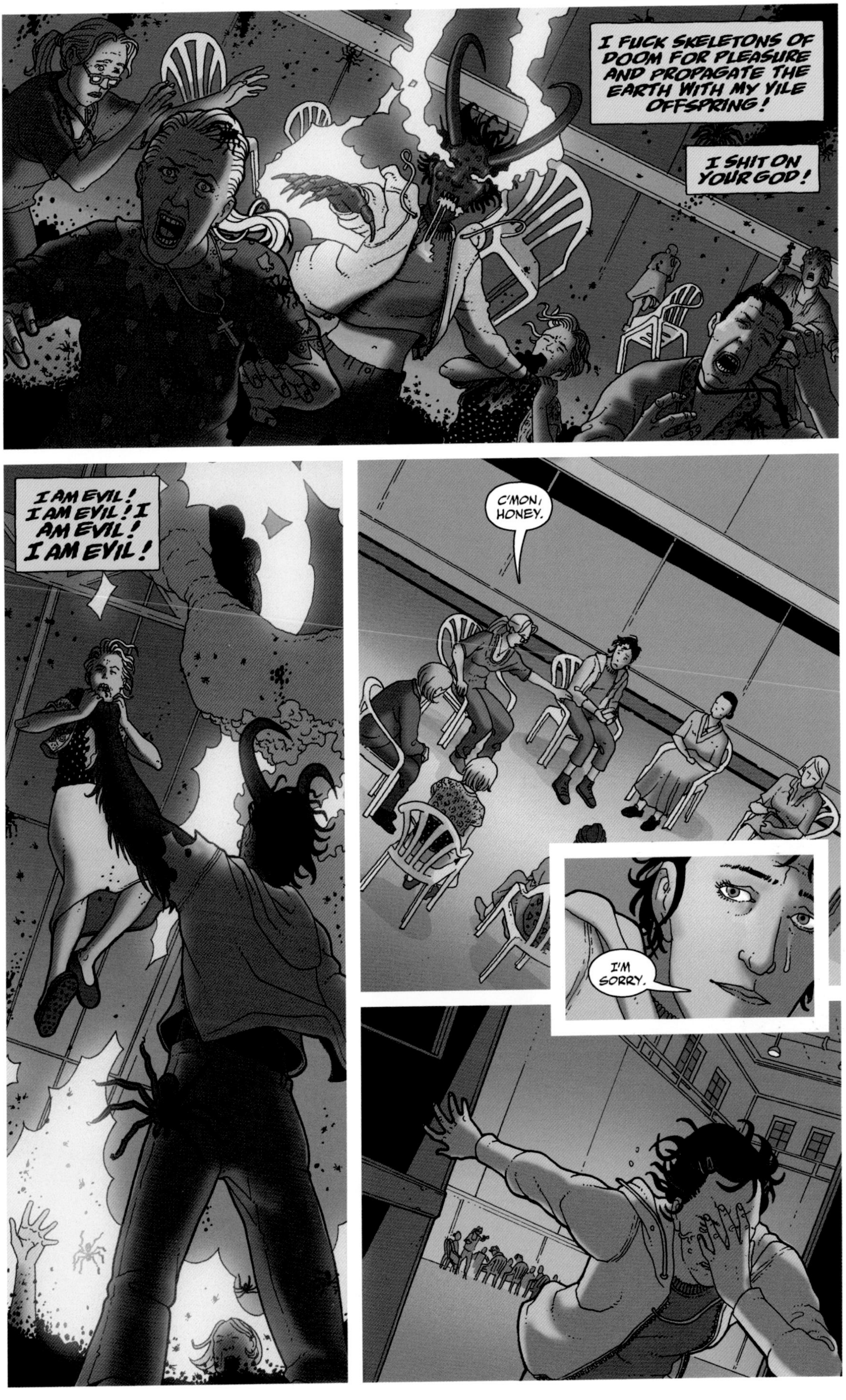
I FUCK SKELETONS OF DOOM FOR PLEASURE AND PROPAGATE THE EARTH WITH MY VILE OFFSPRING!
I SHIT ON YOUR GOD!
I AM EVIL! I AM EVIL! I AM EVIL! I AM EVIL!
C'MON, HONEY.
I'M SORRY.

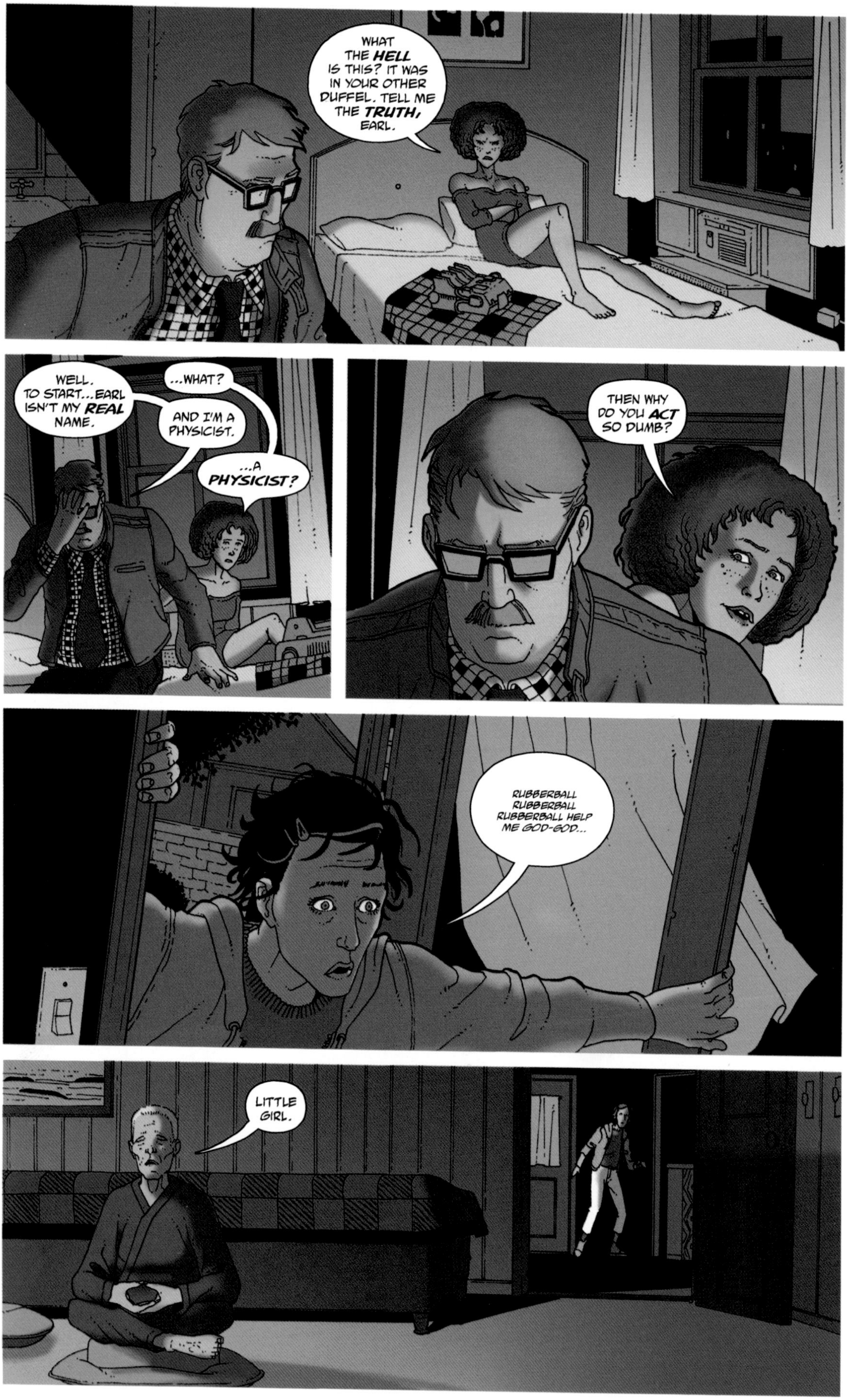
WHAT THE HELL IS THIS? IT WAS IN YOUR OTHER DUFFEL. TELL ME THE TRUTH, EARL.
WELL. TO START... EARL ISN'T MY REAL NAME.
...WHAT?
AND I'M A PHYSICIST.
...A PHYSICIST?
THEN WHY DO YOU ACT SO DUMB?
RUBBERBALL RUBBERBALL RUBBERBALL HELP ME GOD-GOD...
LITTLE GIRL.

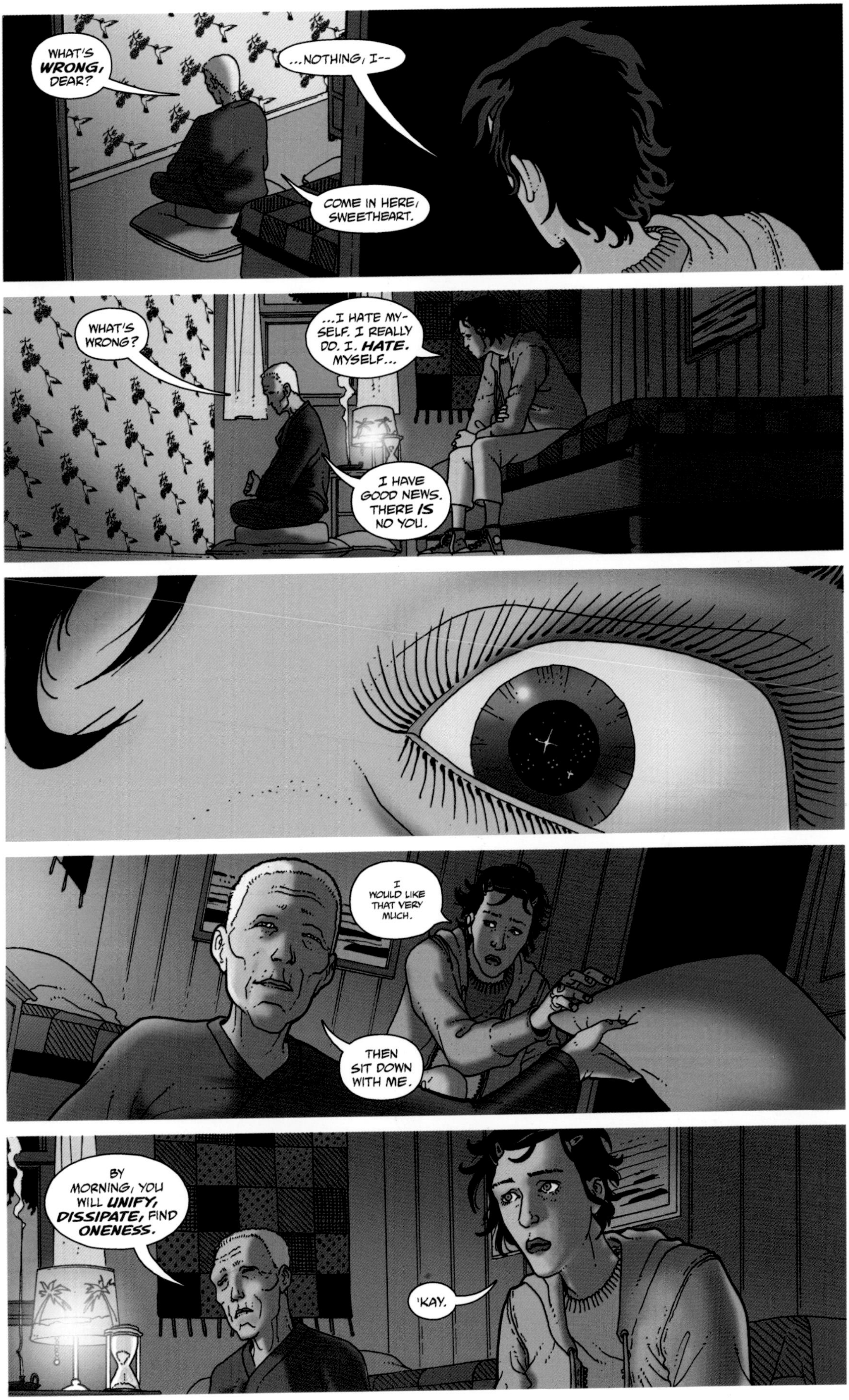
WHAT'S WRONG, DEAR?
...NOTHING, I--
COME IN HERE, SWEETHEART.
WHAT'S WRONG?
...I HATE MY-SELF. I REALLY DO. I. HATE. MYSELF...
I HAVE GOOD NEWS. THERE IS NO YOU.
I WOULD LIKE THAT VERY MUCH.
THEN SIT DOWN WITH ME.
BY MORNING, YOU WILL UNIFY, DISSIPATE, FIND ONENESS.
'KAY.

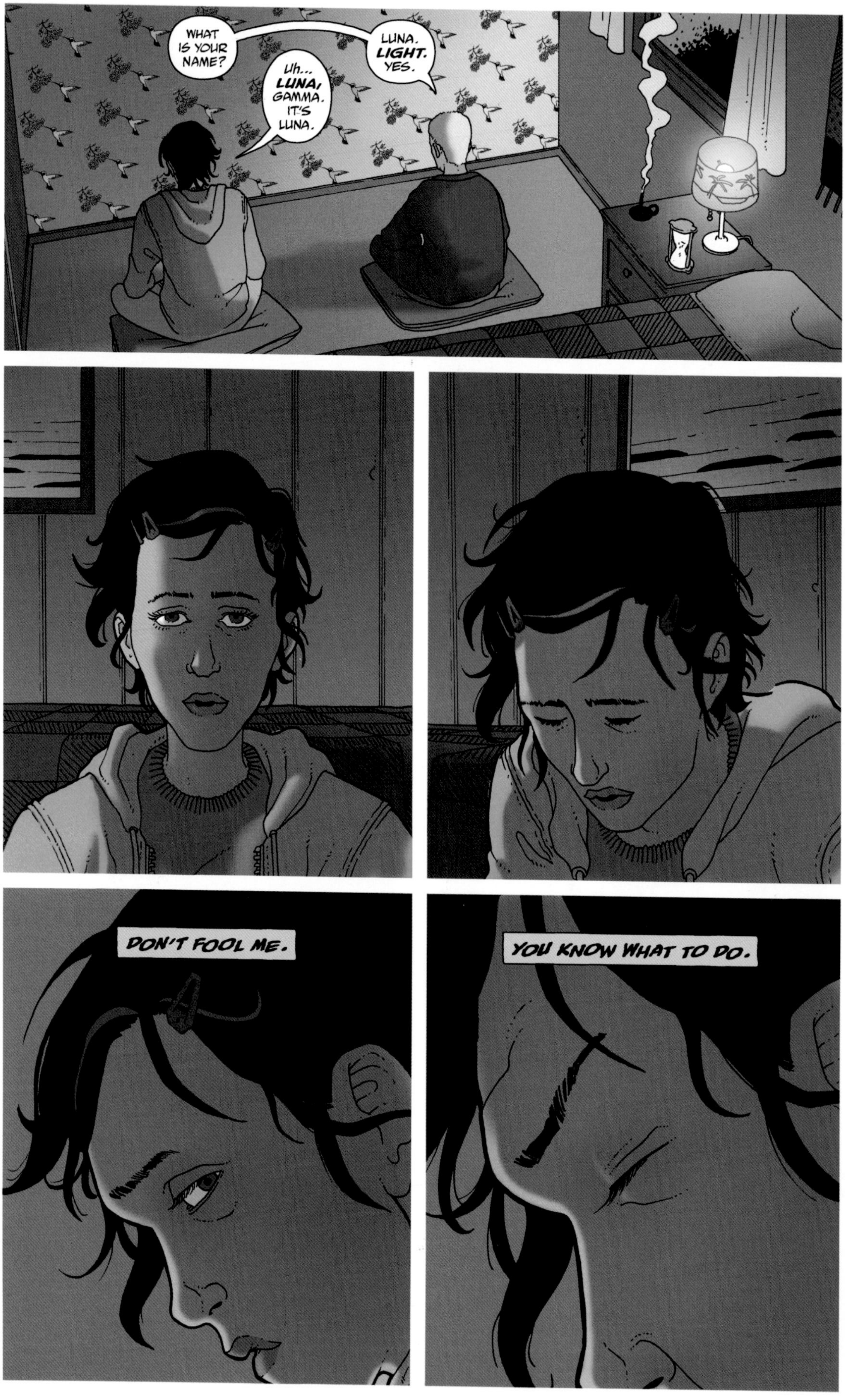
WHAT IS YOUR NAME?
Uh... LUNA, GAMMA. IT'S LUNA.
LUNA. LIGHT. YES.
DON'T FOOL ME.
YOU KNOW WHAT TO DO.

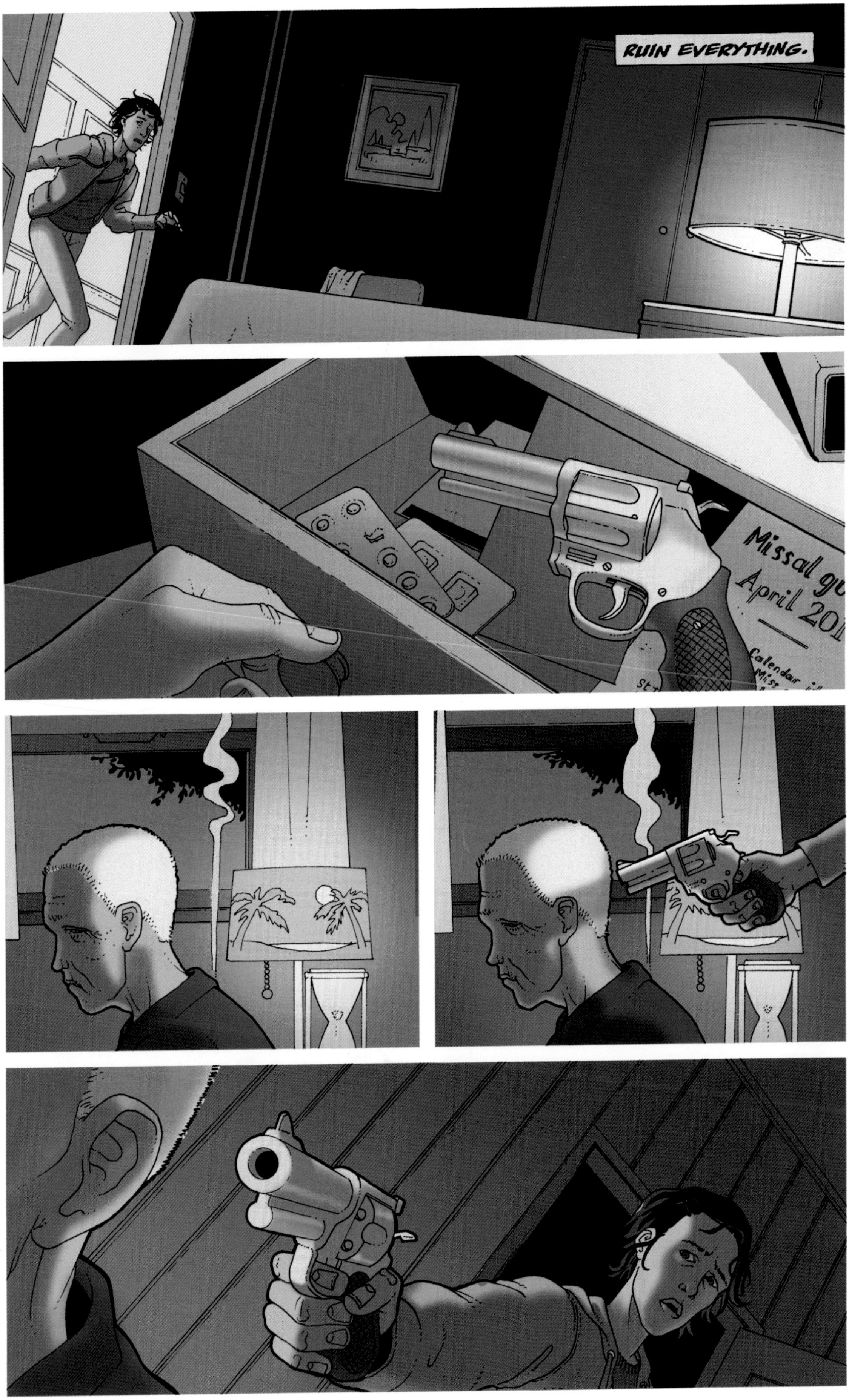
RUIN EVERYTHING.

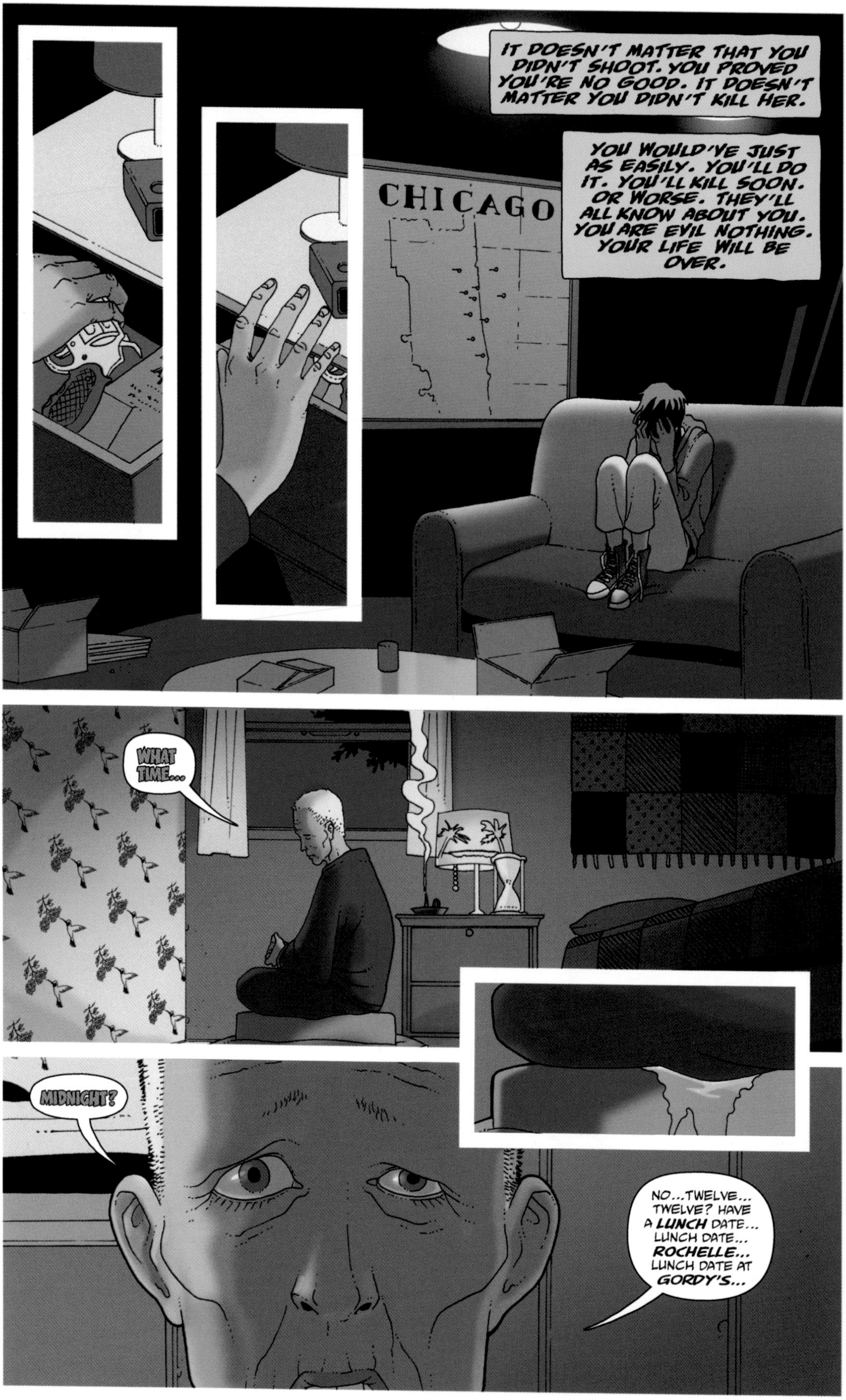
IT DOESN'T MATTER THAT YOU DIDN'T SHOOT. YOU PROVED YOU'RE NO GOOD. IT DOESN'T MATTER YOU DIDN'T KILL HER.
YOU WOULD'VE JUST AS EASILY. YOU'LL DO IT. YOU'LL KILL SOON. OR WORSE. THEY'LL ALL KNOW ABOUT YOU. YOU ARE EVIL NOTHING. YOUR LIFE WILL BE OVER.
CHICAGO
WHAT TIME...
MIDNIGHT?
NO...TWELVE... TWELVE? HAVE A LUNCH DATE... LUNCH DATE... ROCHELLE... LUNCH DATE AT GORDY'S...

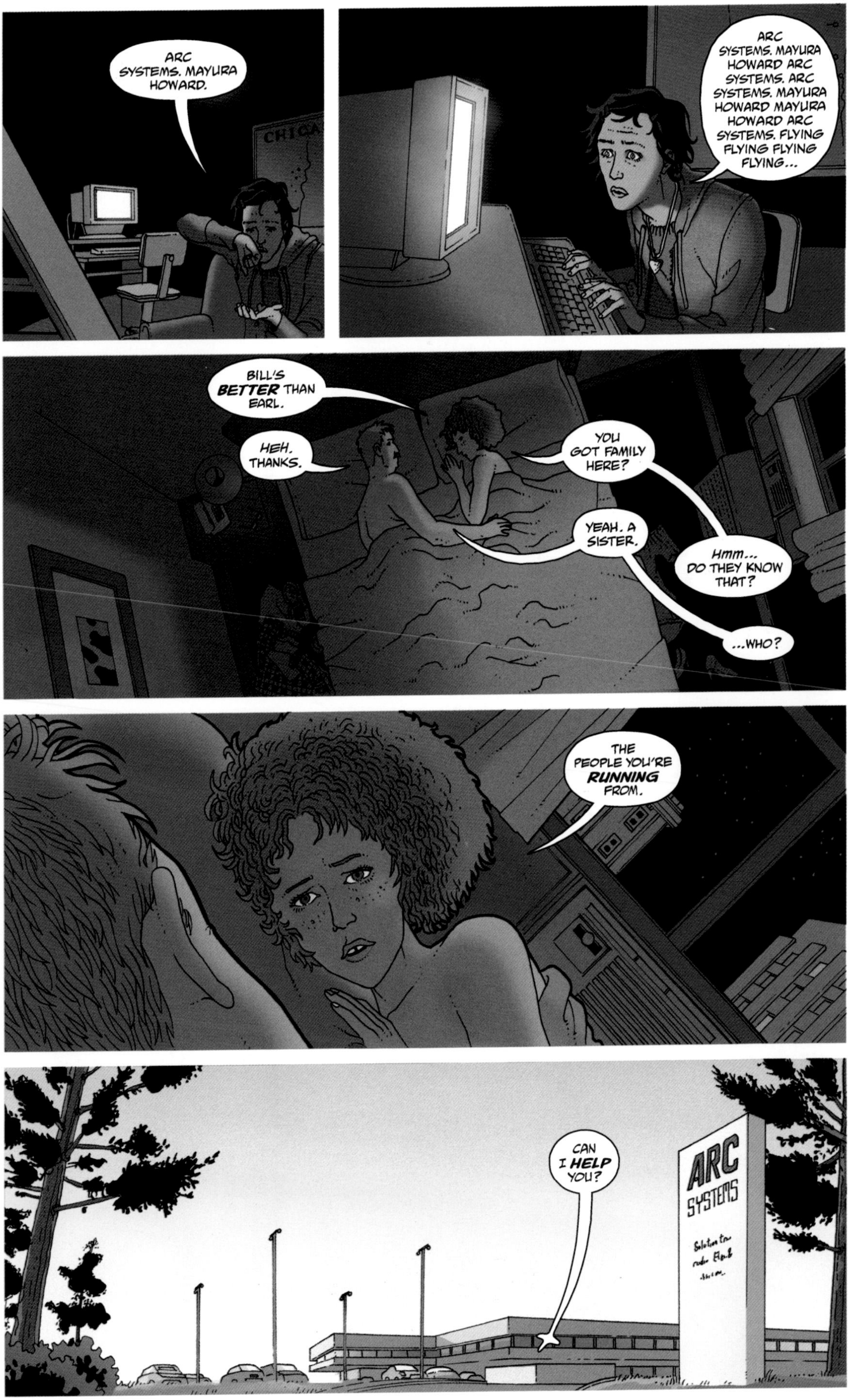
ARC SYSTEMS. MAYURA HOWARD.
ARC SYSTEMS. MAYURA HOWARD ARC SYSTEMS. ARC SYSTEMS. MAYURA HOWARD MAYURA HOWARD ARC SYSTEMS. FLYING FLYING FLYING FLYING...
BILL'S **BETTER** THAN EARL.
HEH. THANKS.
YOU GOT FAMILY HERE?
YEAH. A SISTER.
Hmm... DO THEY KNOW THAT?
...WHO?
THE PEOPLE YOU'RE **RUNNING** FROM.
CAN I **HELP** YOU?
ARC SYSTEMS

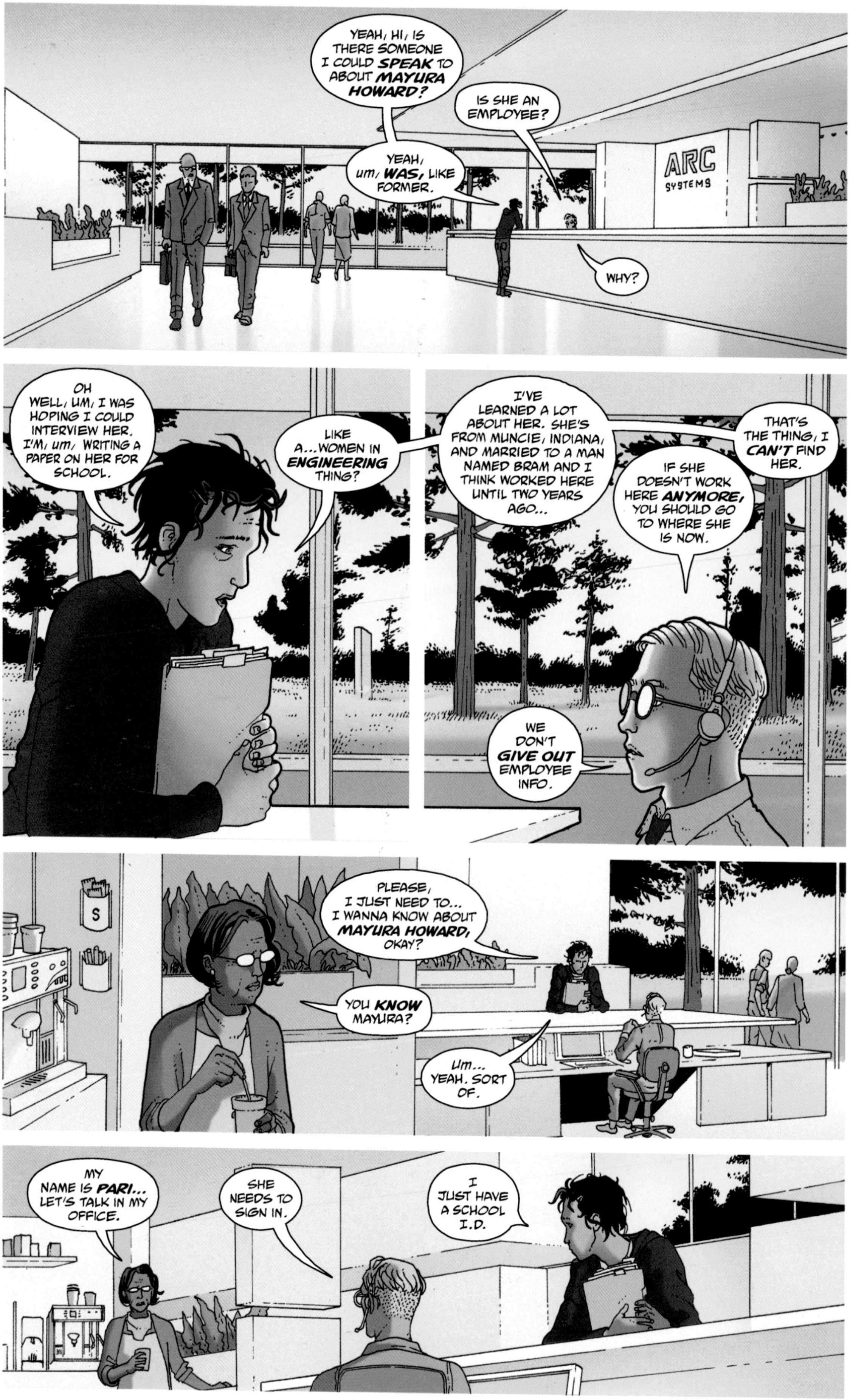
YEAH, HI, IS THERE SOMEONE I COULD SPEAK TO ABOUT MAYURA HOWARD?
IS SHE AN EMPLOYEE?
YEAH, um, WAS, LIKE FORMER.
WHY?
OH WELL, UM, I WAS HOPING I COULD INTERVIEW HER. I'M, um, WRITING A PAPER ON HER FOR SCHOOL.
LIKE A...WOMEN IN ENGINEERING THING?
I'VE LEARNED A LOT ABOUT HER. SHE'S FROM MUNCIE, INDIANA, AND MARRIED TO A MAN NAMED BRAM AND I THINK WORKED HERE UNTIL TWO YEARS AGO...
THAT'S THE THING, I CAN'T FIND HER.
IF SHE DOESN'T WORK HERE ANYMORE, YOU SHOULD GO TO WHERE SHE IS NOW.
WE DON'T GIVE OUT EMPLOYEE INFO.
ARC SYSTEMS
PLEASE, I JUST NEED TO... I WANNA KNOW ABOUT MAYURA HOWARD, OKAY?
YOU KNOW MAYURA?
Um... YEAH. SORT OF.
MY NAME IS PARI... LET'S TALK IN MY OFFICE.
SHE NEEDS TO SIGN IN.
I JUST HAVE A SCHOOL I.D.

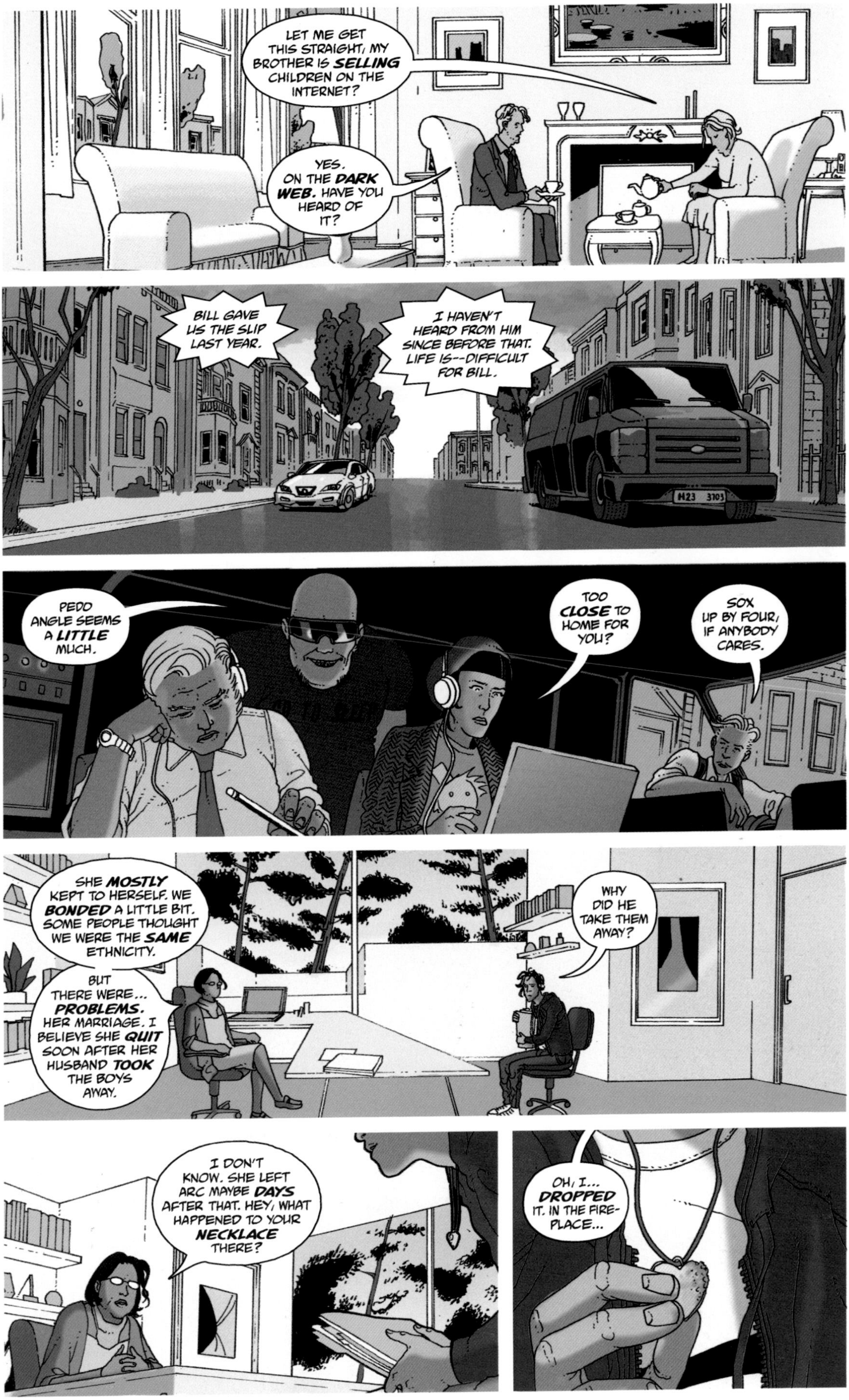

LET ME GET THIS STRAIGHT, MY BROTHER IS SELLING CHILDREN ON THE INTERNET?
YES. ON THE DARK WEB. HAVE YOU HEARD OF IT?
BILL GAVE US THE SLIP LAST YEAR.
I HAVEN'T HEARD FROM HIM SINCE BEFORE THAT. LIFE IS--DIFFICULT FOR BILL.
H23 3103
PEDO ANGLE SEEMS A LITTLE MUCH.
TOO CLOSE TO HOME FOR YOU?
SOX UP BY FOUR, IF ANYBODY CARES.
SHE MOSTLY KEPT TO HERSELF. WE BONDED A LITTLE BIT. SOME PEOPLE THOUGHT WE WERE THE SAME ETHNICITY.
BUT THERE WERE... PROBLEMS. HER MARRIAGE. I BELIEVE SHE QUIT SOON AFTER HER HUSBAND TOOK THE BOYS AWAY.
WHY DID HE TAKE THEM AWAY?
I DON'T KNOW. SHE LEFT ARC MAYBE DAYS AFTER THAT. HEY, WHAT HAPPENED TO YOUR NECKLACE THERE?
OH, I... DROPPED IT. IN THE FIRE-PLACE...

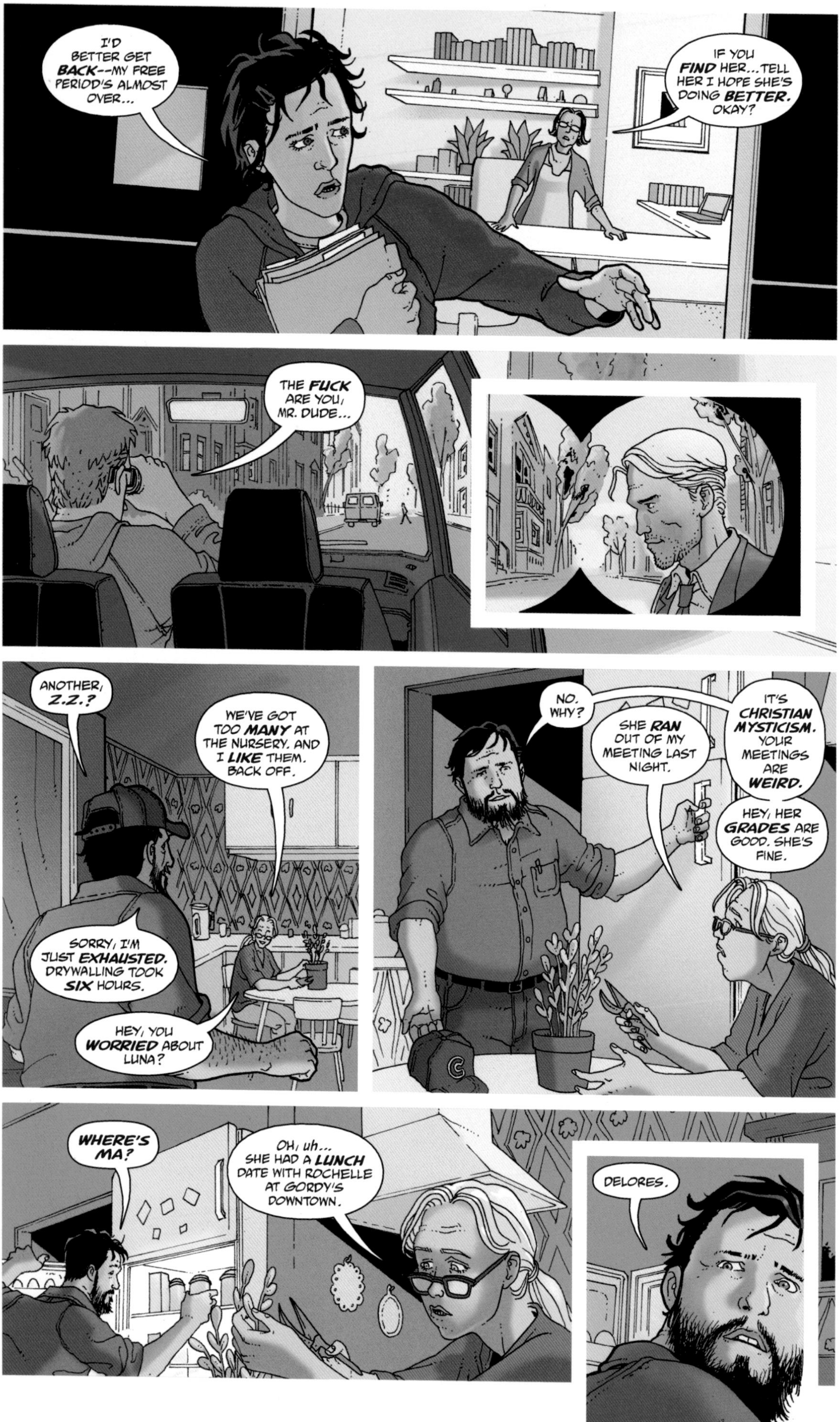
I'D BETTER GET BACK--MY FREE PERIOD'S ALMOST OVER...
IF YOU FIND HER...TELL HER I HOPE SHE'S DOING BETTER. OKAY?
THE FUCK ARE YOU, MR. DUDE...
ANOTHER, Z.Z.?
WE'VE GOT TOO MANY AT THE NURSERY. AND I LIKE THEM. BACK OFF.
SORRY, I'M JUST EXHAUSTED. DRYWALLING TOOK SIX HOURS.
HEY, YOU WORRIED ABOUT LUNA?
NO. WHY?
SHE RAN OUT OF MY MEETING LAST NIGHT.
IT'S CHRISTIAN MYSTICISM. YOUR MEETINGS ARE WEIRD.
HEY, HER GRADES ARE GOOD. SHE'S FINE.
WHERE'S MA?
OH, uh... SHE HAD A LUNCH DATE WITH ROCHELLE AT GORDY'S DOWNTOWN.
DELORES.

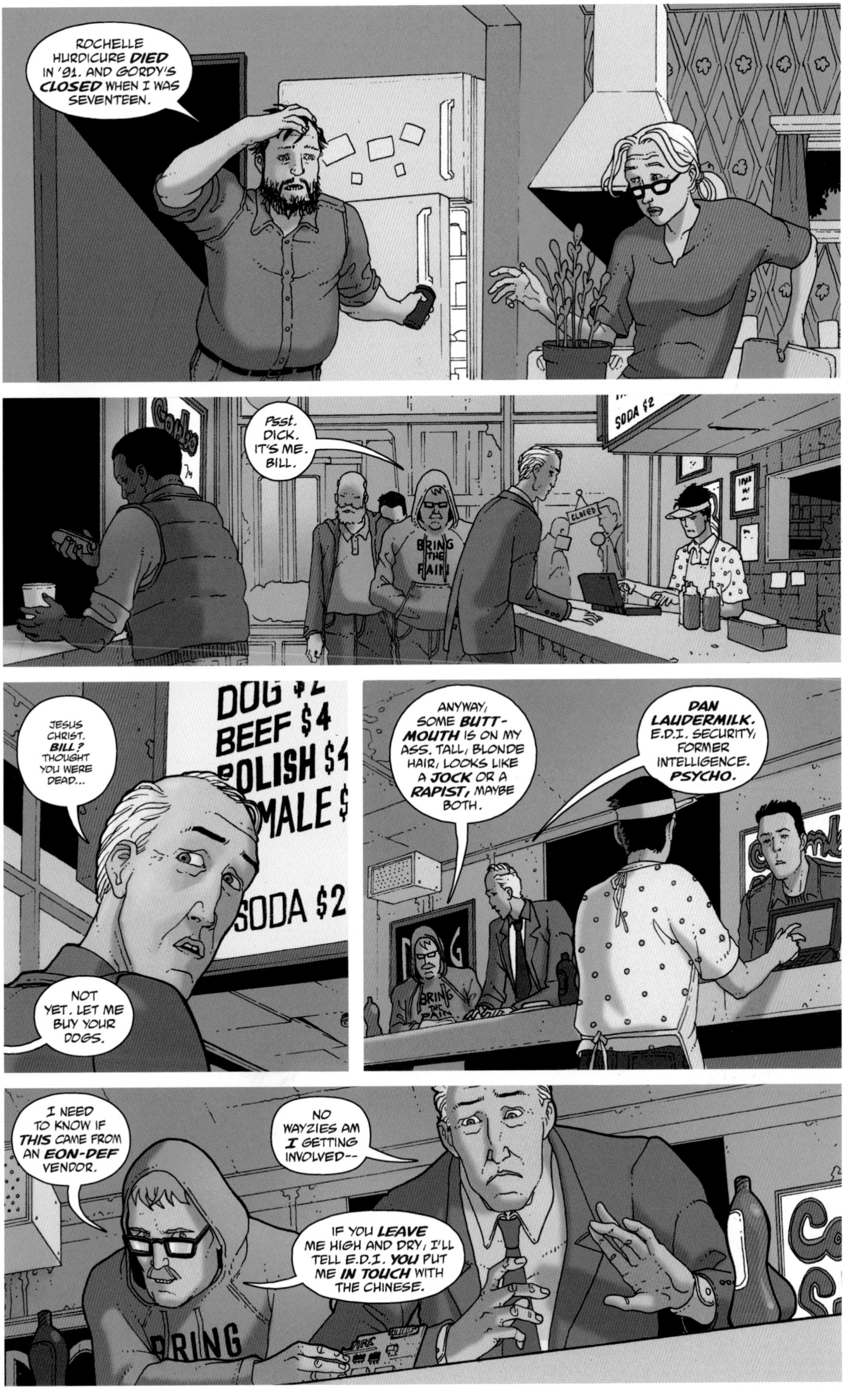
ROCHELLE HURDICURE DIED IN '91. AND GORDY'S CLOSED WHEN I WAS SEVENTEEN.
SODA $2
Psst. DICK. IT'S ME. BILL.
CLOSED
BRING THE PAIN
DOG $2
BEEF $4
POLISH $4
SODA $2
JESUS CHRIST. BILL? THOUGHT YOU WERE DEAD...
NOT YET. LET ME BUY YOUR DOGS.
ANYWAY, SOME BUTT-MOUTH IS ON MY ASS. TALL, BLONDE HAIR, LOOKS LIKE A JOCK OR A RAPIST, MAYBE BOTH.
DAN LAUDERMILK. E.D.I. SECURITY, FORMER INTELLIGENCE. PSYCHO.
I NEED TO KNOW IF THIS CAME FROM AN EON-DEF VENDOR.
NO WAYZIES AM I GETTING INVOLVED--
IF YOU LEAVE ME HIGH AND DRY, I'LL TELL E.D.I. YOU PUT ME IN TOUCH WITH THE CHINESE.

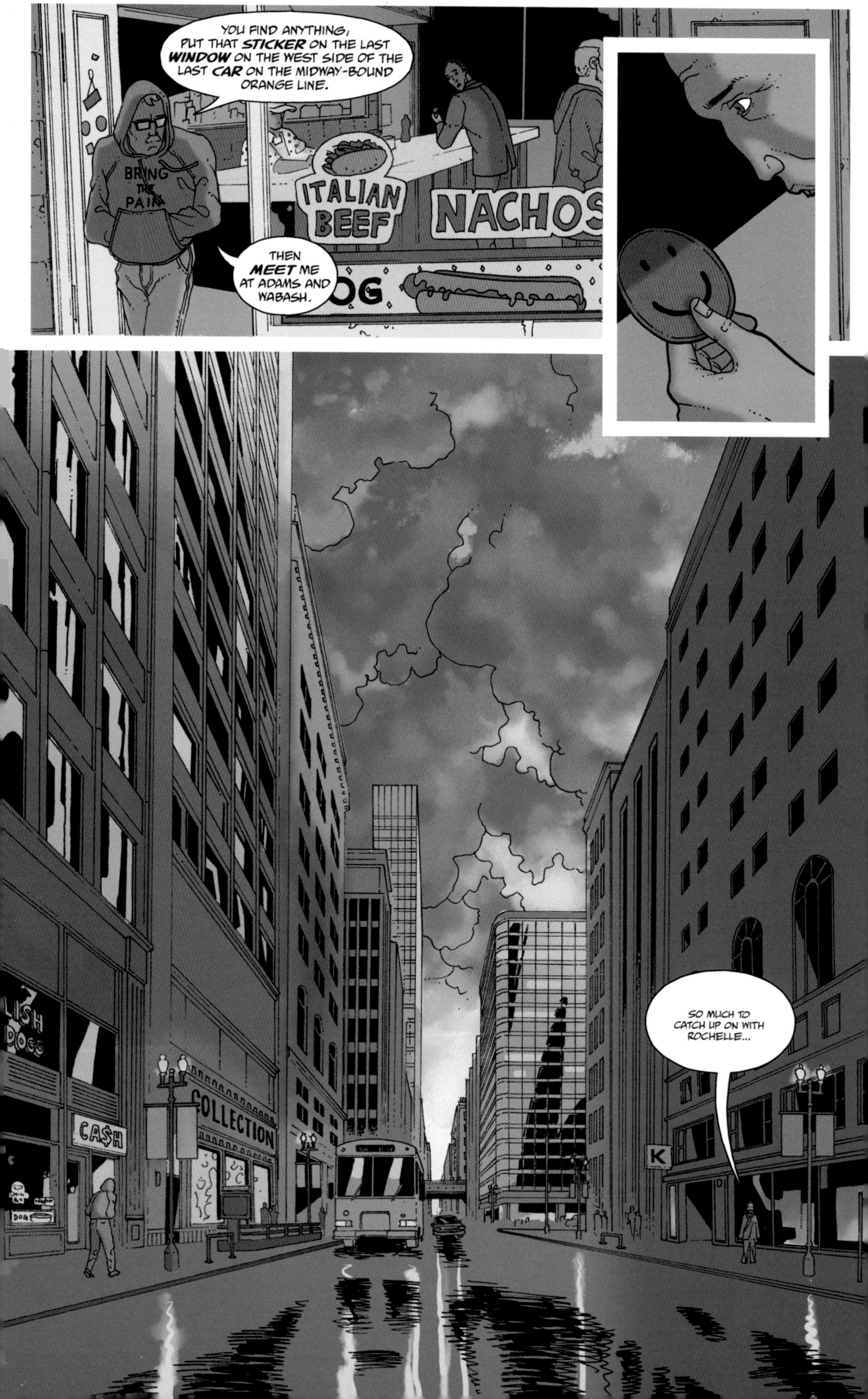
YOU FIND ANYTHING, PUT THAT STICKER ON THE LAST WINDOW ON THE WEST SIDE OF THE LAST CAR ON THE MIDWAY-BOUND ORANGE LINE.
BRING THE PAIN
ITALIAN BEEF
NACHOS
THEN MEET ME AT ADAMS AND WABASH.
CA$H
COLLECTION
K
SO MUCH TO CATCH UP ON WITH ROCHELLE...

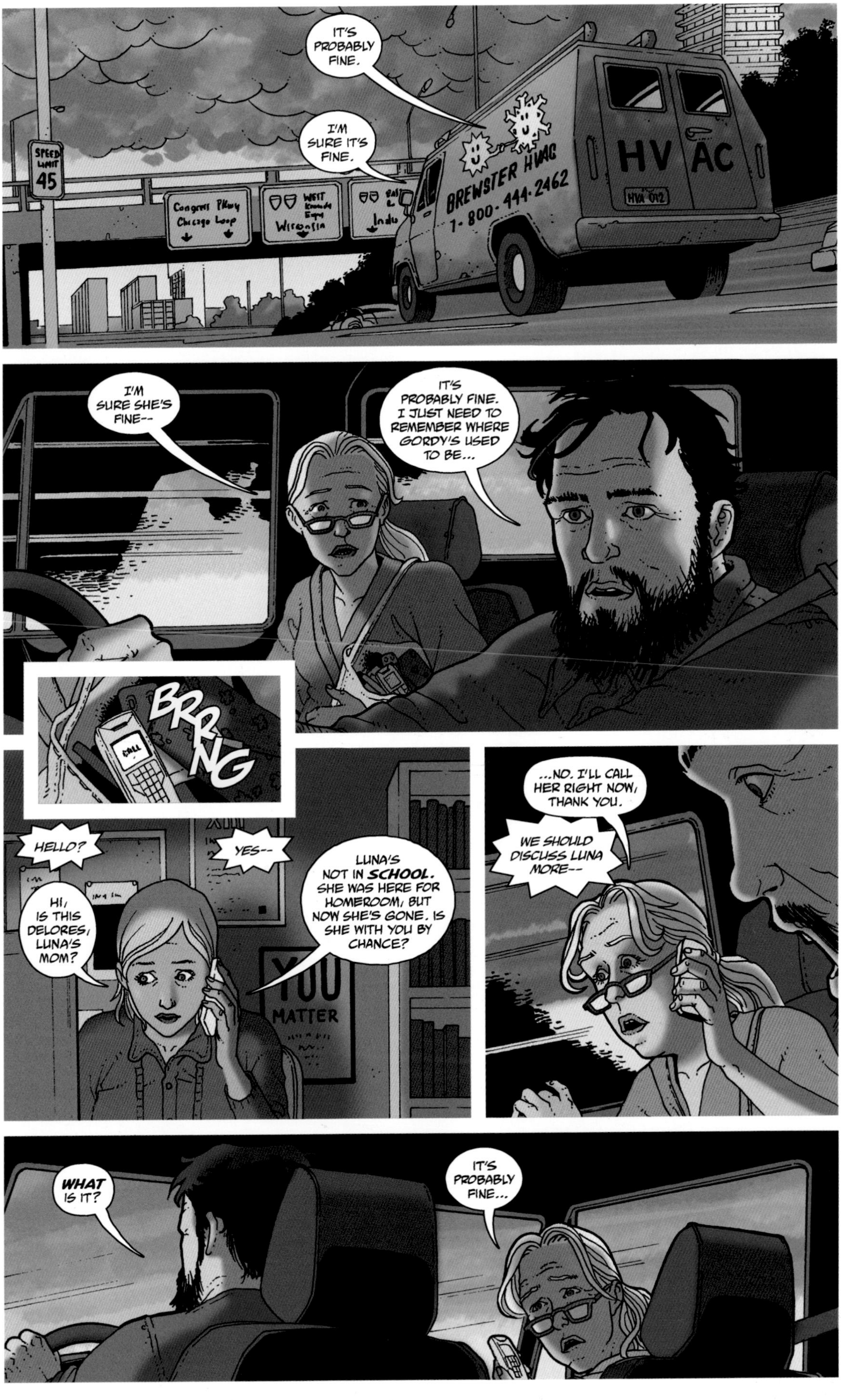
SPEED LIMIT 45
Congress Pkwy Chicago Loop
BREWSTER HVAC
1-800-444-2462
HV AC
IT'S PROBABLY FINE.
I'M SURE IT'S FINE.
I'M SURE SHE'S FINE--
IT'S PROBABLY FINE. I JUST NEED TO REMEMBER WHERE GORDY'S USED TO BE...
BRRRNG
HELLO?
HI, IS THIS DELORES, LUNA'S MOM?
YES--
LUNA'S NOT IN SCHOOL. SHE WAS HERE FOR HOMEROOM, BUT NOW SHE'S GONE. IS SHE WITH YOU BY CHANCE?
YOU MATTER
...NO. I'LL CALL HER RIGHT NOW, THANK YOU.
WE SHOULD DISCUSS LUNA MORE--
WHAT IS IT?
IT'S PROBABLY FINE...

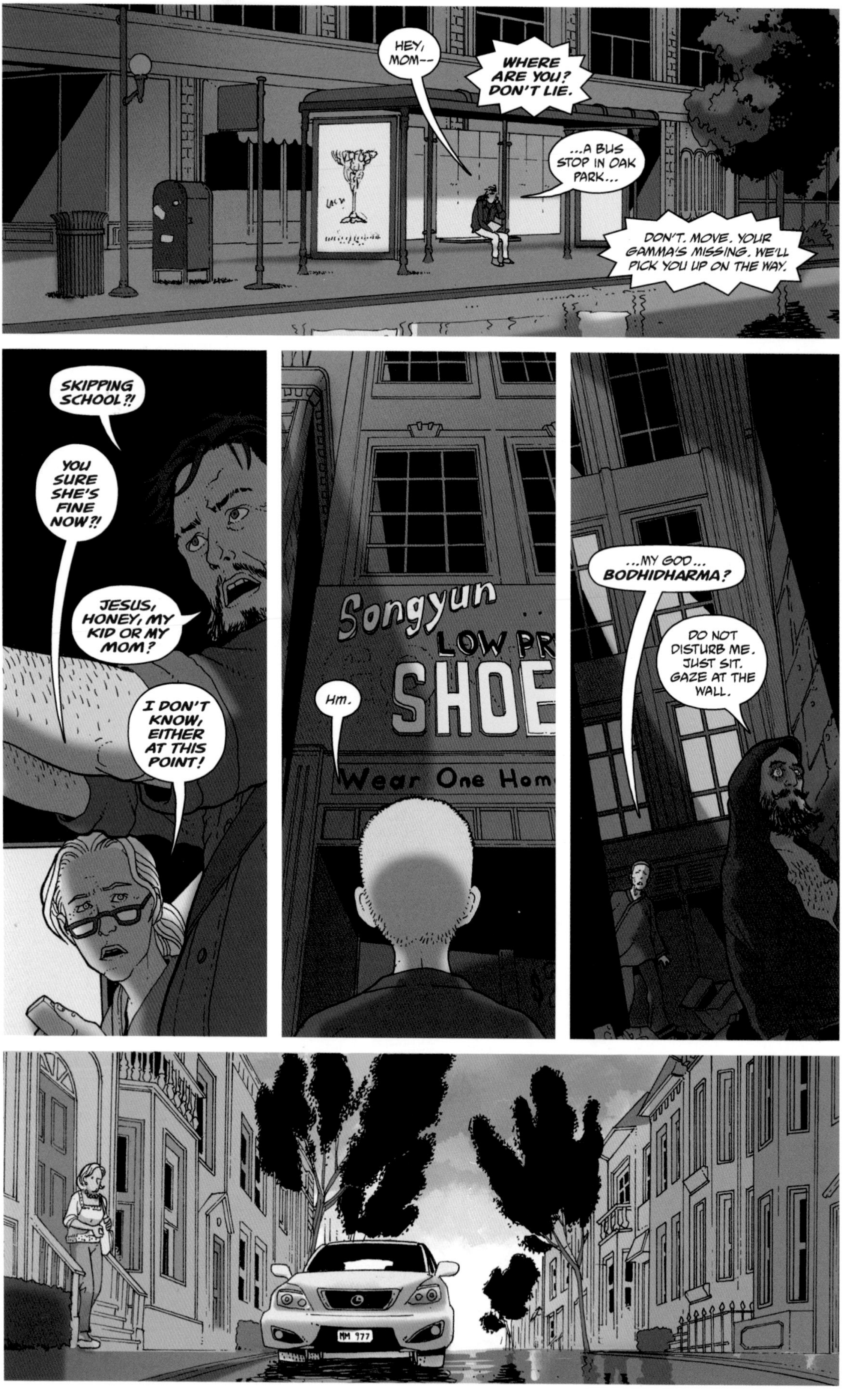
HEY, MOM--
WHERE ARE YOU? DON'T LIE.
...A BUS STOP IN OAK PARK...
DON'T. MOVE. YOUR GAMMA'S MISSING. WE'LL PICK YOU UP ON THE WAY.
SKIPPING SCHOOL?!
YOU SURE SHE'S FINE NOW?!
JESUS, HONEY, MY KID OR MY MOM?
I DON'T KNOW, EITHER AT THIS POINT!
Songyun
LOW PR
SHOE
Wear One Hom
Hm.
...MY GOD... BODHIDHARMA?
DO NOT DISTURB ME. JUST SIT. GAZE AT THE WALL.
MM 977

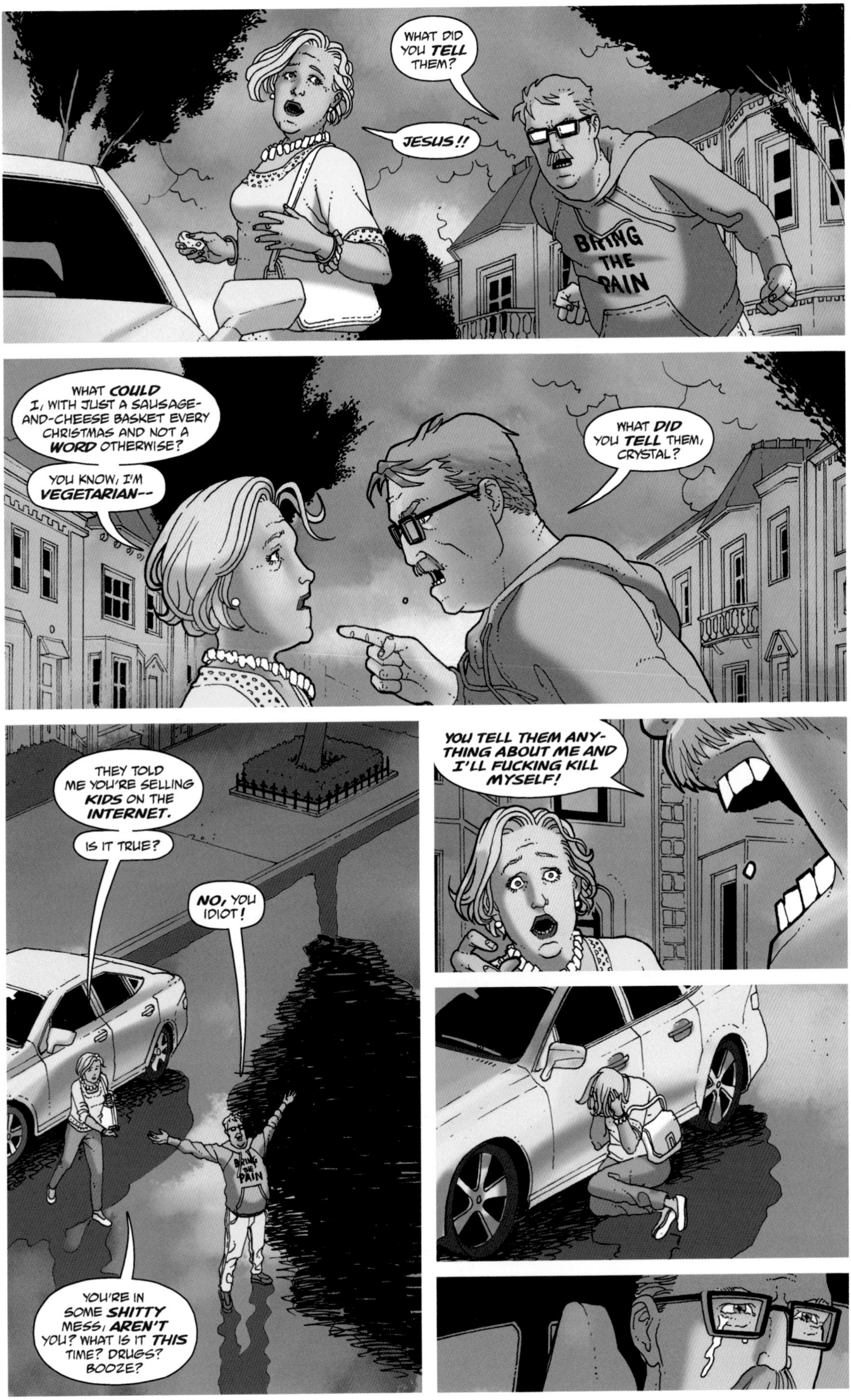
WHAT DID YOU TELL THEM?
JESUS!!
BRING THE PAIN
WHAT COULD I, WITH JUST A SAUSAGE-AND-CHEESE BASKET EVERY CHRISTMAS AND NOT A WORD OTHERWISE?
YOU KNOW, I'M VEGETARIAN--
WHAT DID YOU TELL THEM, CRYSTAL?
THEY TOLD ME YOU'RE SELLING KIDS ON THE INTERNET.
IS IT TRUE?
NO, YOU IDIOT!
YOU'RE IN SOME SHITTY MESS, AREN'T YOU? WHAT IS IT THIS TIME? DRUGS? BOOZE?
YOU TELL THEM ANYTHING ABOUT ME AND I'LL FUCKING KILL MYSELF!

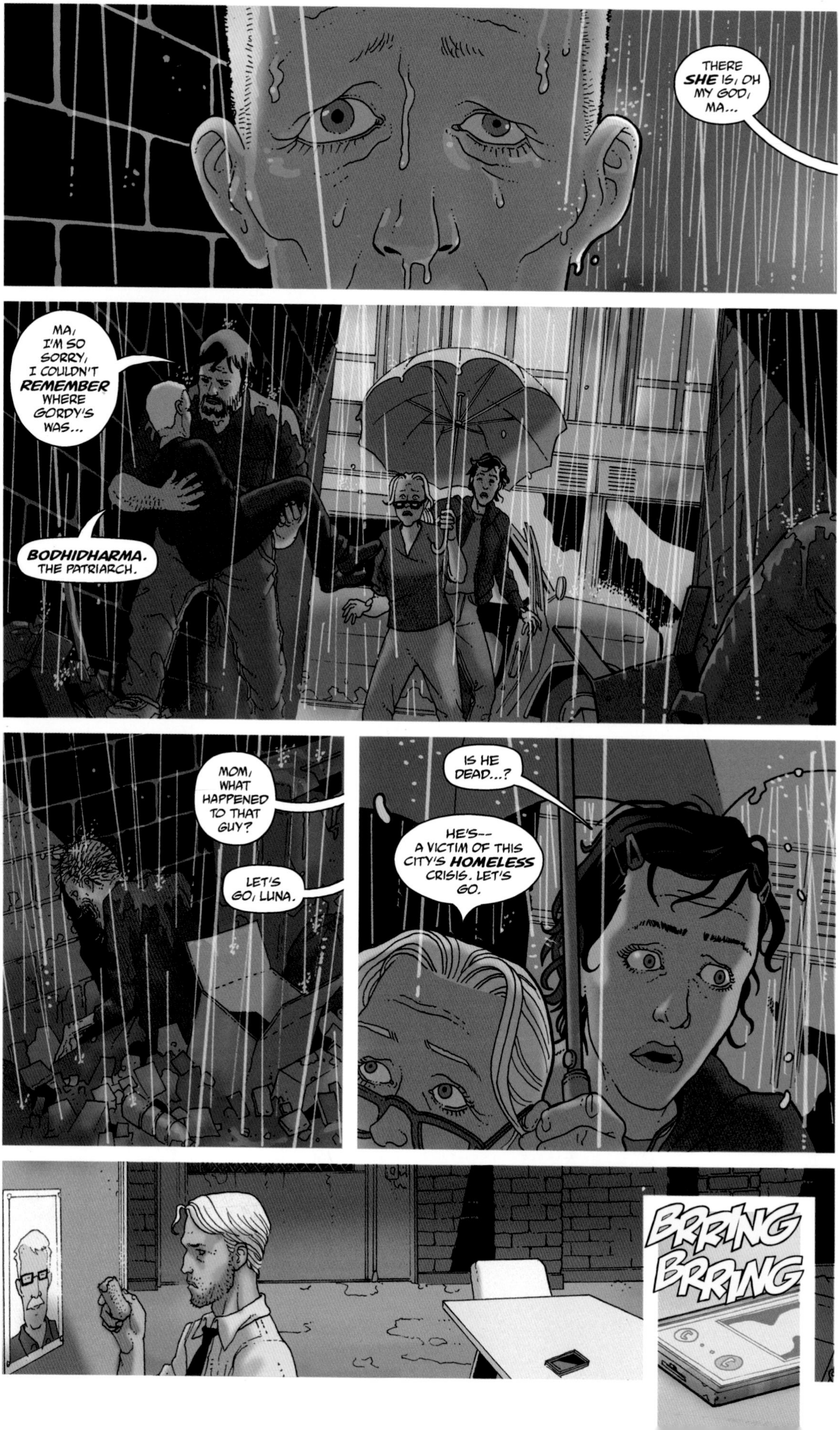
THERE SHE IS, OH MY GOD, MA...
MA, I'M SO SORRY, I COULDN'T REMEMBER WHERE GORDY'S WAS...
BODHIDHARMA. THE PATRIARCH.
MOM, WHAT HAPPENED TO THAT GUY?
LET'S GO, LUNA.
IS HE DEAD...?
HE'S-- A VICTIM OF THIS CITY'S HOMELESS CRISIS. LET'S GO.
BRRING BRRING

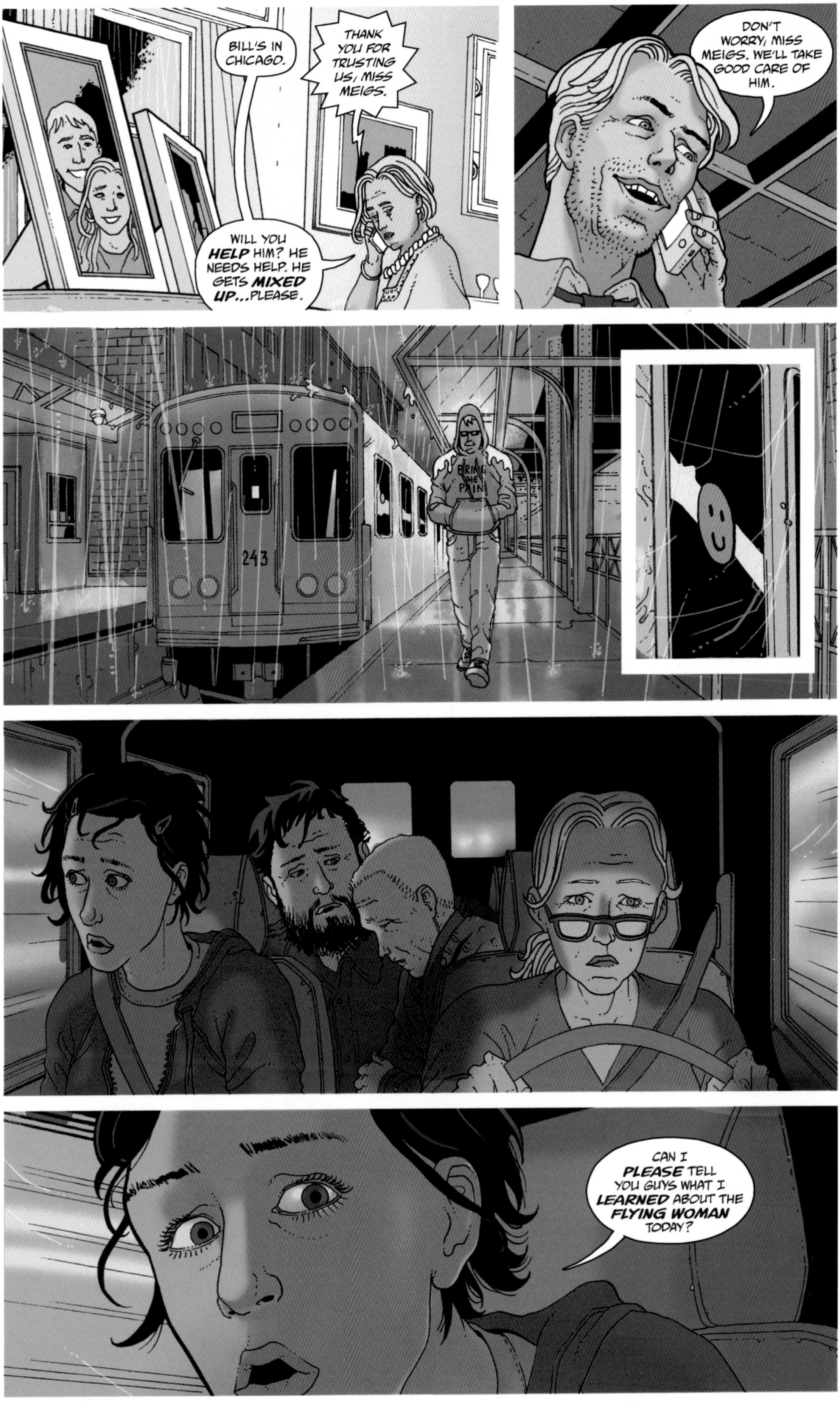
BILL'S IN CHICAGO.
THANK YOU FOR TRUSTING US, MISS MEIGS.
WILL YOU HELP HIM? HE NEEDS HELP. HE GETS MIXED UP... PLEASE.
DON'T WORRY, MISS MEIGS. WE'LL TAKE GOOD CARE OF HIM.
243
CAN I PLEASE TELL YOU GUYS WHAT I LEARNED ABOUT THE FLYING WOMAN TODAY?

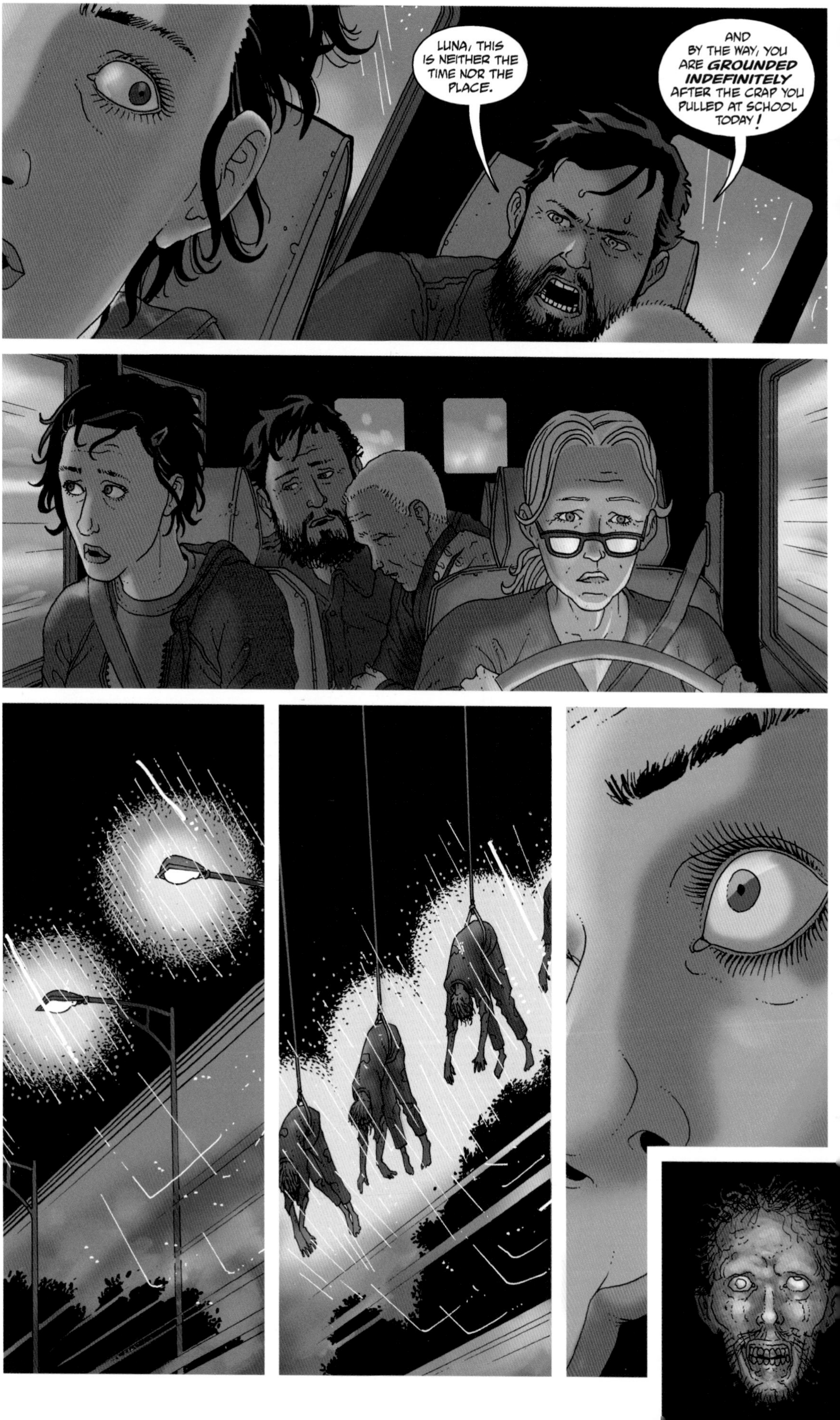
LUNA, THIS IS NEITHER THE TIME NOR THE PLACE.
AND BY THE WAY, YOU ARE GROUNDED INDEFINITELY AFTER THE CRAP YOU PULLED AT SCHOOL TODAY!

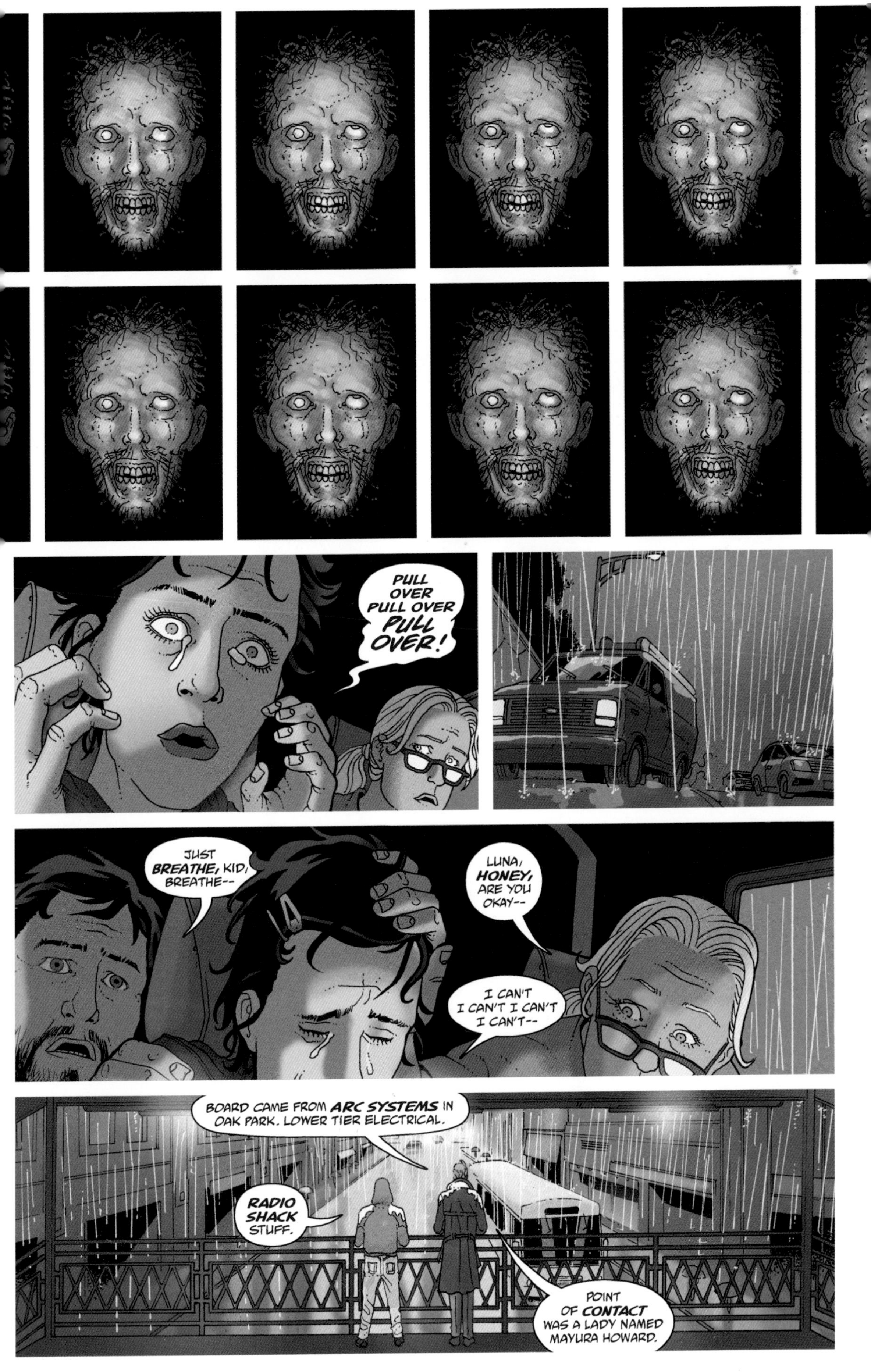
PULL OVER PULL OVER PULL OVER!
JUST BREATHE, KID, BREATHE--
LUNA, HONEY, ARE YOU OKAY--
I CAN'T I CAN'T I CAN'T I CAN'T--
BOARD CAME FROM ARC SYSTEMS IN OAK PARK. LOWER TIER ELECTRICAL.
RADIO SHACK STUFF.
POINT OF CONTACT WAS A LADY NAMED MAYURA HOWARD.

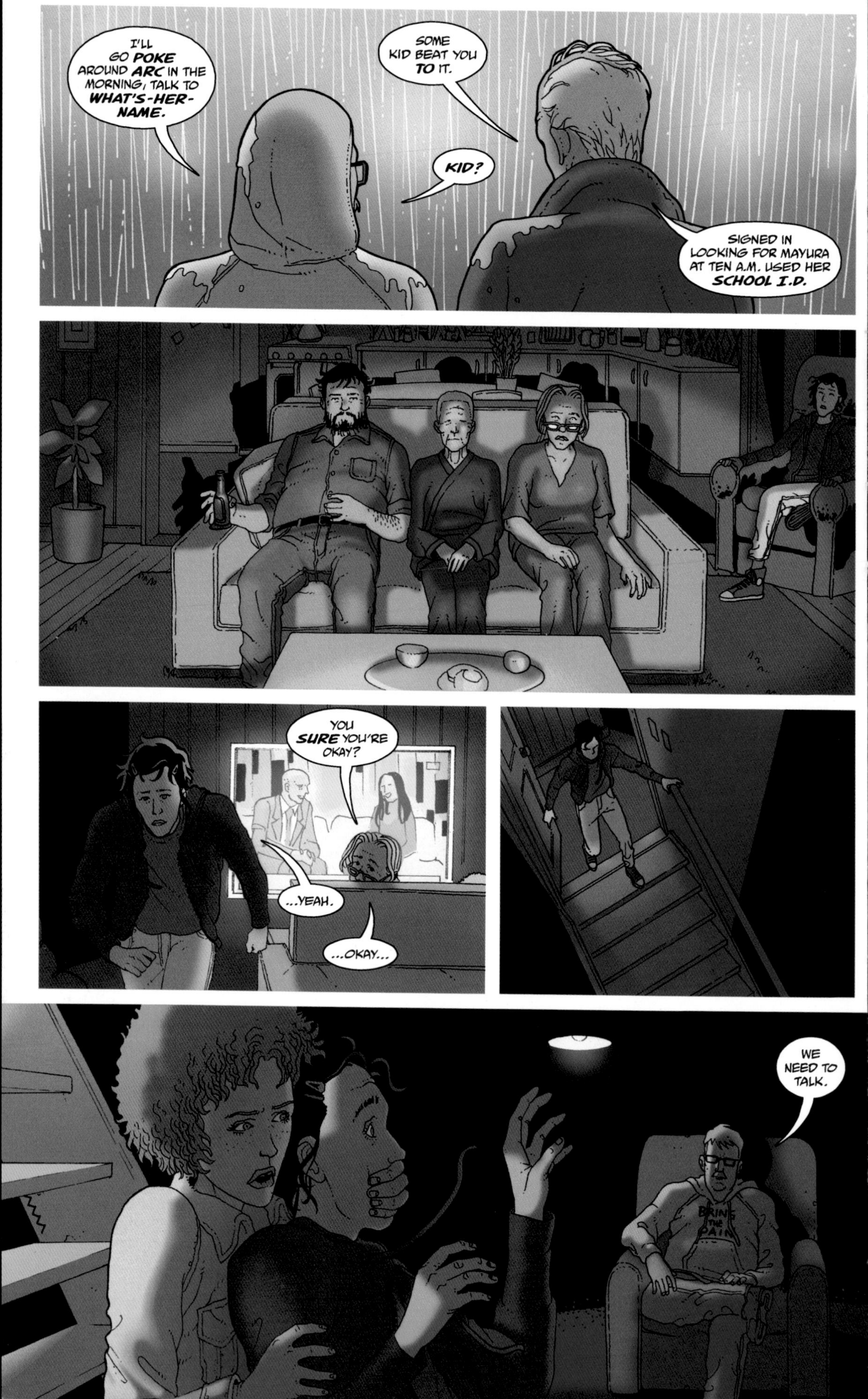
I'LL GO POKE AROUND ARC IN THE MORNING, TALK TO WHAT'S-HER-NAME.
SOME KID BEAT YOU TO IT.
KID?
SIGNED IN LOOKING FOR MAYURA AT TEN A.M. USED HER SCHOOL I.D.
YOU SURE YOU'RE OKAY?
...YEAH.
...OKAY...
WE NEED TO TALK.
BRING THE PAIN

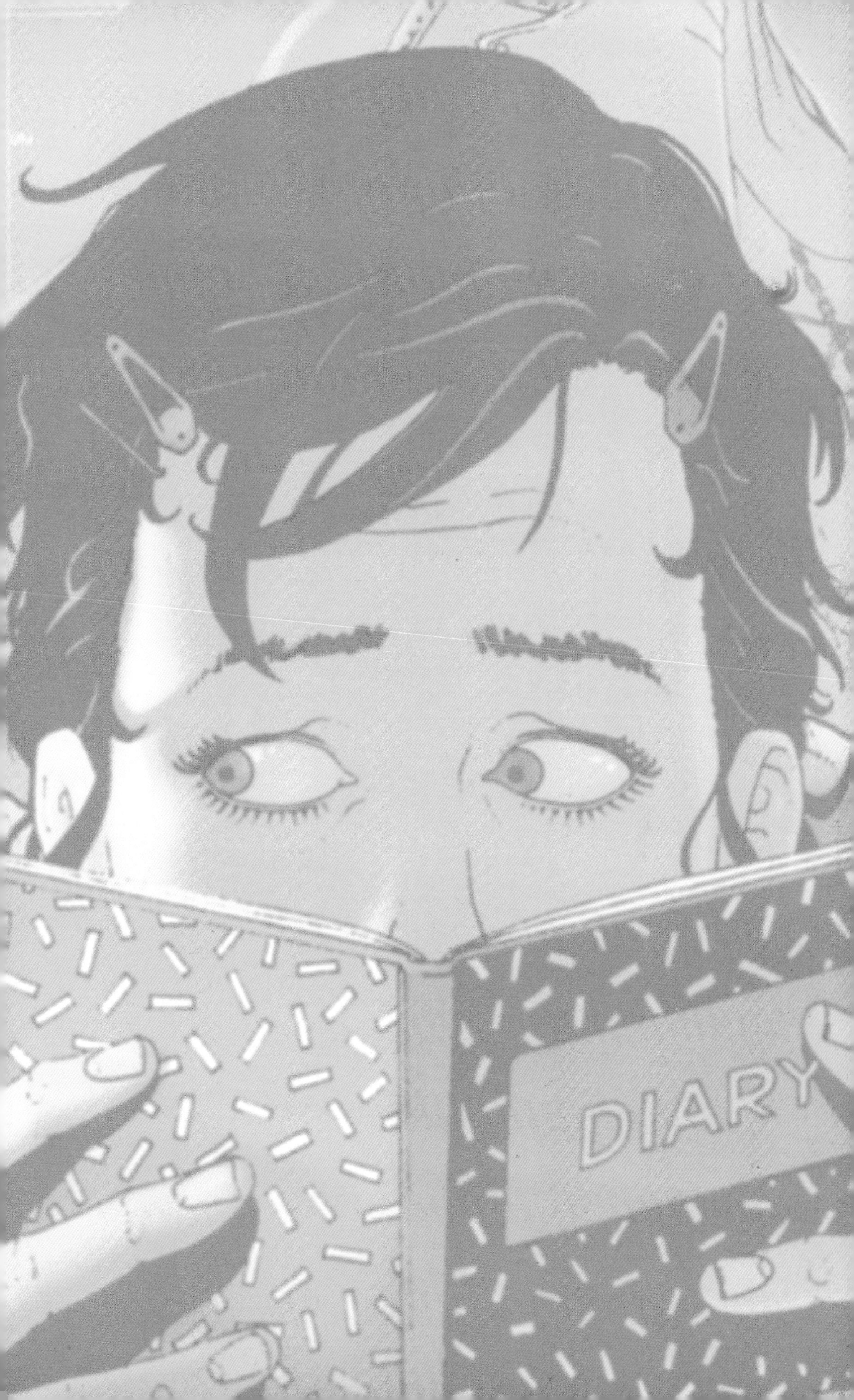
DIARY

CHAPTER III
"Just the place for a Snark"

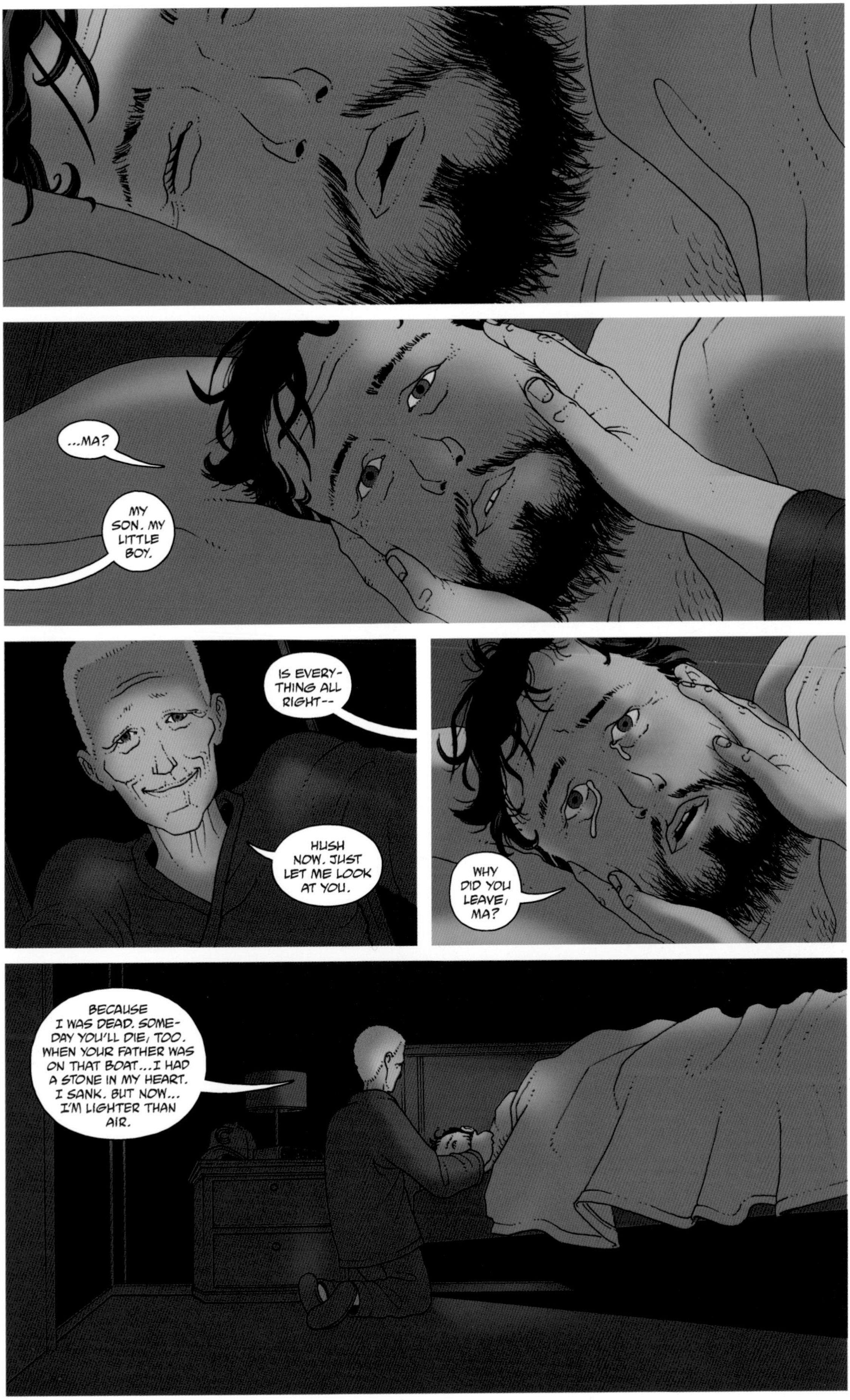
...MA?
MY SON. MY LITTLE BOY.
IS EVERY-THING ALL RIGHT--
HUSH NOW. JUST LET ME LOOK AT YOU.
WHY DID YOU LEAVE, MA?
BECAUSE I WAS DEAD. SOME-DAY YOU'LL DIE, TOO. WHEN YOUR FATHER WAS ON THAT BOAT...I HAD A STONE IN MY HEART. I SANK. BUT NOW... I'M LIGHTER THAN AIR.

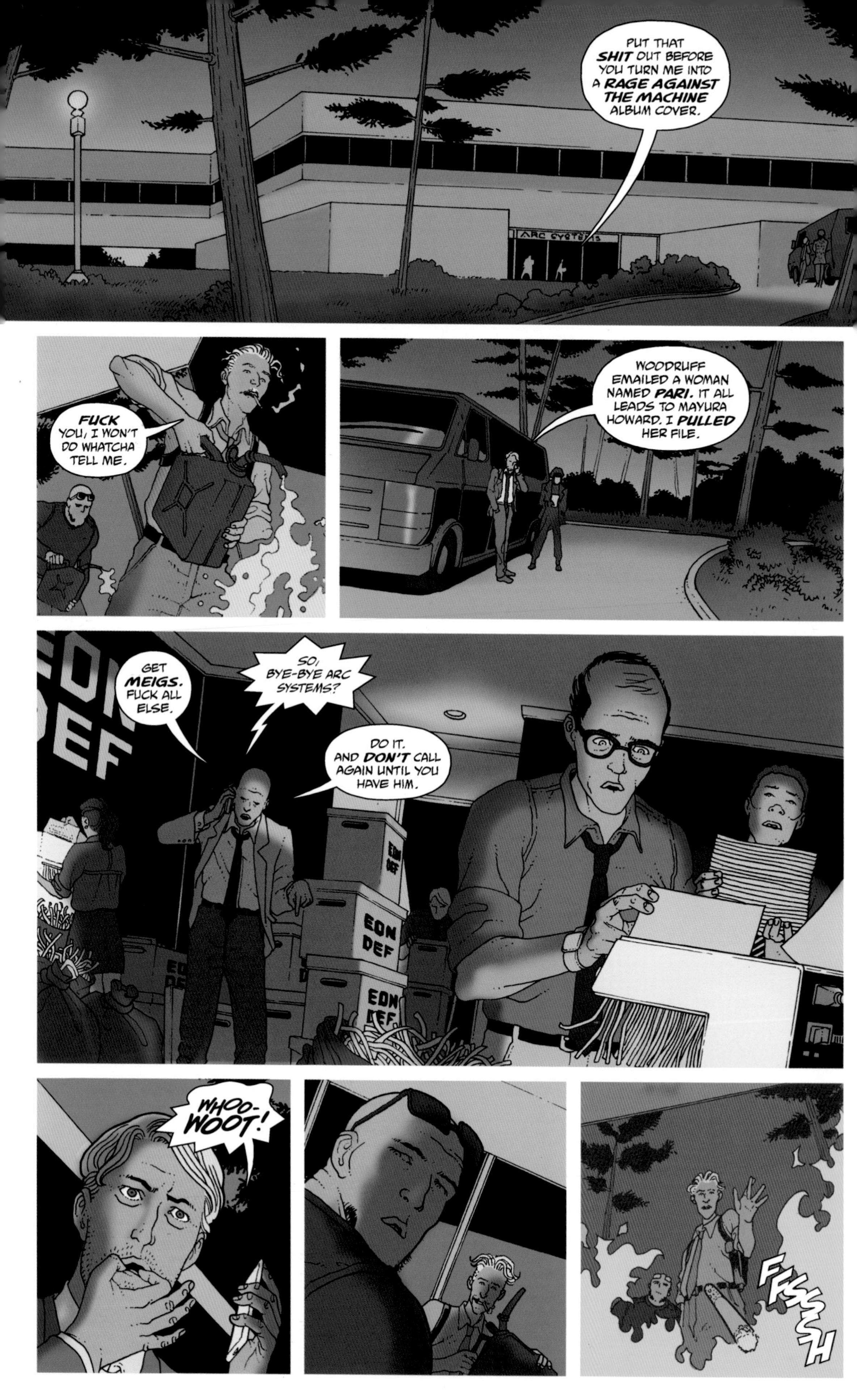
PUT THAT SHIT OUT BEFORE YOU TURN ME INTO A RAGE AGAINST THE MACHINE ALBUM COVER.
ARC SYSTEMS
FUCK YOU, I WON'T DO WHATCHA TELL ME.
WOODRUFF EMAILED A WOMAN NAMED PARI. IT ALL LEADS TO MAYURA HOWARD. I PULLED HER FILE.
EON DEF
GET MEIGS. FUCK ALL ELSE.
SO, BYE-BYE ARC SYSTEMS?
DO IT. AND DON'T CALL AGAIN UNTIL YOU HAVE HIM.
EON DEF
EON DEF
EON DEF
WHOO-WOOT!
FFSSSH

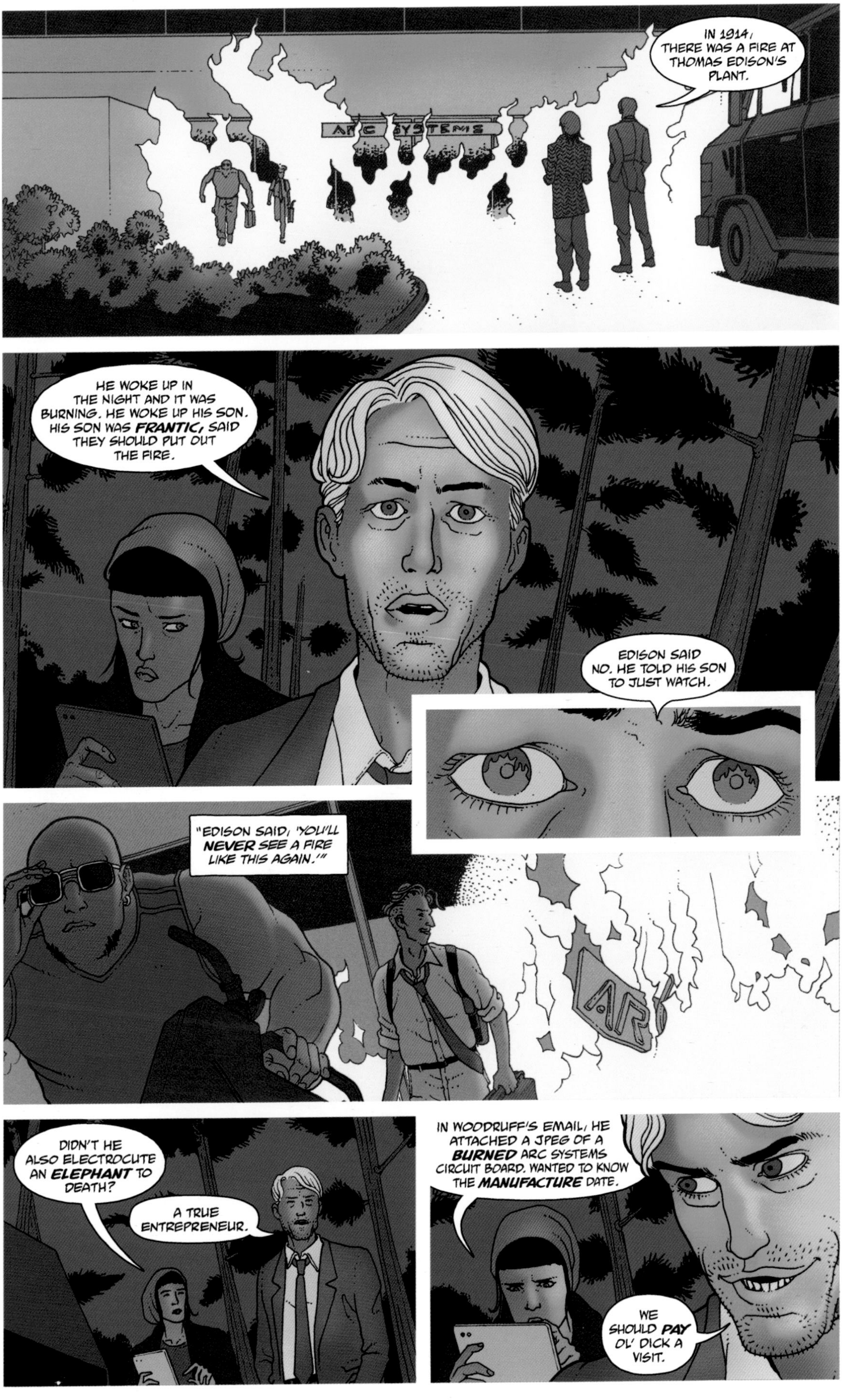
IN 1914, THERE WAS A FIRE AT THOMAS EDISON'S PLANT.
ARC SYSTEMS
HE WOKE UP IN THE NIGHT AND IT WAS BURNING. HE WOKE UP HIS SON. HIS SON WAS FRANTIC, SAID THEY SHOULD PUT OUT THE FIRE.
EDISON SAID NO. HE TOLD HIS SON TO JUST WATCH.
"EDISON SAID, 'YOU'LL NEVER SEE A FIRE LIKE THIS AGAIN.'"
DIDN'T HE ALSO ELECTROCUTE AN ELEPHANT TO DEATH?
A TRUE ENTREPRENEUR.
IN WOODRUFF'S EMAIL, HE ATTACHED A JPEG OF A BURNED ARC SYSTEMS CIRCUIT BOARD. WANTED TO KNOW THE MANUFACTURE DATE.
WE SHOULD PAY OL' DICK A VISIT.

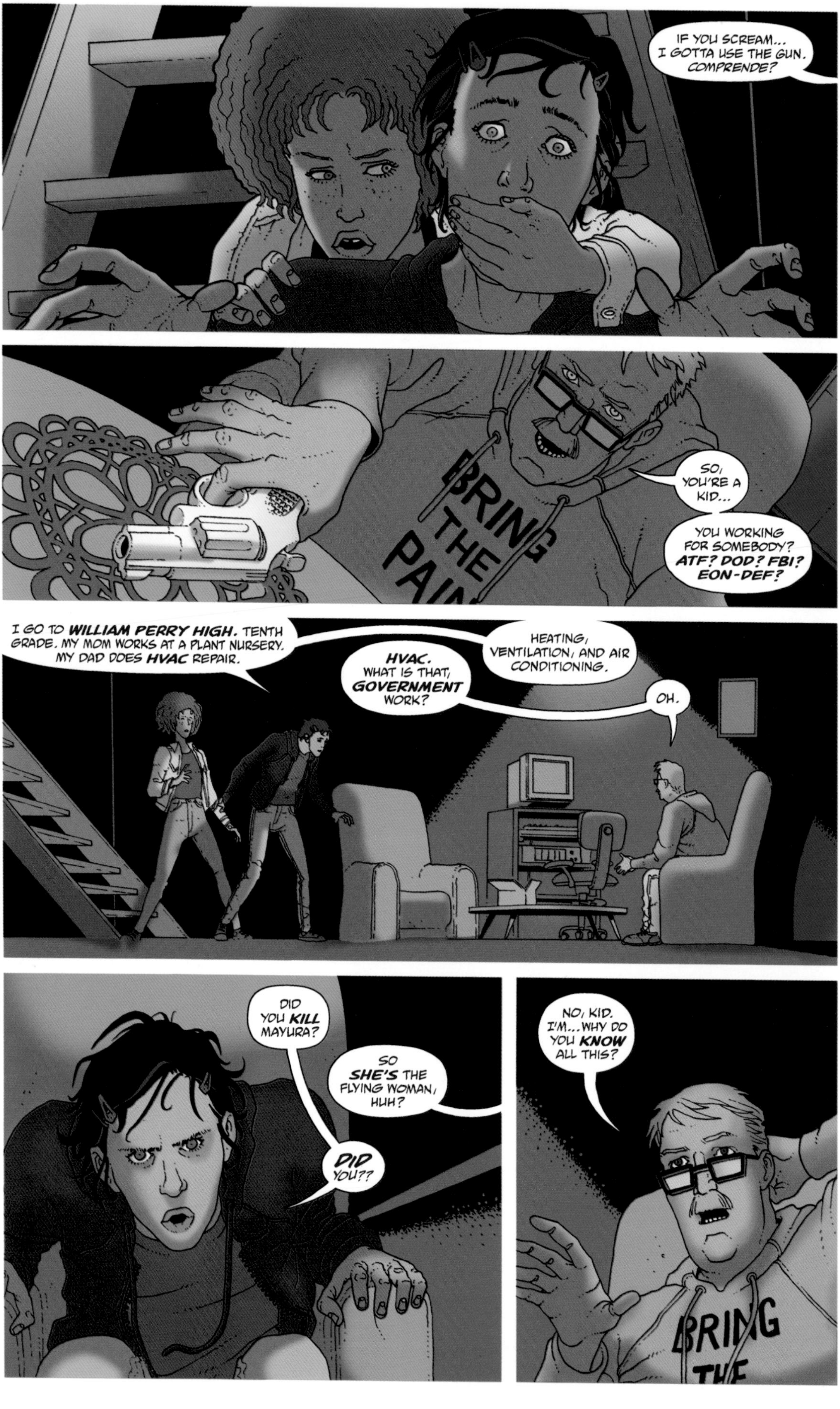
IF YOU SCREAM... I GOTTA USE THE GUN. COMPRENDE?
SO, YOU'RE A KID...
YOU WORKING FOR SOMEBODY? ATF? DOD? FBI? EON-DEF?
BRING THE PAIN
I GO TO WILLIAM PERRY HIGH. TENTH GRADE. MY MOM WORKS AT A PLANT NURSERY. MY DAD DOES HVAC REPAIR.
HVAC. WHAT IS THAT, GOVERNMENT WORK?
HEATING, VENTILATION, AND AIR CONDITIONING.
OH.
DID YOU KILL MAYURA?
SO SHE'S THE FLYING WOMAN, HUH?
DID YOU??
NO, KID. I'M...WHY DO YOU KNOW ALL THIS?
BRING

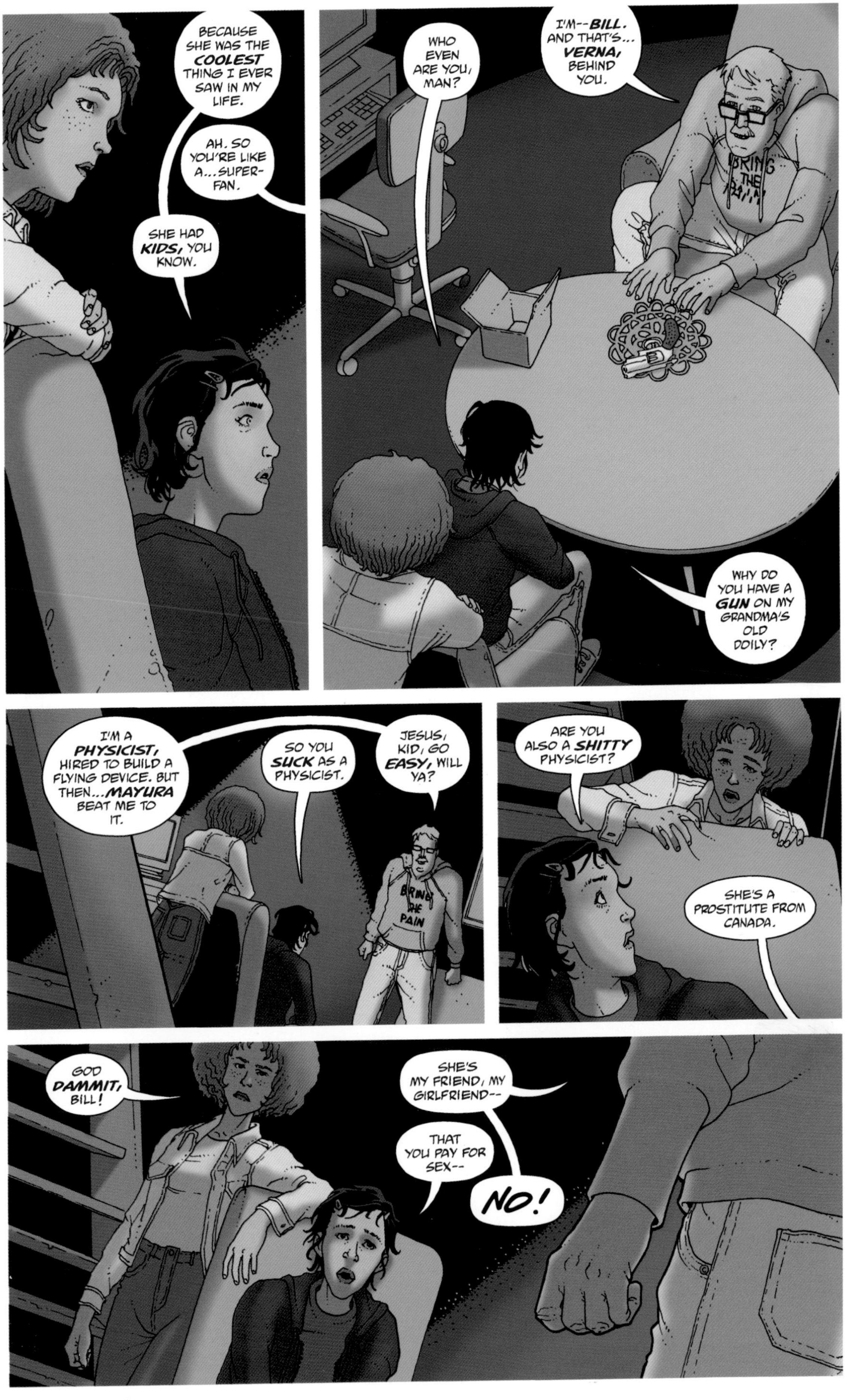
BECAUSE SHE WAS THE COOLEST THING I EVER SAW IN MY LIFE.
AH. SO YOU'RE LIKE A...SUPER-FAN.
SHE HAD KIDS, YOU KNOW.
WHO EVEN ARE YOU, MAN?
I'M--BILL. AND THAT'S... VERNA, BEHIND YOU.
WHY DO YOU HAVE A GUN ON MY GRANDMA'S OLD DOILY?
I'M A PHYSICIST, HIRED TO BUILD A FLYING DEVICE. BUT THEN...MAYURA BEAT ME TO IT.
SO YOU SUCK AS A PHYSICIST.
JESUS, KID, GO EASY, WILL YA?
ARE YOU ALSO A SHITTY PHYSICIST?
SHE'S A PROSTITUTE FROM CANADA.
GOD DAMMIT, BILL!
SHE'S MY FRIEND, MY GIRLFRIEND--
THAT YOU PAY FOR SEX--
NO!

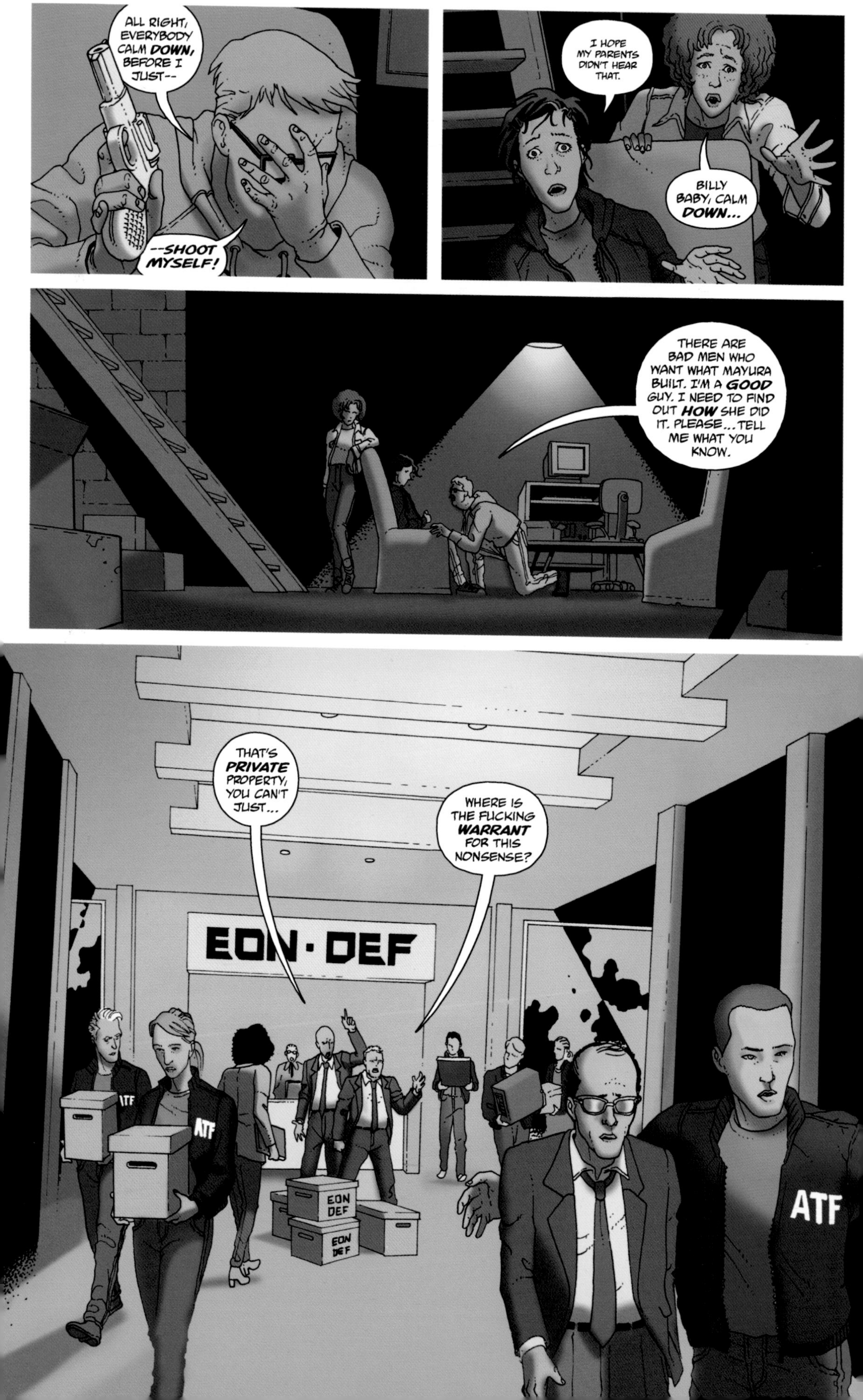
ALL RIGHT, EVERYBODY CALM DOWN, BEFORE I JUST--
--SHOOT MYSELF!
I HOPE MY PARENTS DIDN'T HEAR THAT.
BILLY BABY, CALM DOWN...
THERE ARE BAD MEN WHO WANT WHAT MAYURA BUILT. I'M A GOOD GUY. I NEED TO FIND OUT HOW SHE DID IT. PLEASE... TELL ME WHAT YOU KNOW.
THAT'S PRIVATE PROPERTY, YOU CAN'T JUST...
WHERE IS THE FUCKING WARRANT FOR THIS NONSENSE?
EON · DEF
EON DEF
EON DEF
ATF
ATF
ATF

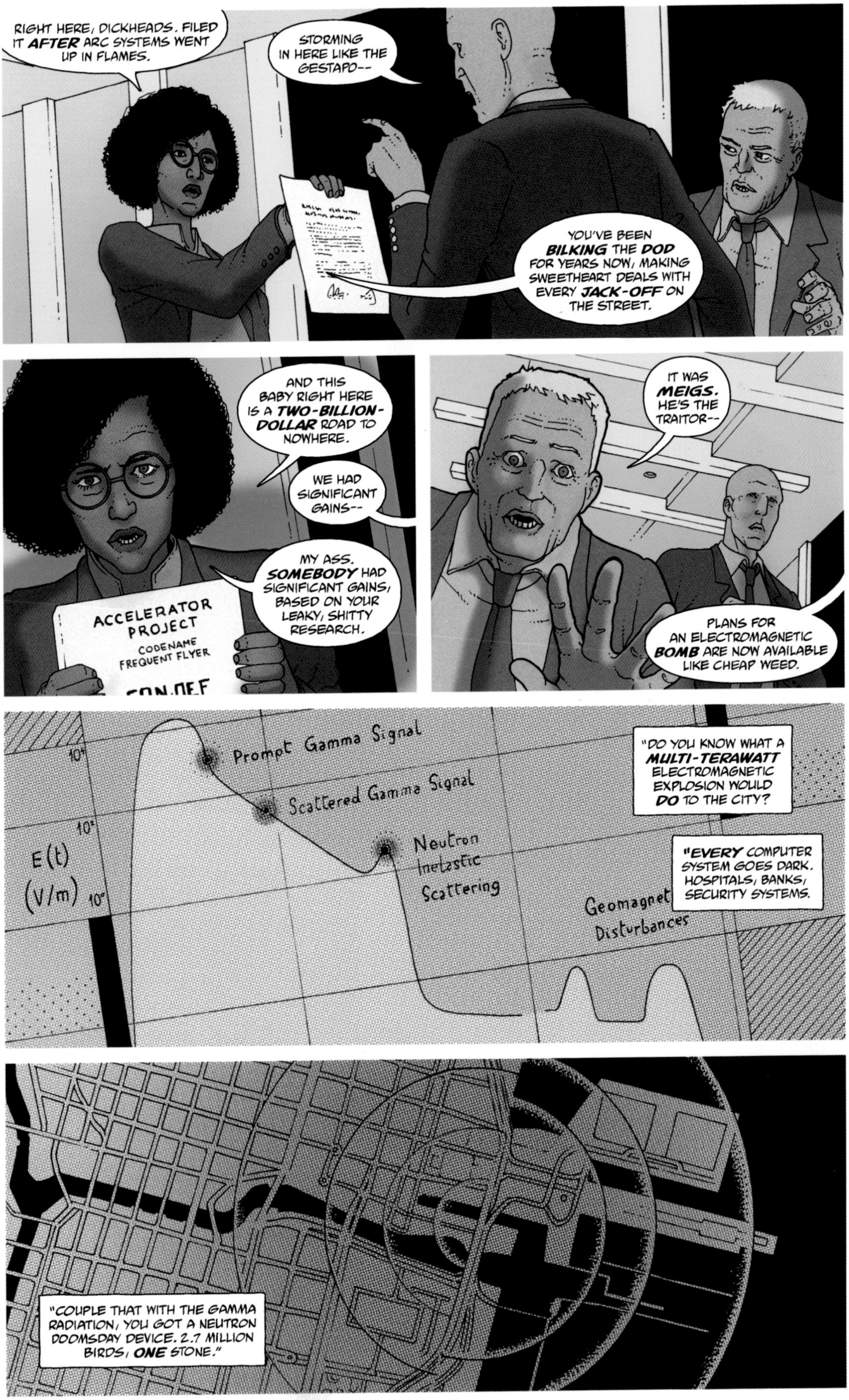
RIGHT HERE, DICKHEADS. FILED IT **AFTER** ARC SYSTEMS WENT UP IN FLAMES.
STORMING IN HERE LIKE THE GESTAPO--
YOU'VE BEEN **BILKING** THE **DOD** FOR YEARS NOW, MAKING SWEETHEART DEALS WITH EVERY **JACK-OFF** ON THE STREET.
AND THIS BABY RIGHT HERE IS A **TWO-BILLION-DOLLAR** ROAD TO NOWHERE.
WE HAD SIGNIFICANT GAINS--
MY ASS. **SOMEBODY** HAD SIGNIFICANT GAINS, BASED ON YOUR LEAKY, SHITTY RESEARCH.
ACCELERATOR PROJECT
CODENAME FREQUENT FLYER
IT WAS **MEIGS.** HE'S THE TRAITOR--
PLANS FOR AN ELECTROMAGNETIC **BOMB** ARE NOW AVAILABLE LIKE CHEAP WEED.
Prompt Gamma Signal
Scattered Gamma Signal
Neutron Inelastic Scattering
Geomagnet Disturbances
E(t) (V/m)
"DO YOU KNOW WHAT A **MULTI-TERAWATT** ELECTROMAGNETIC EXPLOSION WOULD **DO** TO THE CITY?
"**EVERY** COMPUTER SYSTEM GOES DARK. HOSPITALS, BANKS, SECURITY SYSTEMS.
"COUPLE THAT WITH THE GAMMA RADIATION, YOU GOT A NEUTRON DOOMSDAY DEVICE. 2.7 MILLION BIRDS, **ONE** STONE."

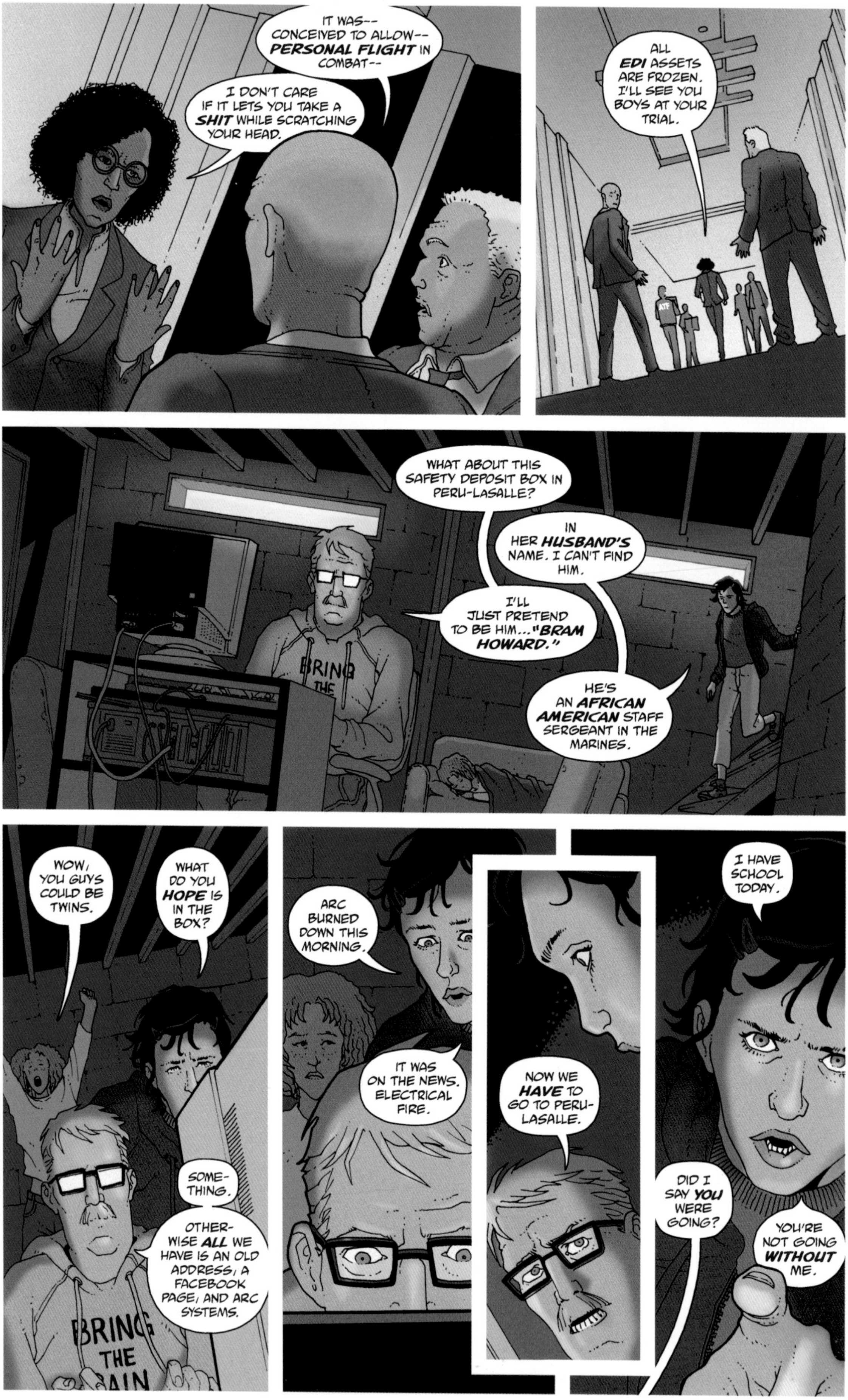
IT WAS-- CONCEIVED TO ALLOW-- **PERSONAL FLIGHT** IN COMBAT--
I DON'T CARE IF IT LETS YOU TAKE A **SHIT** WHILE SCRATCHING YOUR HEAD.
ALL **EDI** ASSETS ARE FROZEN. I'LL SEE YOU BOYS AT YOUR TRIAL.
ATF
WHAT ABOUT THIS SAFETY DEPOSIT BOX IN PERU-LASALLE?
IN HER **HUSBAND'S** NAME. I CAN'T FIND HIM.
I'LL JUST PRETEND TO BE HIM..."**BRAM HOWARD.**"
BRING THE
HE'S AN **AFRICAN AMERICAN** STAFF SERGEANT IN THE MARINES.
WOW, YOU GUYS COULD BE TWINS.
WHAT DO YOU **HOPE** IS IN THE BOX?
SOME-THING.
OTHER-WISE **ALL** WE HAVE IS AN OLD ADDRESS, A FACEBOOK PAGE, AND ARC SYSTEMS.
BRING THE
ARC BURNED DOWN THIS MORNING.
IT WAS ON THE NEWS. ELECTRICAL FIRE.
NOW WE **HAVE** TO GO TO PERU-LASALLE.
I HAVE SCHOOL TODAY.
DID I SAY **YOU** WERE GOING?
YOU'RE NOT GOING **WITHOUT** ME.

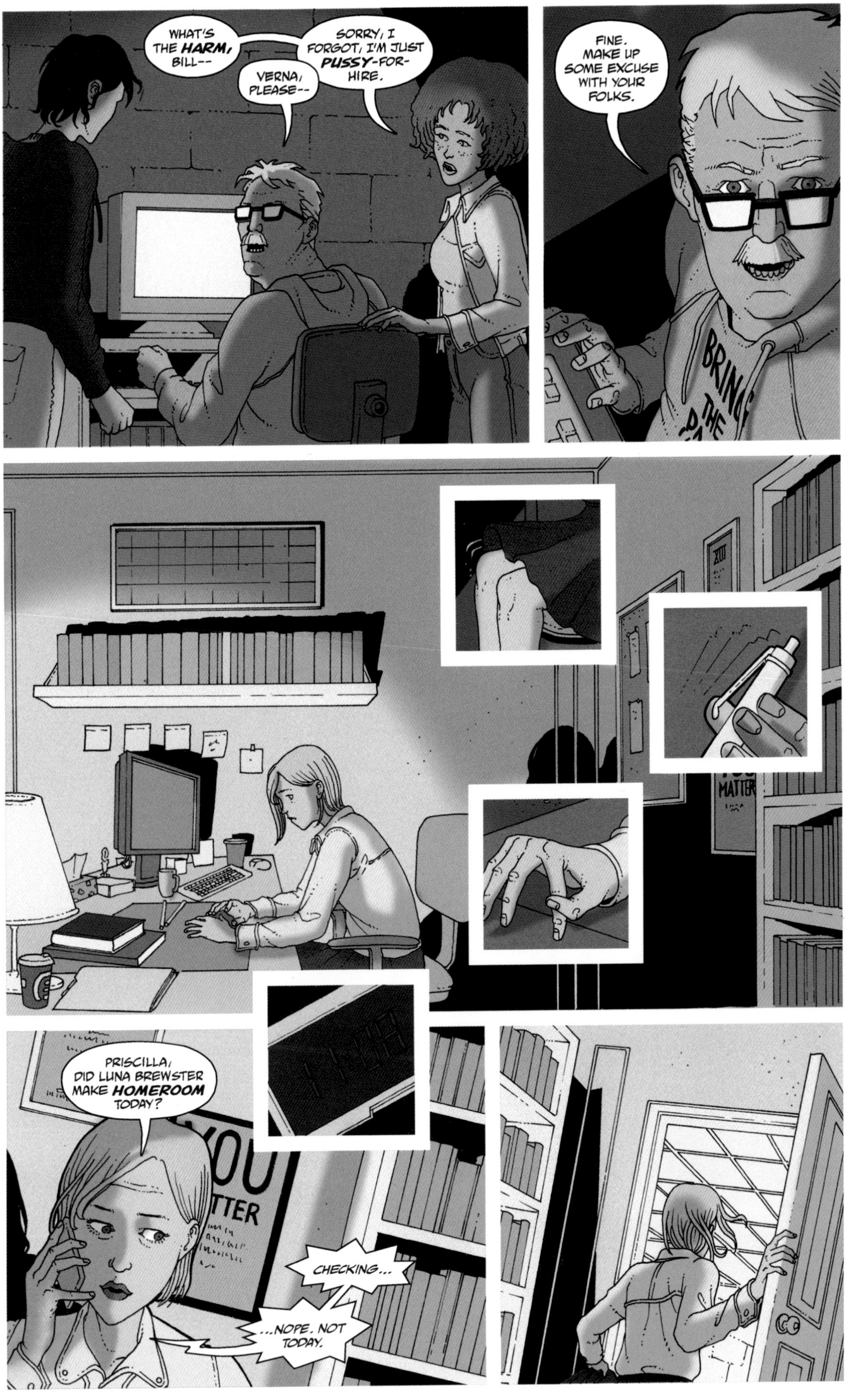

WHAT'S THE **HARM,** BILL--
VERNA, PLEASE--
SORRY, I FORGOT, I'M JUST **PUSSY**-FOR-HIRE.
FINE. MAKE UP SOME EXCUSE WITH YOUR FOLKS.
PRISCILLA, DID LUNA BREWSTER MAKE **HOMEROOM** TODAY?
CHECKING...
...NOPE. NOT TODAY.

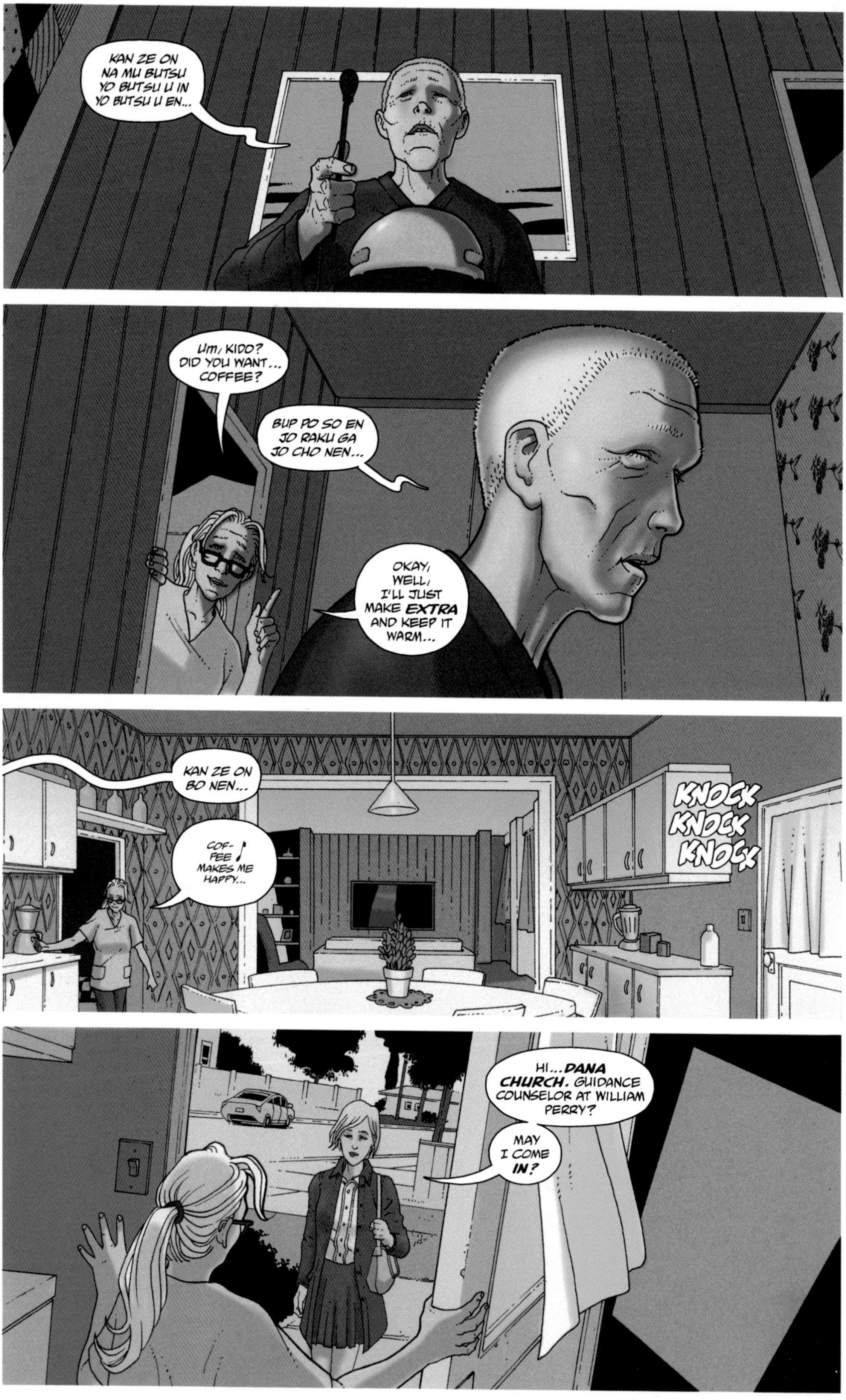
KAN ZE ON NA MU BUTSU YO BUTSU U IN YO BUTSU U EN...
UM, KIDO? DID YOU WANT... COFFEE?
BUP PO SO EN JO RAKU GA JO CHO NEN...
OKAY, WELL, I'LL JUST MAKE **EXTRA** AND KEEP IT WARM...
KAN ZE ON BO NEN...
COF- FEE ♪ MAKES ME HAPPY...
KNOCK KNOCK KNOCK
HI... **DANA CHURCH.** GUIDANCE COUNSELOR AT WILLIAM PERRY?
MAY I COME **IN?**

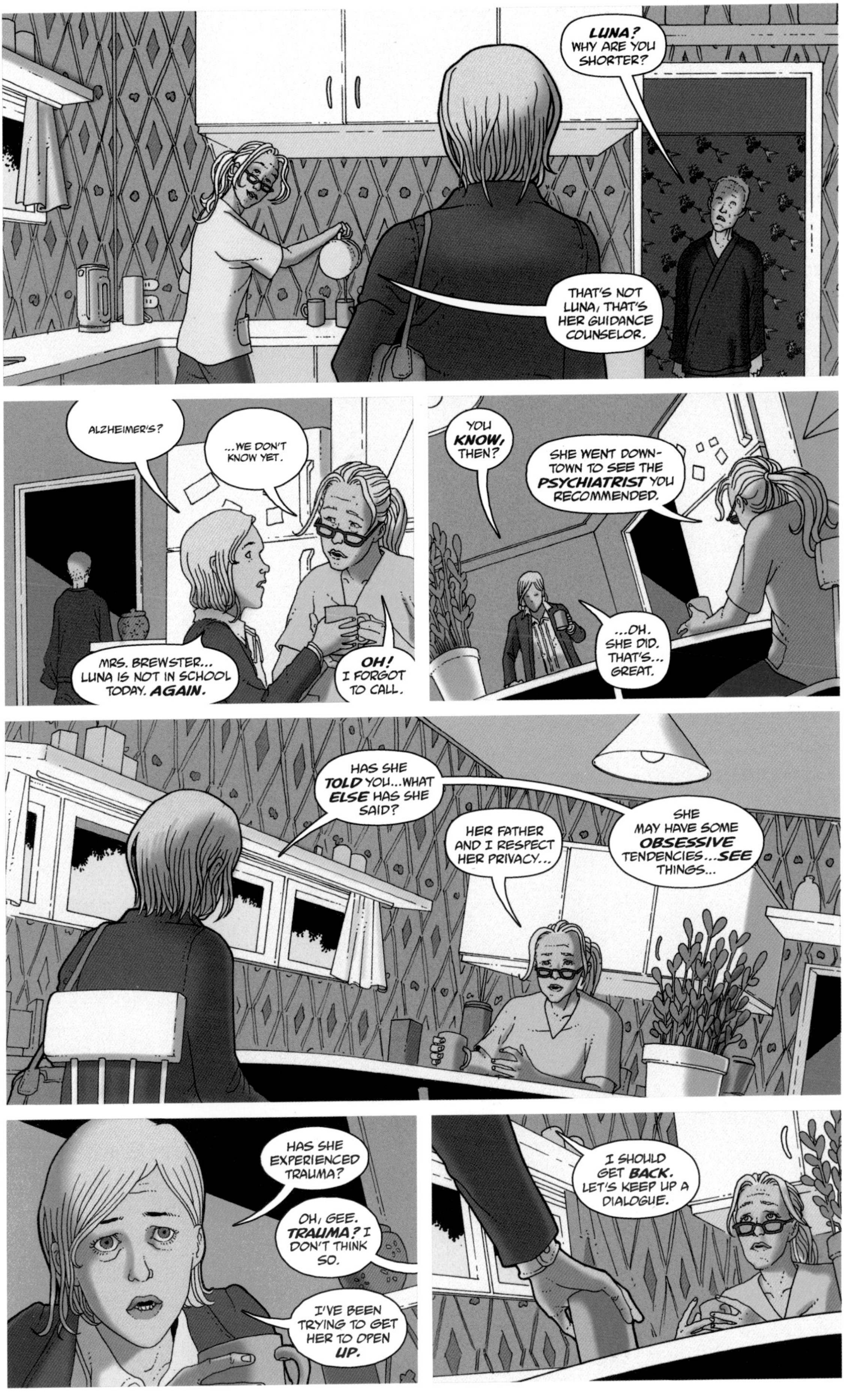
LUNA? WHY ARE YOU SHORTER?
THAT'S NOT LUNA, THAT'S HER GUIDANCE COUNSELOR.
ALZHEIMER'S?
...WE DON'T KNOW YET.
MRS. BREWSTER... LUNA IS NOT IN SCHOOL TODAY. AGAIN.
OH! I FORGOT TO CALL.
YOU KNOW, THEN?
SHE WENT DOWN-TOWN TO SEE THE PSYCHIATRIST YOU RECOMMENDED.
...OH. SHE DID. THAT'S... GREAT.
HAS SHE TOLD YOU...WHAT ELSE HAS SHE SAID?
HER FATHER AND I RESPECT HER PRIVACY...
SHE MAY HAVE SOME OBSESSIVE TENDENCIES...SEE THINGS...
HAS SHE EXPERIENCED TRAUMA?
OH, GEE. TRAUMA? I DON'T THINK SO.
I'VE BEEN TRYING TO GET HER TO OPEN UP.
I SHOULD GET BACK. LET'S KEEP UP A DIALOGUE.

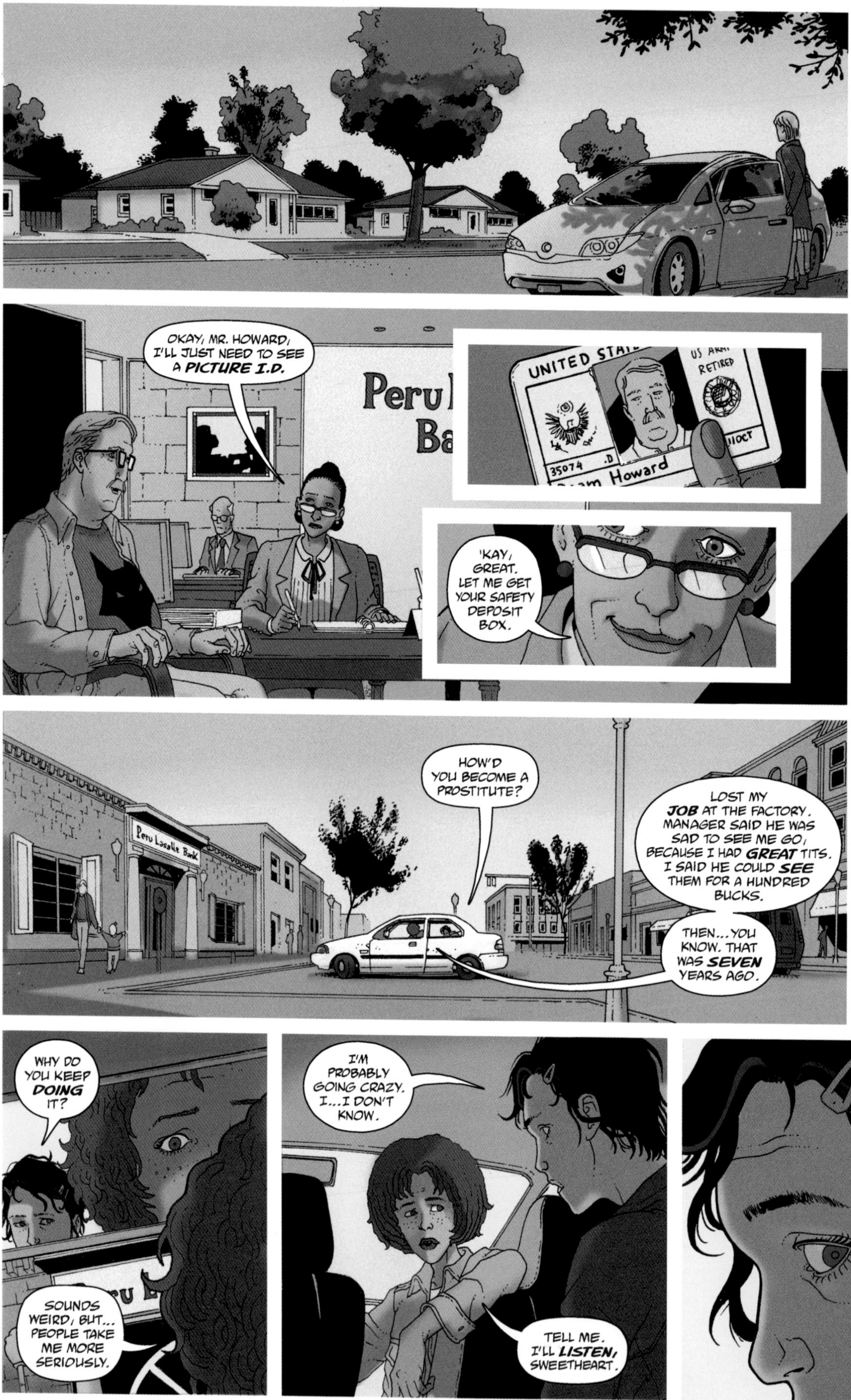
OKAY, MR. HOWARD, I'LL JUST NEED TO SEE A PICTURE I.D.
Peru
Ba
UNITED STATE
US ARMY RETIRED
35074
Howard
'KAY, GREAT. LET ME GET YOUR SAFETY DEPOSIT BOX.
Peru Lasalle Bank
HOW'D YOU BECOME A PROSTITUTE?
LOST MY JOB AT THE FACTORY. MANAGER SAID HE WAS SAD TO SEE ME GO, BECAUSE I HAD GREAT TITS. I SAID HE COULD SEE THEM FOR A HUNDRED BUCKS.
THEN... YOU KNOW. THAT WAS SEVEN YEARS AGO.
WHY DO YOU KEEP DOING IT?
SOUNDS WEIRD, BUT... PEOPLE TAKE ME MORE SERIOUSLY.
I'M PROBABLY GOING CRAZY. I... I DON'T KNOW.
TELL ME. I'LL LISTEN, SWEETHEART.

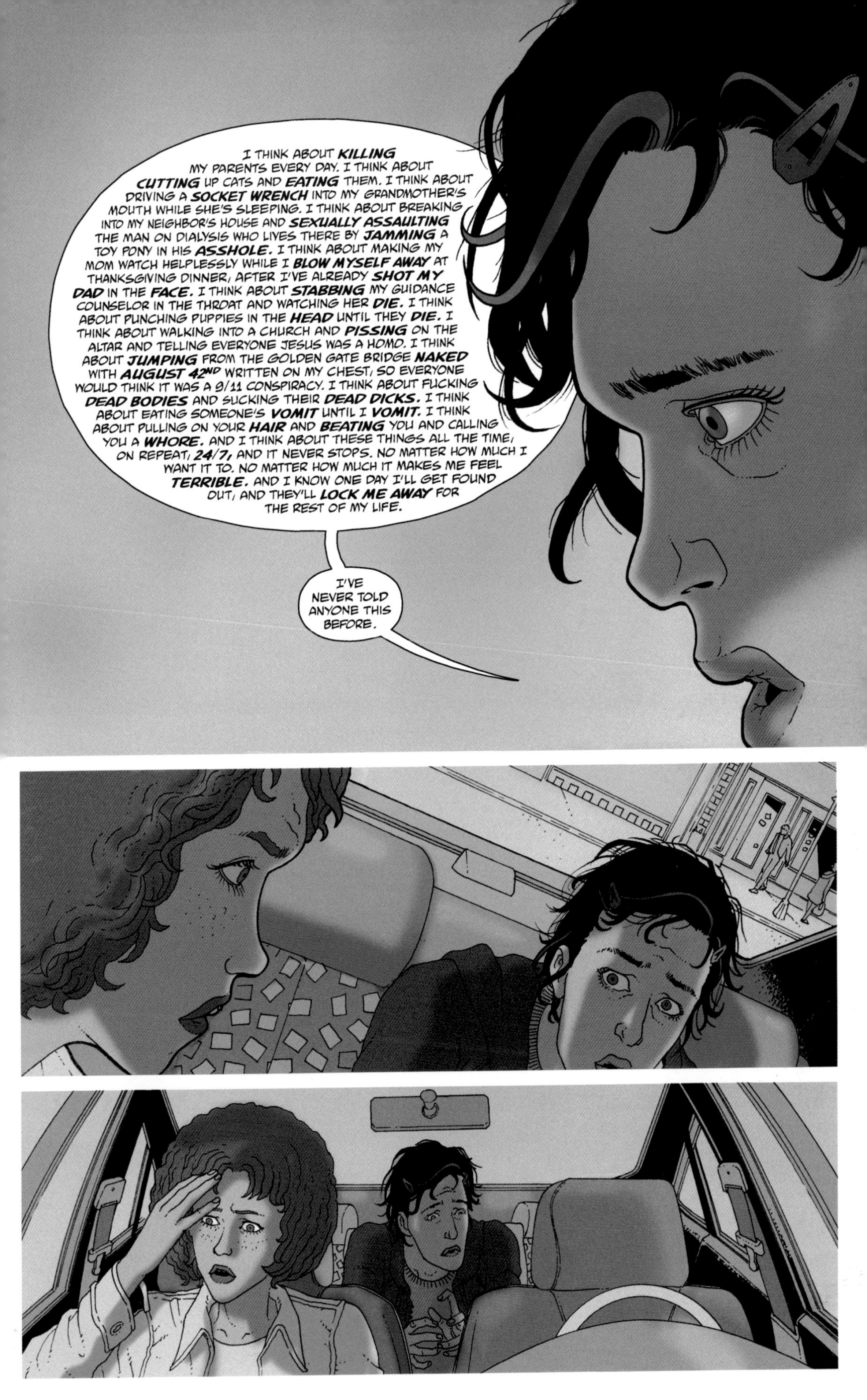
I THINK ABOUT KILLING MY PARENTS EVERY DAY. I THINK ABOUT CUTTING UP CATS AND EATING THEM. I THINK ABOUT DRIVING A SOCKET WRENCH INTO MY GRANDMOTHER'S MOUTH WHILE SHE'S SLEEPING. I THINK ABOUT BREAKING INTO MY NEIGHBOR'S HOUSE AND SEXUALLY ASSAULTING THE MAN ON DIALYSIS WHO LIVES THERE BY JAMMING A TOY PONY IN HIS ASSHOLE. I THINK ABOUT MAKING MY MOM WATCH HELPLESSLY WHILE I BLOW MYSELF AWAY AT THANKSGIVING DINNER, AFTER I'VE ALREADY SHOT MY DAD IN THE FACE. I THINK ABOUT STABBING MY GUIDANCE COUNSELOR IN THE THROAT AND WATCHING HER DIE. I THINK ABOUT PUNCHING PUPPIES IN THE HEAD UNTIL THEY DIE. I THINK ABOUT WALKING INTO A CHURCH AND PISSING ON THE ALTAR AND TELLING EVERYONE JESUS WAS A HOMO. I THINK ABOUT JUMPING FROM THE GOLDEN GATE BRIDGE NAKED WITH AUGUST 42ND WRITTEN ON MY CHEST, SO EVERYONE WOULD THINK IT WAS A 9/11 CONSPIRACY. I THINK ABOUT FUCKING DEAD BODIES AND SUCKING THEIR DEAD DICKS. I THINK ABOUT EATING SOMEONE'S VOMIT UNTIL I VOMIT. I THINK ABOUT PULLING ON YOUR HAIR AND BEATING YOU AND CALLING YOU A WHORE. AND I THINK ABOUT THESE THINGS ALL THE TIME, ON REPEAT, 24/7, AND IT NEVER STOPS. NO MATTER HOW MUCH I WANT IT TO. NO MATTER HOW MUCH IT MAKES ME FEEL TERRIBLE. AND I KNOW ONE DAY I'LL GET FOUND OUT, AND THEY'LL LOCK ME AWAY FOR THE REST OF MY LIFE.
I'VE NEVER TOLD ANYONE THIS BEFORE.

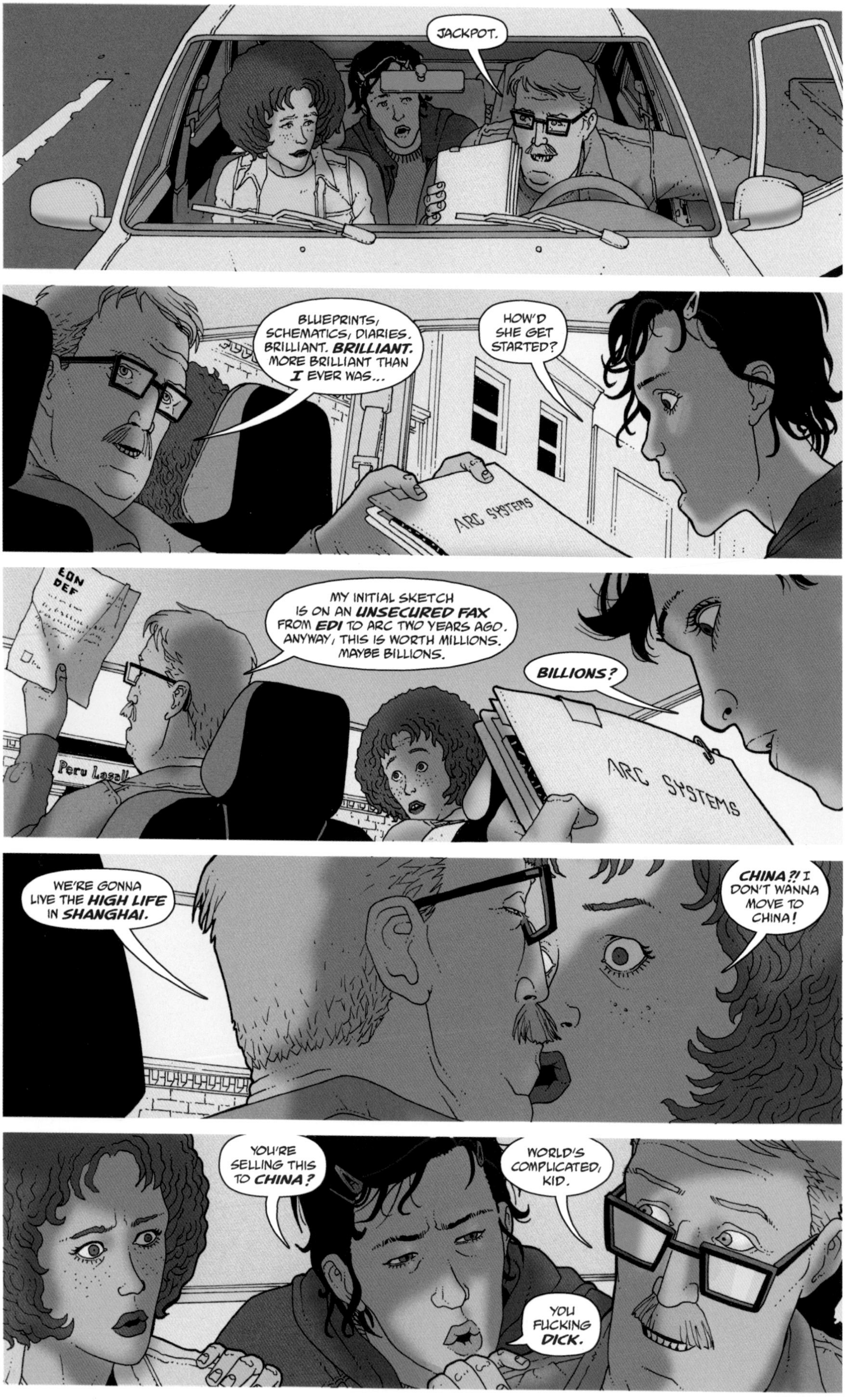
JACKPOT.
BLUEPRINTS, SCHEMATICS, DIARIES. BRILLIANT. **BRILLIANT.** MORE BRILLIANT THAN ***I*** EVER WAS...
HOW'D SHE GET STARTED?
ARC SYSTEMS
MY INITIAL SKETCH IS ON AN **UNSECURED FAX** FROM **EDI** TO ARC TWO YEARS AGO. ANYWAY, THIS IS WORTH MILLIONS. MAYBE BILLIONS.
BILLIONS?
Peru Lasall
ARC SYSTEMS
WE'RE GONNA LIVE THE **HIGH LIFE** IN **SHANGHAI.**
CHINA?! I DON'T WANNA MOVE TO CHINA**!**
YOU'RE SELLING THIS TO **CHINA?**
WORLD'S COMPLICATED, KID.
YOU FUCKING **DICK.**

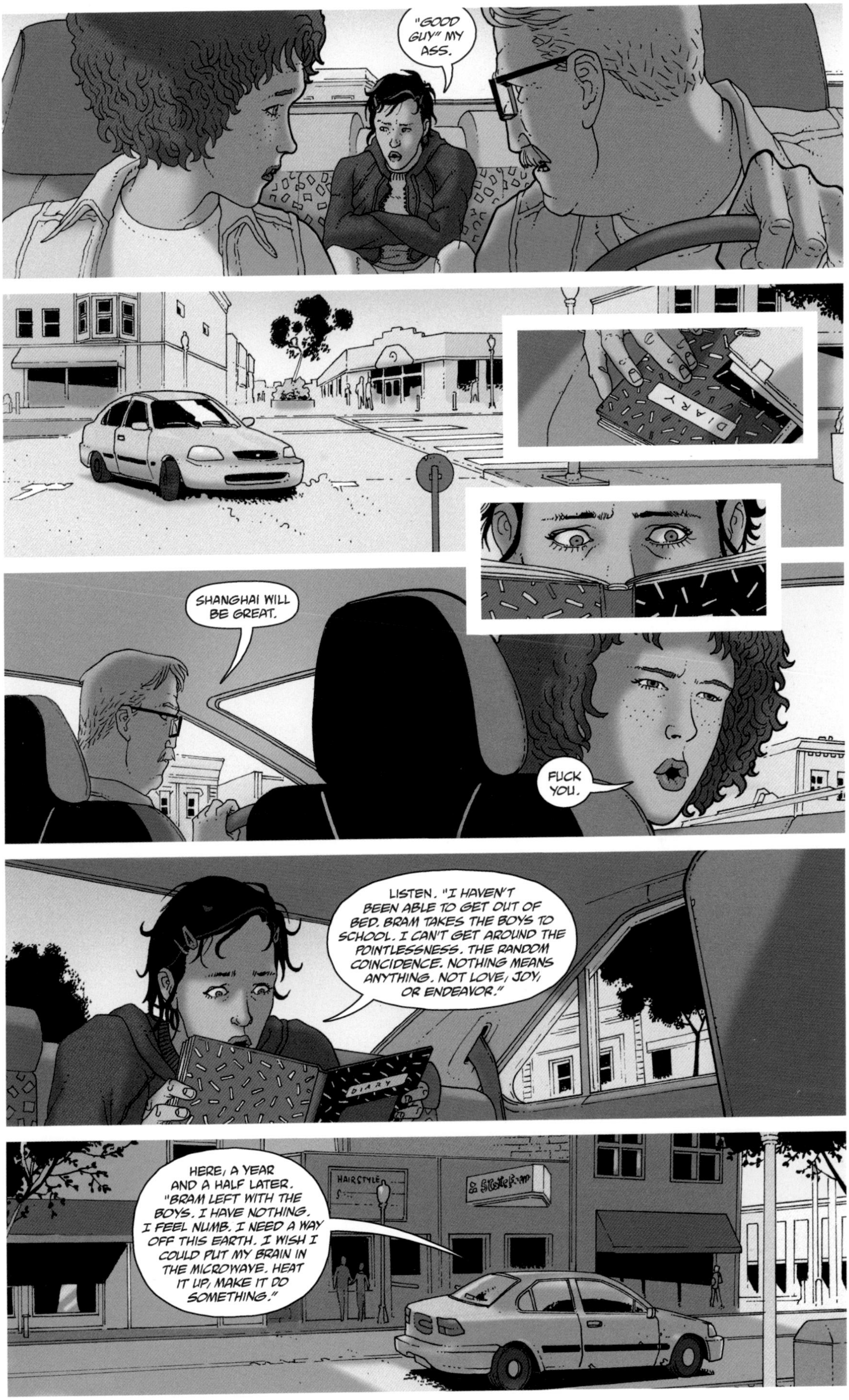
"GOOD GUY" MY ASS.
DIARY
SHANGHAI WILL BE GREAT.
FUCK YOU.
LISTEN. "I HAVEN'T BEEN ABLE TO GET OUT OF BED. BRAM TAKES THE BOYS TO SCHOOL. I CAN'T GET AROUND THE POINTLESSNESS. THE RANDOM COINCIDENCE. NOTHING MEANS ANYTHING. NOT LOVE, JOY, OR ENDEAVOR."
DIARY
HAIRSTYLE
HERE, A YEAR AND A HALF LATER. "BRAM LEFT WITH THE BOYS. I HAVE NOTHING. I FEEL NUMB. I NEED A WAY OFF THIS EARTH. I WISH I COULD PUT MY BRAIN IN THE MICROWAVE. HEAT IT UP, MAKE IT DO SOMETHING."

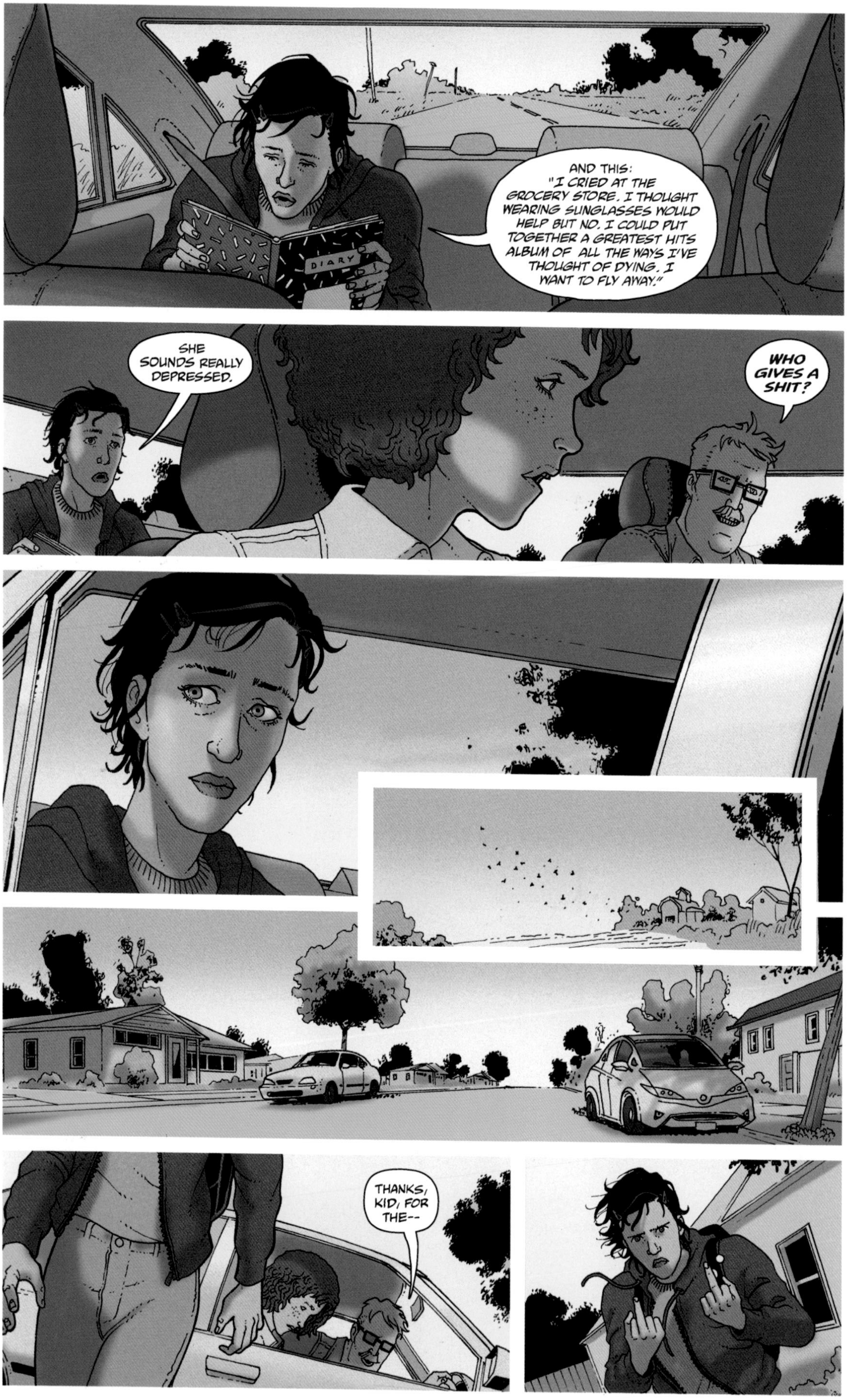
AND THIS: "I CRIED AT THE GROCERY STORE. I THOUGHT WEARING SUNGLASSES WOULD HELP BUT NO. I COULD PUT TOGETHER A GREATEST HITS ALBUM OF ALL THE WAYS I'VE THOUGHT OF DYING. I WANT TO FLY AWAY."
SHE SOUNDS REALLY DEPRESSED.
WHO GIVES A SHIT?
THANKS, KID, FOR THE--

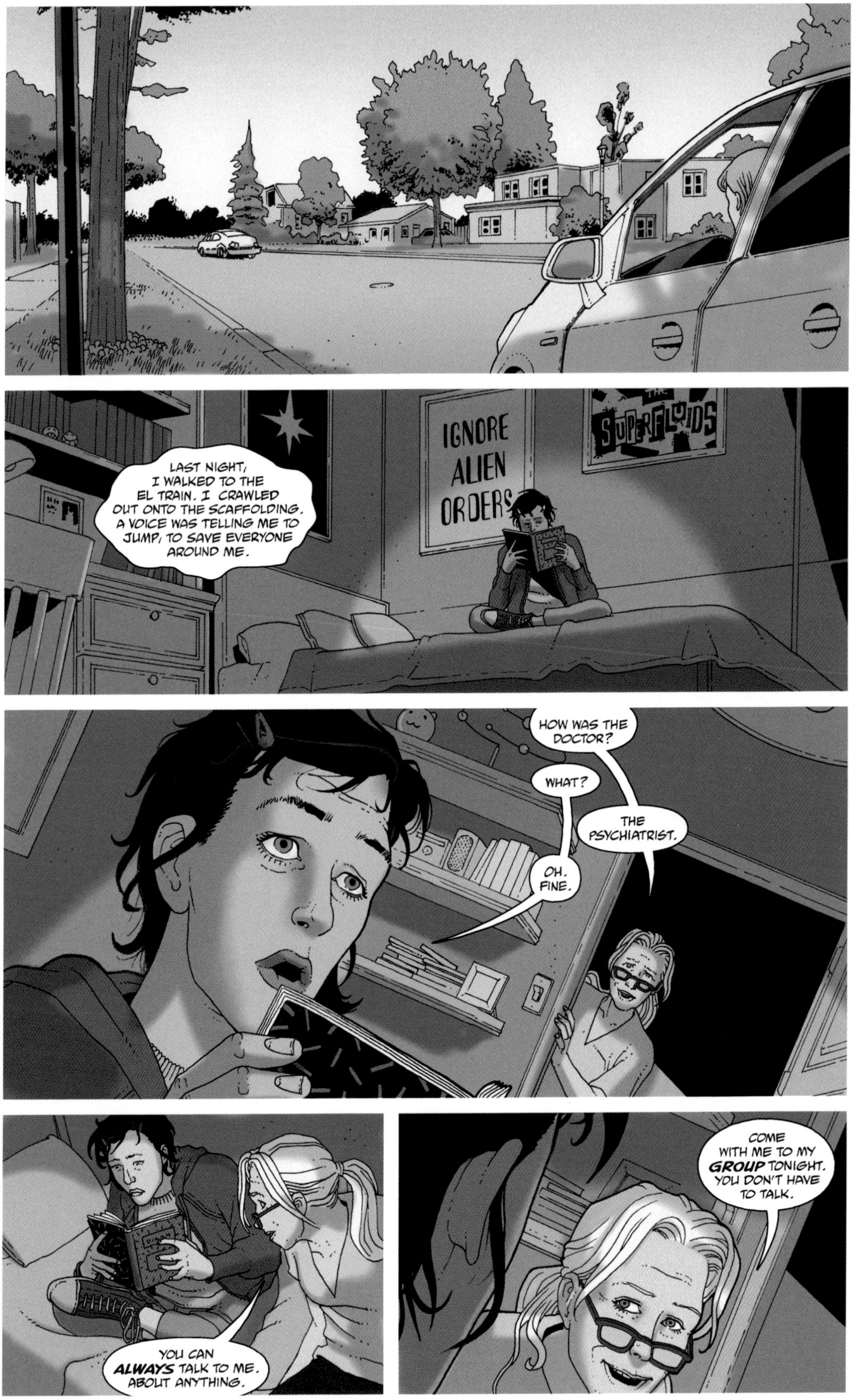
IGNORE ALIEN ORDERS
SUPERFLUIDS
LAST NIGHT, I WALKED TO THE EL TRAIN. I CRAWLED OUT ONTO THE SCAFFOLDING. A VOICE WAS TELLING ME TO JUMP, TO SAVE EVERYONE AROUND ME.
HOW WAS THE DOCTOR?
WHAT?
THE PSYCHIATRIST.
OH. FINE.
YOU CAN ALWAYS TALK TO ME. ABOUT ANYTHING.
COME WITH ME TO MY GROUP TONIGHT. YOU DON'T HAVE TO TALK.

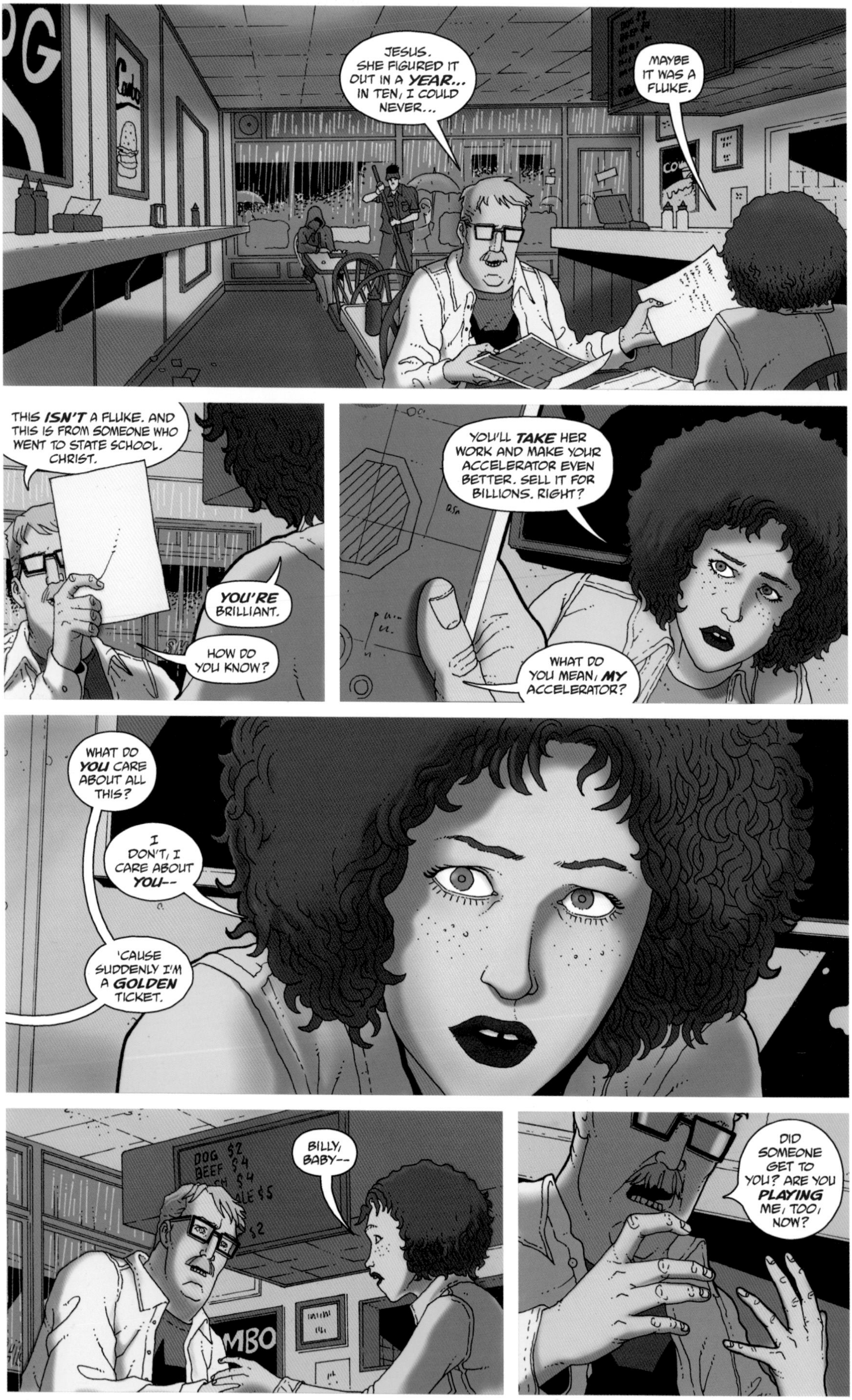
JESUS. SHE FIGURED IT OUT IN A **YEAR...** IN TEN, I COULD NEVER...
MAYBE IT WAS A FLUKE.
THIS **ISN'T** A FLUKE. AND THIS IS FROM SOMEONE WHO WENT TO STATE SCHOOL. CHRIST.
YOU'RE BRILLIANT.
HOW DO YOU KNOW?
YOU'LL **TAKE** HER WORK AND MAKE YOUR ACCELERATOR EVEN BETTER. SELL IT FOR BILLIONS. RIGHT?
WHAT DO YOU MEAN, **MY** ACCELERATOR?
WHAT DO **YOU** CARE ABOUT ALL THIS?
I DON'T, I CARE ABOUT **YOU**--
'CAUSE SUDDENLY I'M A **GOLDEN** TICKET.
DOG $2
BEEF $4
BILLY, BABY--
DID SOMEONE GET TO YOU? ARE YOU **PLAYING** ME, TOO, NOW?

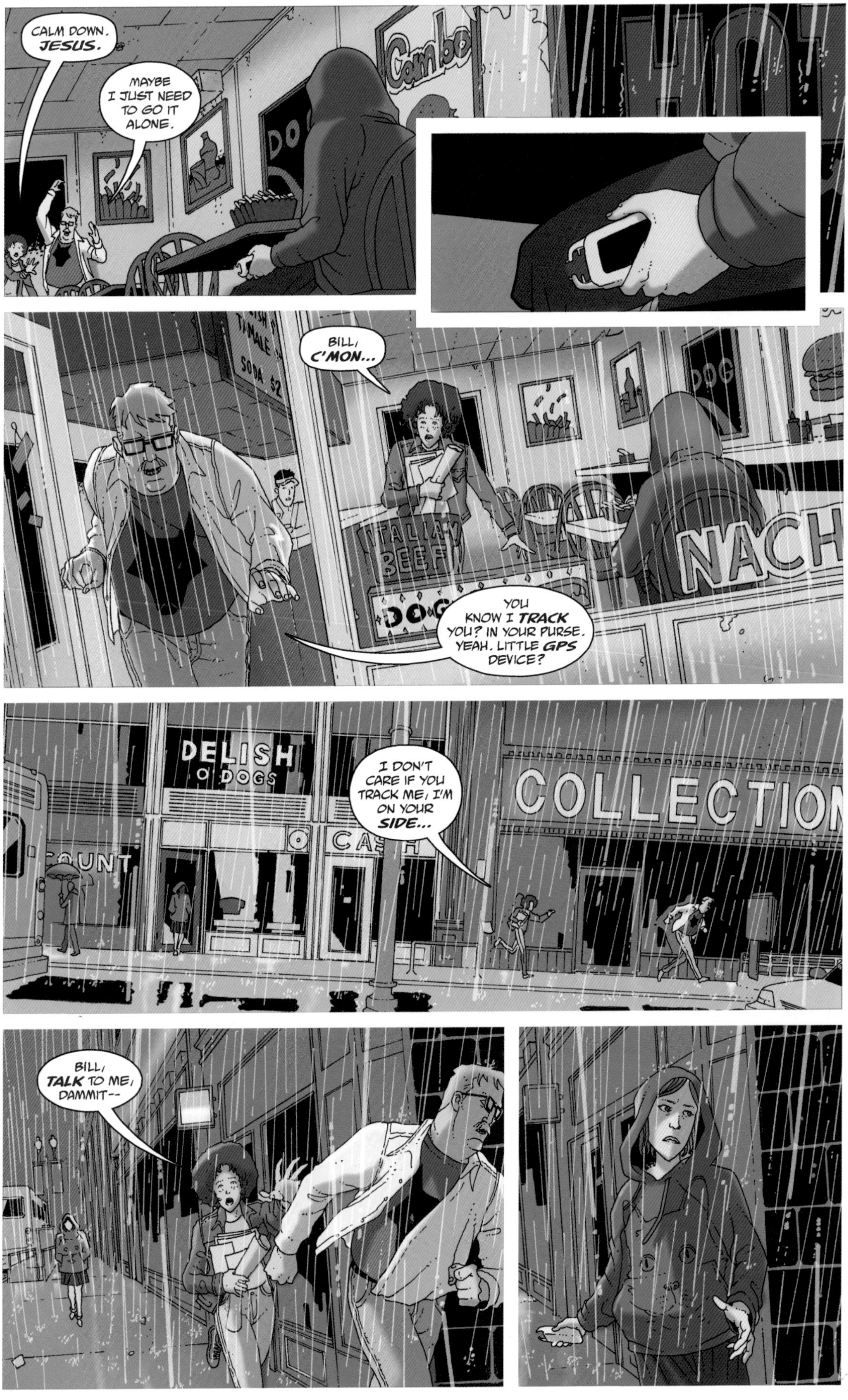
CALM DOWN. JESUS.
MAYBE I JUST NEED TO GO IT ALONE.
Combo
DOG
TAMALE
SODA $2
BILL, C'MON...
ITALIAN BEEF
NACH
YOU KNOW I TRACK YOU? IN YOUR PURSE. YEAH. LITTLE GPS DEVICE?
DELISH DOGS
COUNT
CASH
COLLECTION
I DON'T CARE IF YOU TRACK ME, I'M ON YOUR SIDE...
BILL, TALK TO ME, DAMMIT--

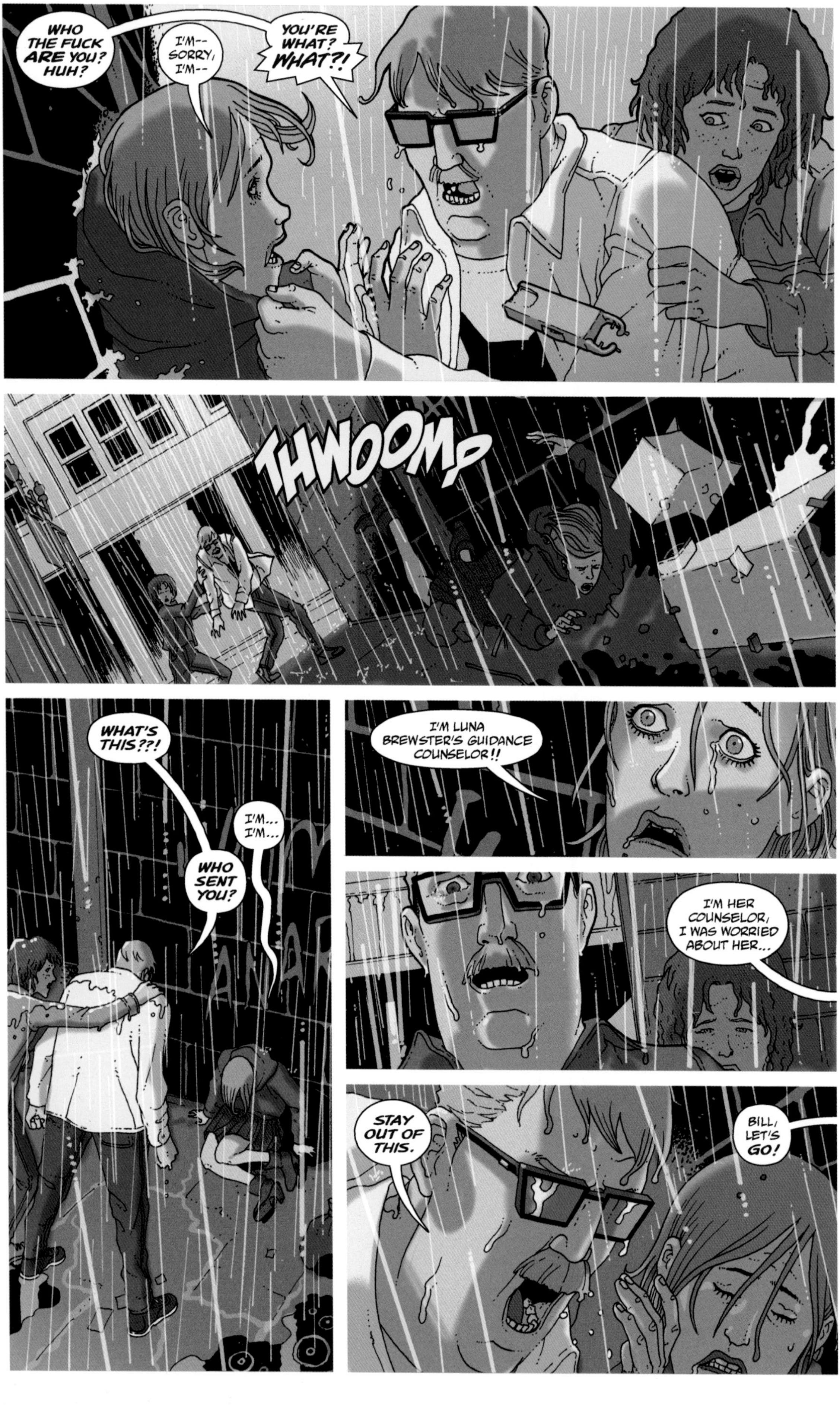
WHO THE FUCK ARE YOU? HUH?
I'M-- SORRY, I'M--
YOU'RE WHAT? WHAT?!
THWOOMP
WHAT'S THIS??!
I'M... I'M...
WHO SENT YOU?
I'M LUNA BREWSTER'S GUIDANCE COUNSELOR!!
I'M HER COUNSELOR, I WAS WORRIED ABOUT HER...
STAY OUT OF THIS.
BILL, LET'S GO!

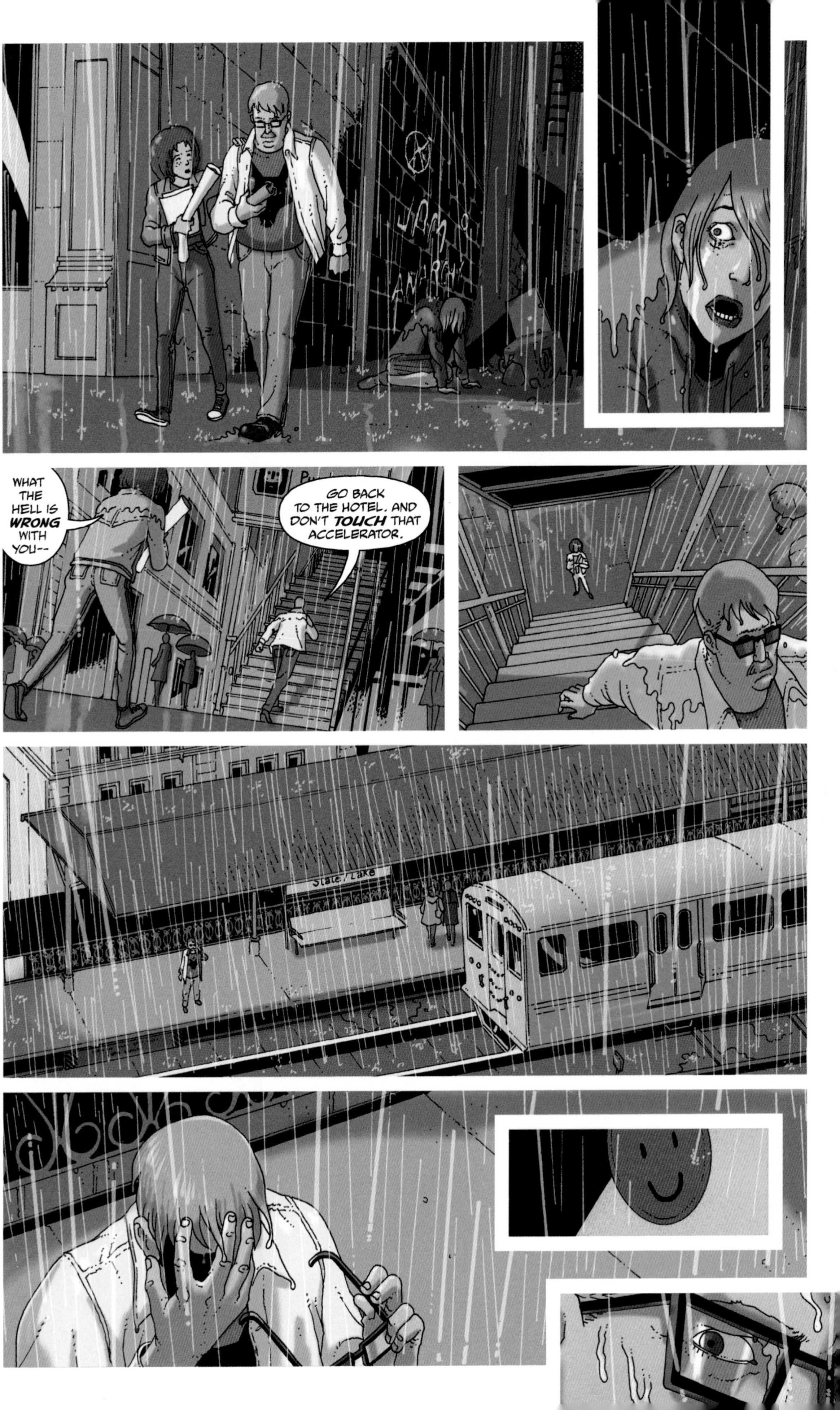
WHAT THE HELL IS WRONG WITH YOU--
GO BACK TO THE HOTEL. AND DON'T TOUCH THAT ACCELERATOR.
State / Lake

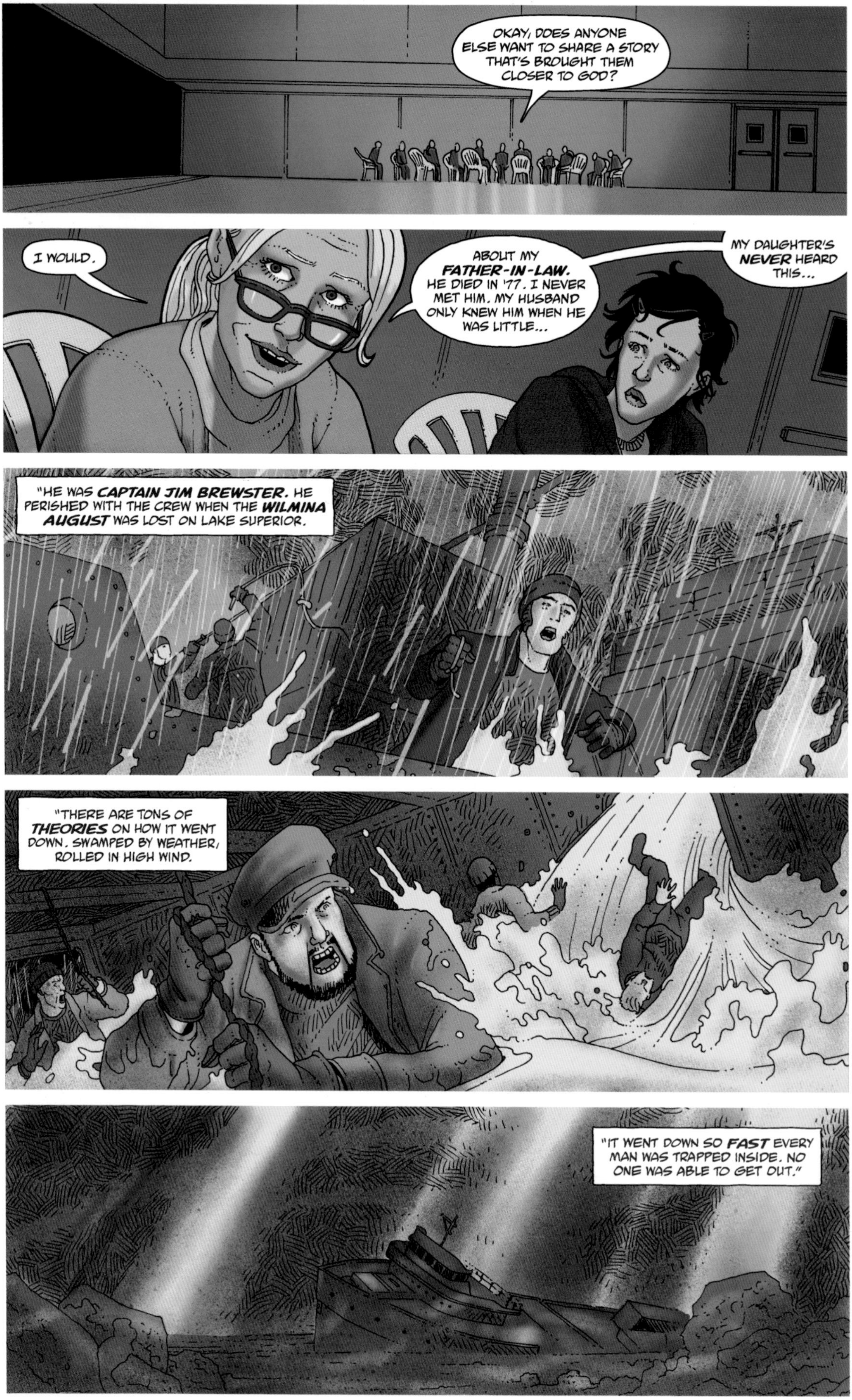
OKAY, DOES ANYONE ELSE WANT TO SHARE A STORY THAT'S BROUGHT THEM CLOSER TO GOD?
I WOULD.
ABOUT MY FATHER-IN-LAW. HE DIED IN '77. I NEVER MET HIM. MY HUSBAND ONLY KNEW HIM WHEN HE WAS LITTLE...
MY DAUGHTER'S NEVER HEARD THIS...
"HE WAS CAPTAIN JIM BREWSTER. HE PERISHED WITH THE CREW WHEN THE WILMINA AUGUST WAS LOST ON LAKE SUPERIOR.
"THERE ARE TONS OF THEORIES ON HOW IT WENT DOWN. SWAMPED BY WEATHER, ROLLED IN HIGH WIND.
"IT WENT DOWN SO FAST EVERY MAN WAS TRAPPED INSIDE. NO ONE WAS ABLE TO GET OUT."

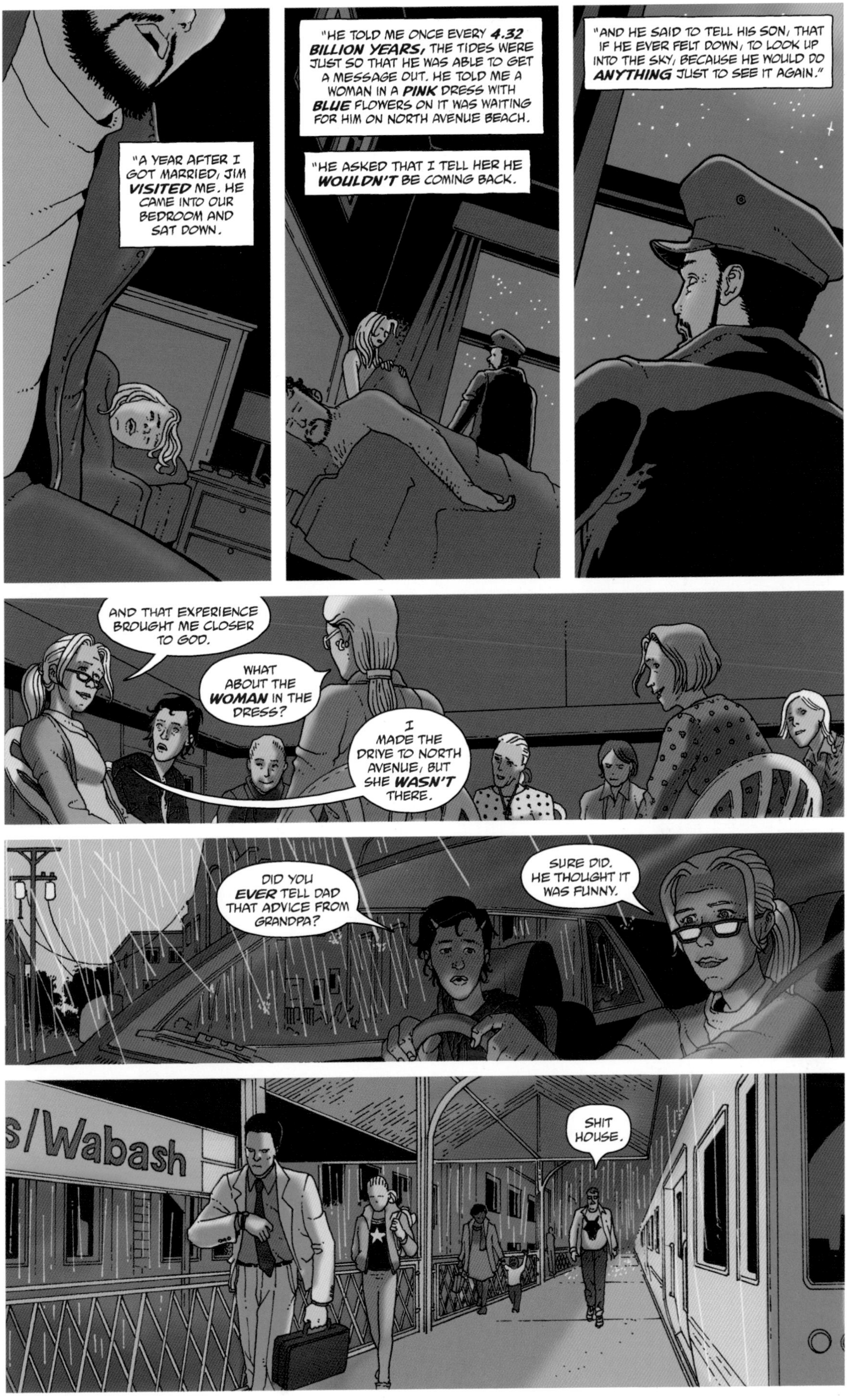
"A YEAR AFTER I GOT MARRIED, JIM VISITED ME. HE CAME INTO OUR BEDROOM AND SAT DOWN.
"HE TOLD ME ONCE EVERY 4.32 BILLION YEARS, THE TIDES WERE JUST SO THAT HE WAS ABLE TO GET A MESSAGE OUT. HE TOLD ME A WOMAN IN A PINK DRESS WITH BLUE FLOWERS ON IT WAS WAITING FOR HIM ON NORTH AVENUE BEACH.
"HE ASKED THAT I TELL HER HE WOULDN'T BE COMING BACK.
"AND HE SAID TO TELL HIS SON, THAT IF HE EVER FELT DOWN, TO LOOK UP INTO THE SKY, BECAUSE HE WOULD DO ANYTHING JUST TO SEE IT AGAIN."
AND THAT EXPERIENCE BROUGHT ME CLOSER TO GOD.
WHAT ABOUT THE WOMAN IN THE DRESS?
I MADE THE DRIVE TO NORTH AVENUE, BUT SHE WASN'T THERE.
DID YOU EVER TELL DAD THAT ADVICE FROM GRANDPA?
SURE DID. HE THOUGHT IT WAS FUNNY.
s/Wabash
SHIT HOUSE.

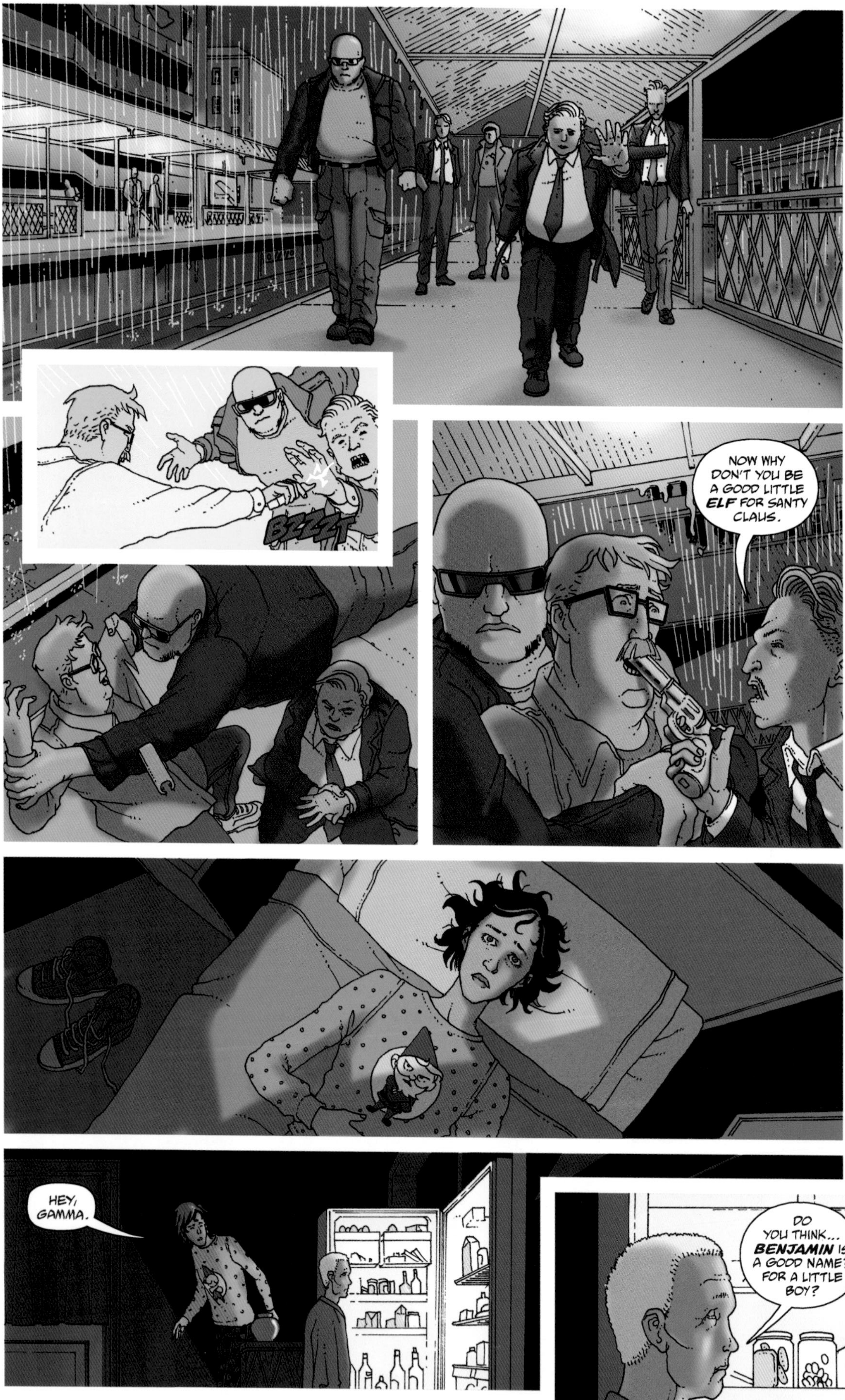
BZZZT
NOW WHY DON'T YOU BE A GOOD LITTLE ELF FOR SANTY CLAUS.
HEY, GAMMA.
DO YOU THINK... BENJAMIN IS A GOOD NAME? FOR A LITTLE BOY?

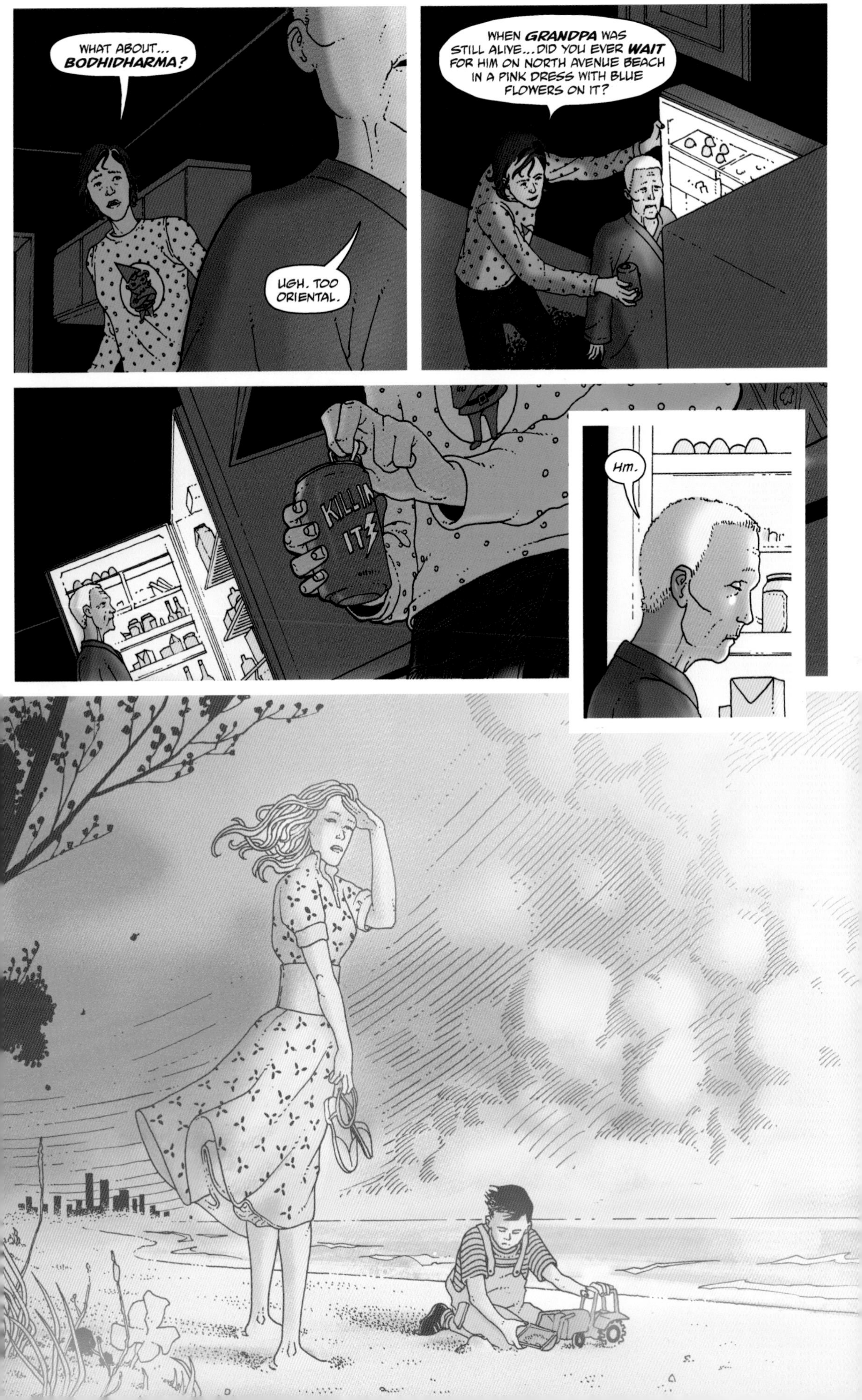
WHAT ABOUT... **BODHIDHARMA?**
UGH. TOO ORIENTAL.
WHEN **GRANDPA** WAS STILL ALIVE... DID YOU EVER **WAIT** FOR HIM ON NORTH AVENUE BEACH IN A PINK DRESS WITH BLUE FLOWERS ON IT?
KILLIN IT
Hm.

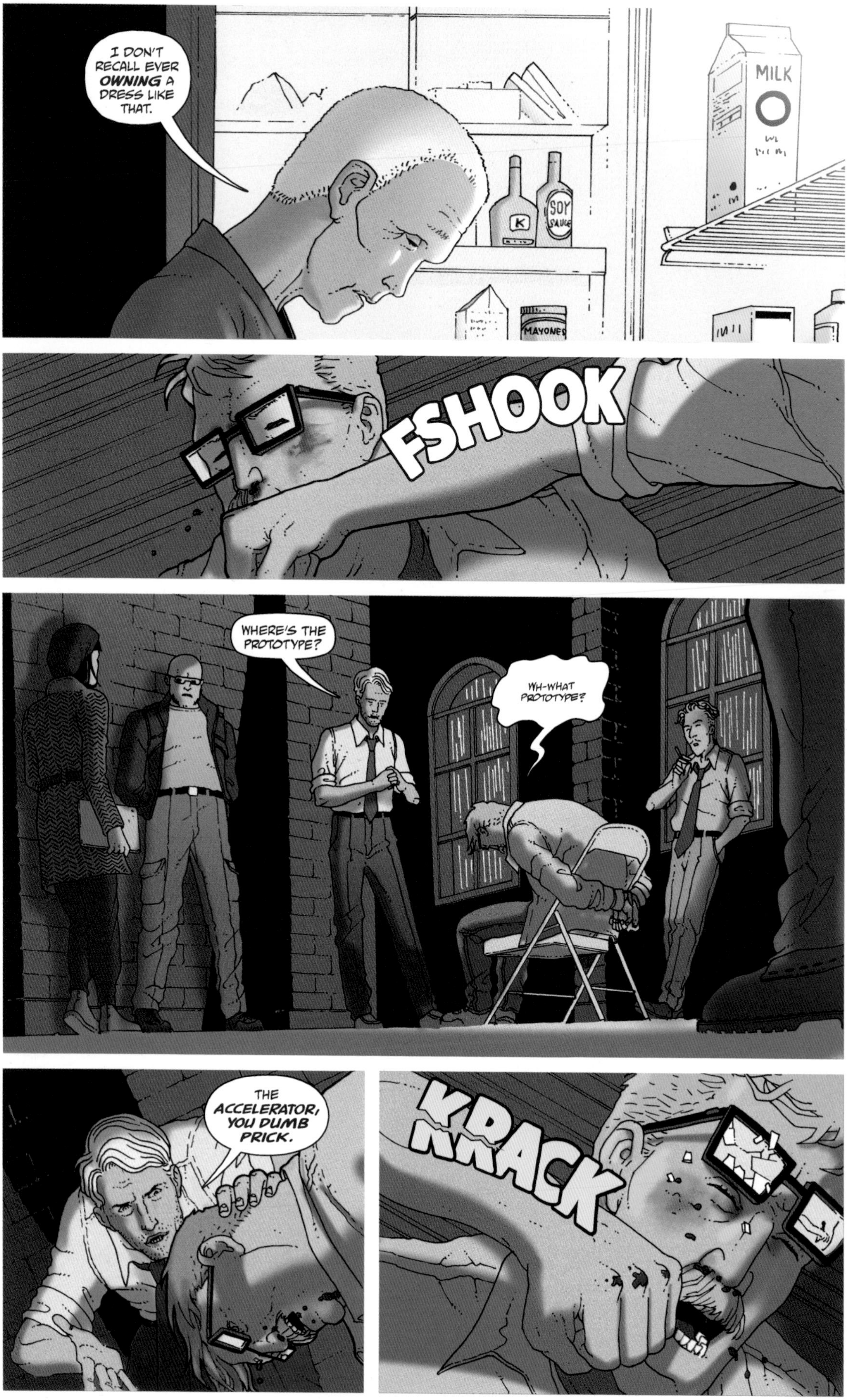
I DON'T RECALL EVER OWNING A DRESS LIKE THAT.
MILK
SOY SAUCE
MAYONE
FSHOOK
WHERE'S THE PROTOTYPE?
WH-WHAT PROTOTYPE?
THE ACCELERATOR, YOU DUMB PRICK.
KRACK

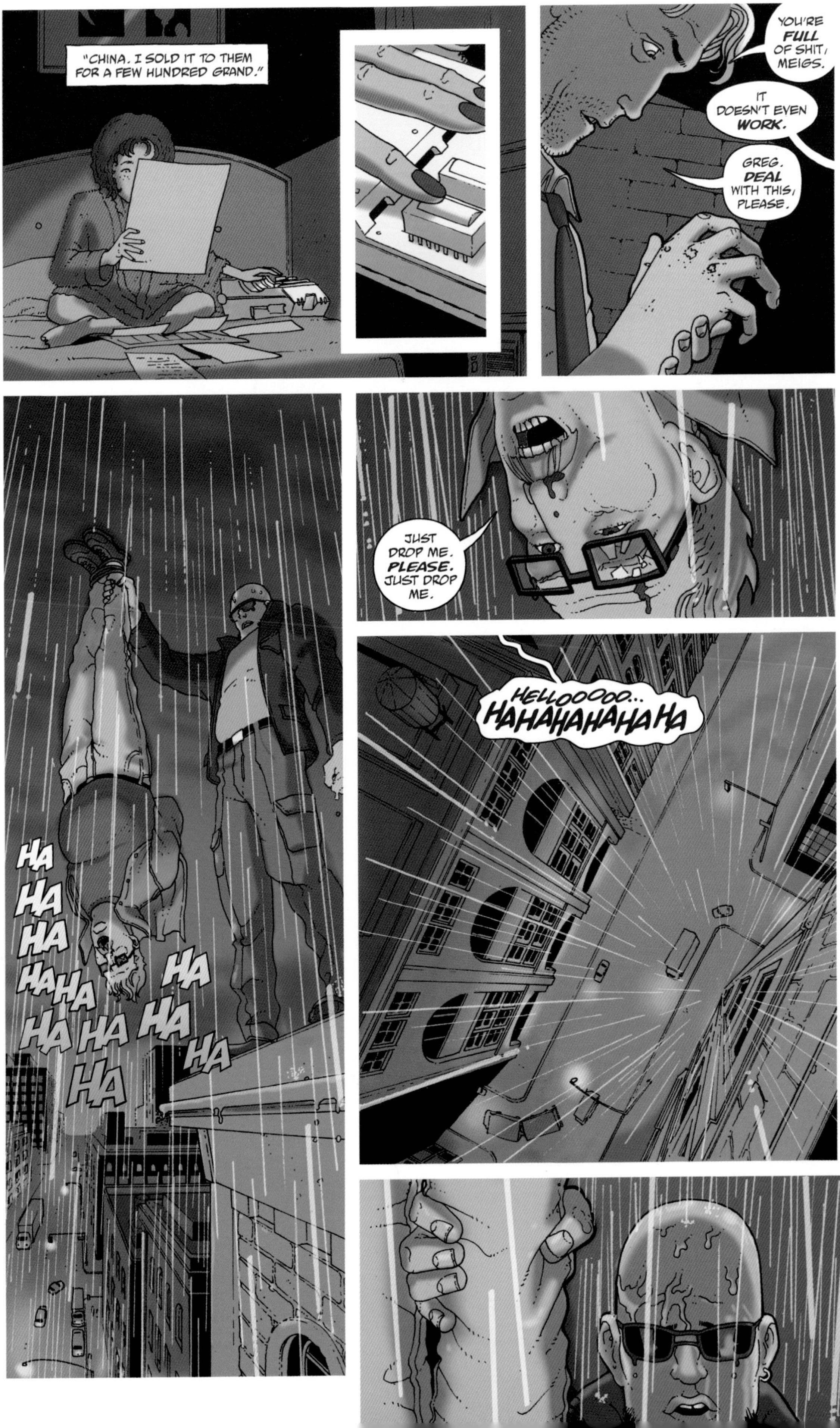
"CHINA. I SOLD IT TO THEM FOR A FEW HUNDRED GRAND."
YOU'RE FULL OF SHIT, MEIGS.
IT DOESN'T EVEN WORK.
GREG. DEAL WITH THIS, PLEASE.
JUST DROP ME. PLEASE. JUST DROP ME.
HA HA HA HAHA HA HA HA HA HA HA HA
HELLOOOOO... HAHAHAHAHAHAHA

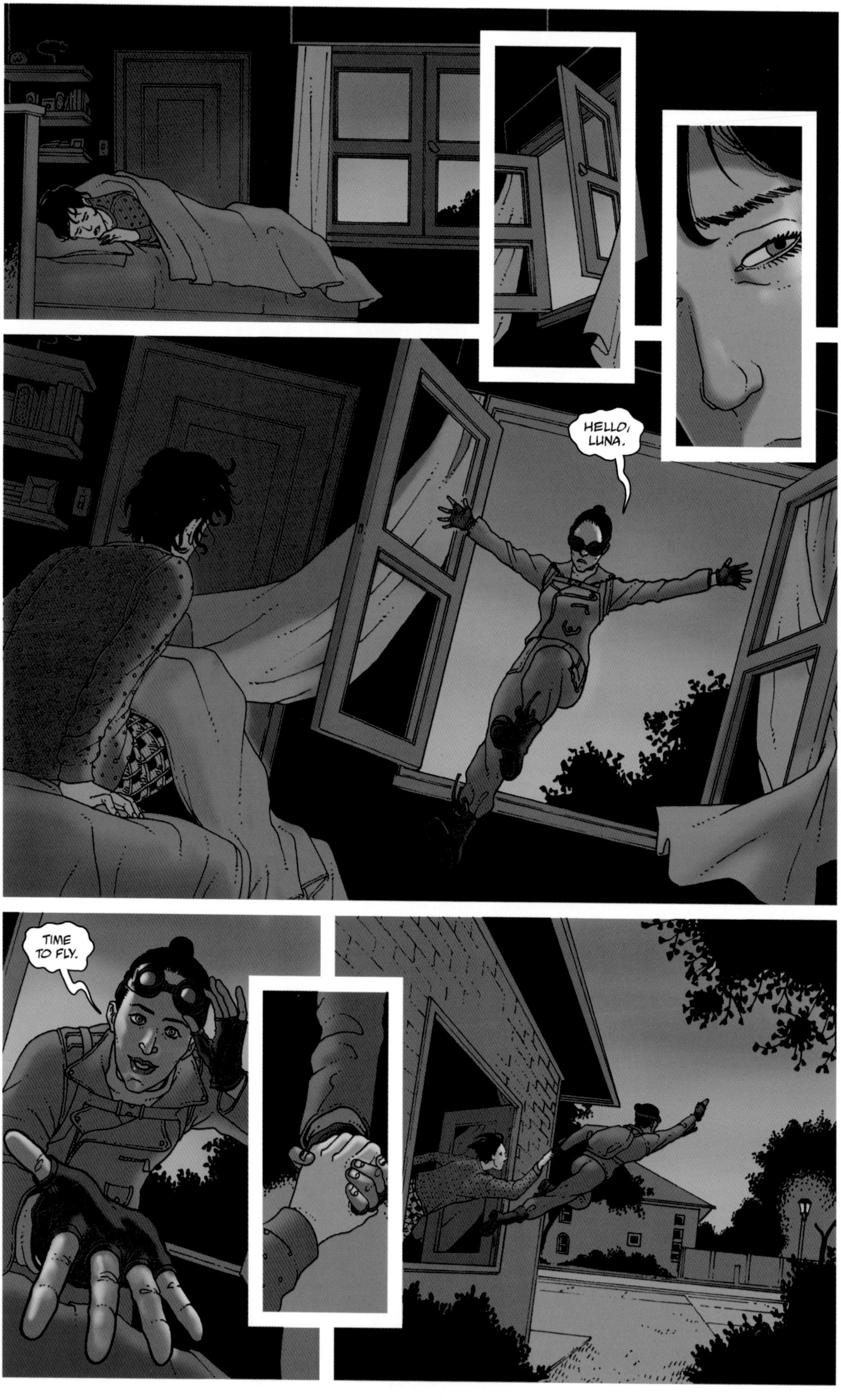
HELLO, LUNA.
TIME TO FLY.

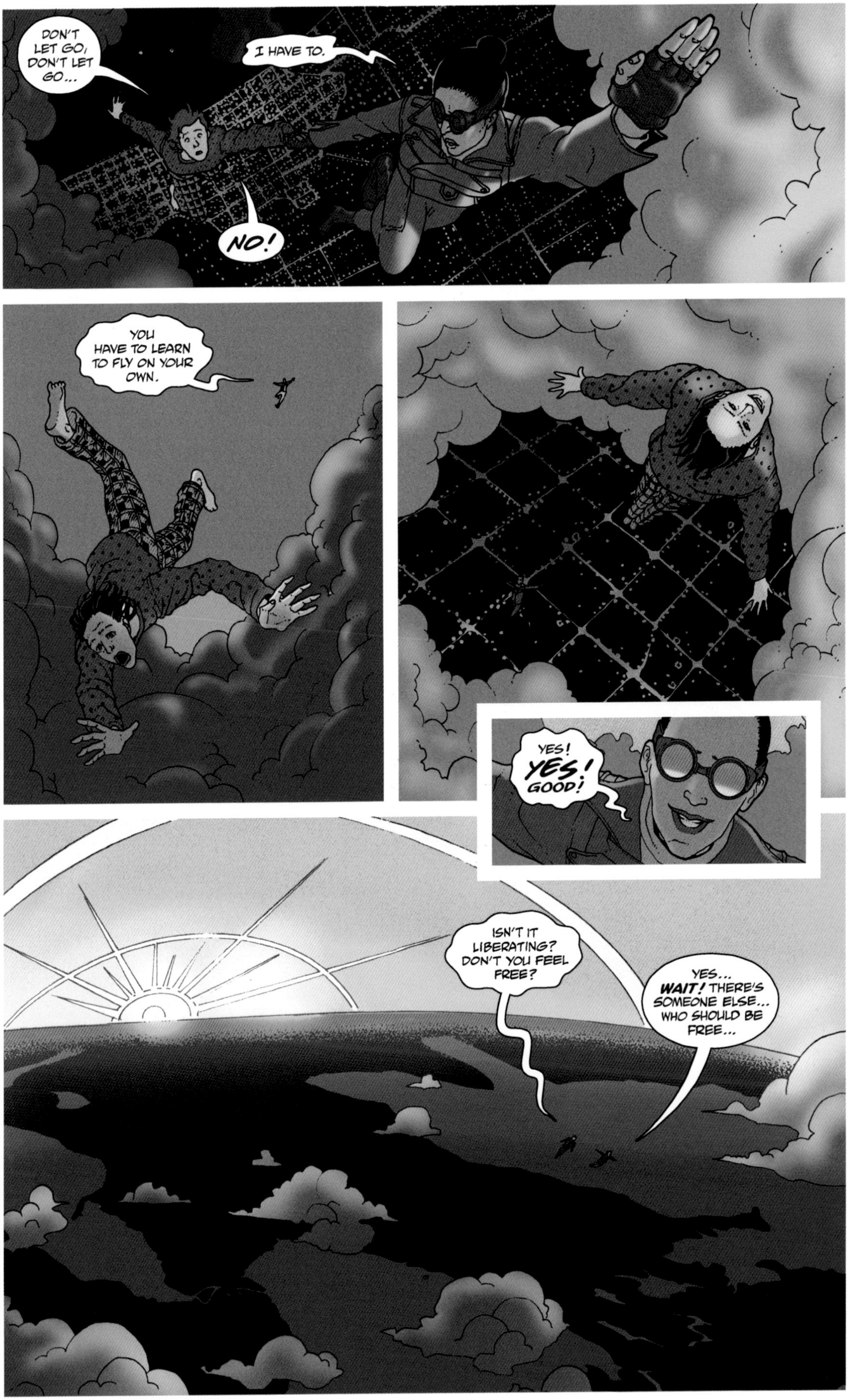
DON'T LET GO, DON'T LET GO...
I HAVE TO.
NO!
YOU HAVE TO LEARN TO FLY ON YOUR OWN.
YES! YES! GOOD!
ISN'T IT LIBERATING? DON'T YOU FEEL FREE?
YES... WAIT! THERE'S SOMEONE ELSE... WHO SHOULD BE FREE...

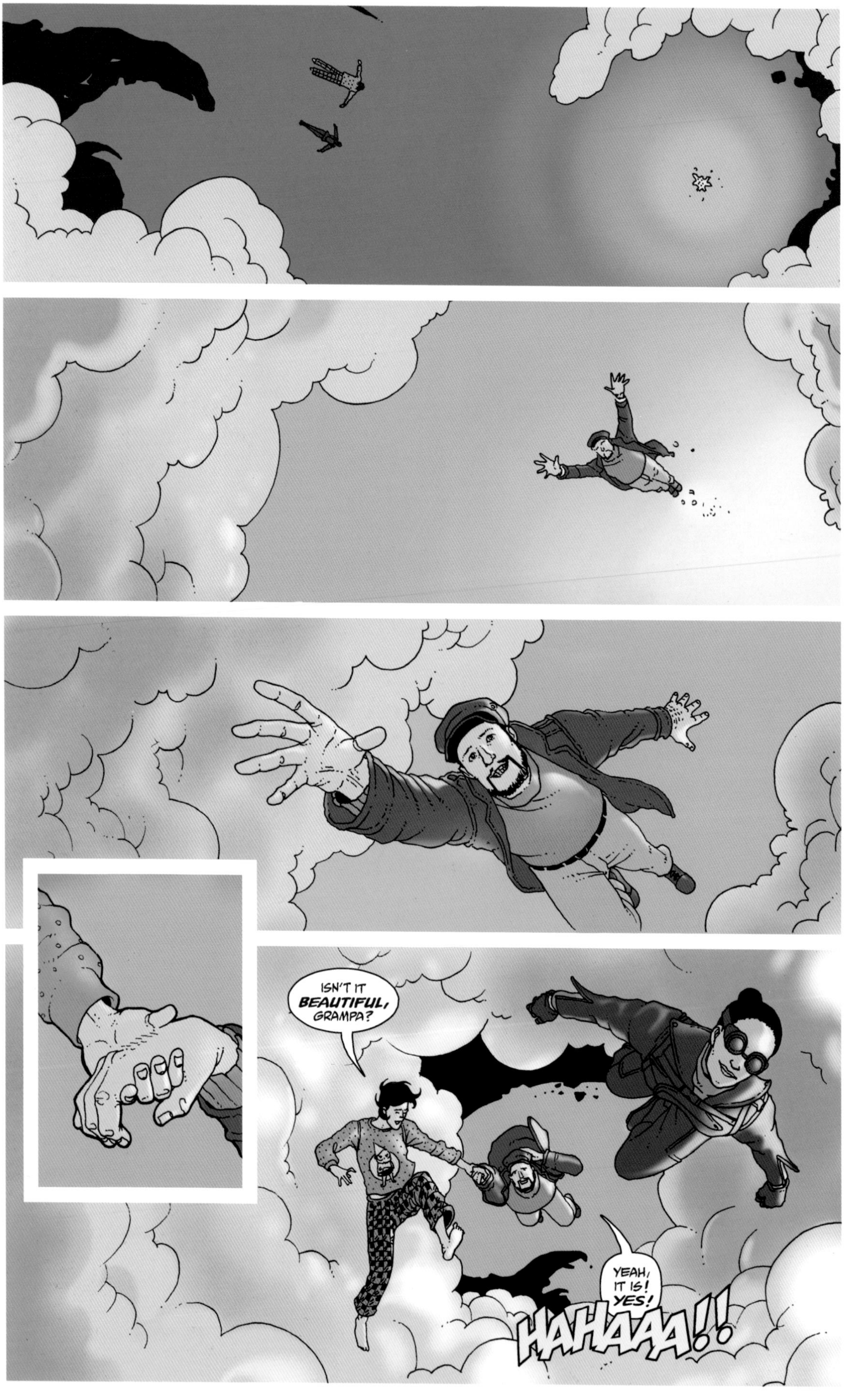
ISN'T IT BEAUTIFUL, GRAMPA?
YEAH, IT IS! YES!
HAHAAA!!

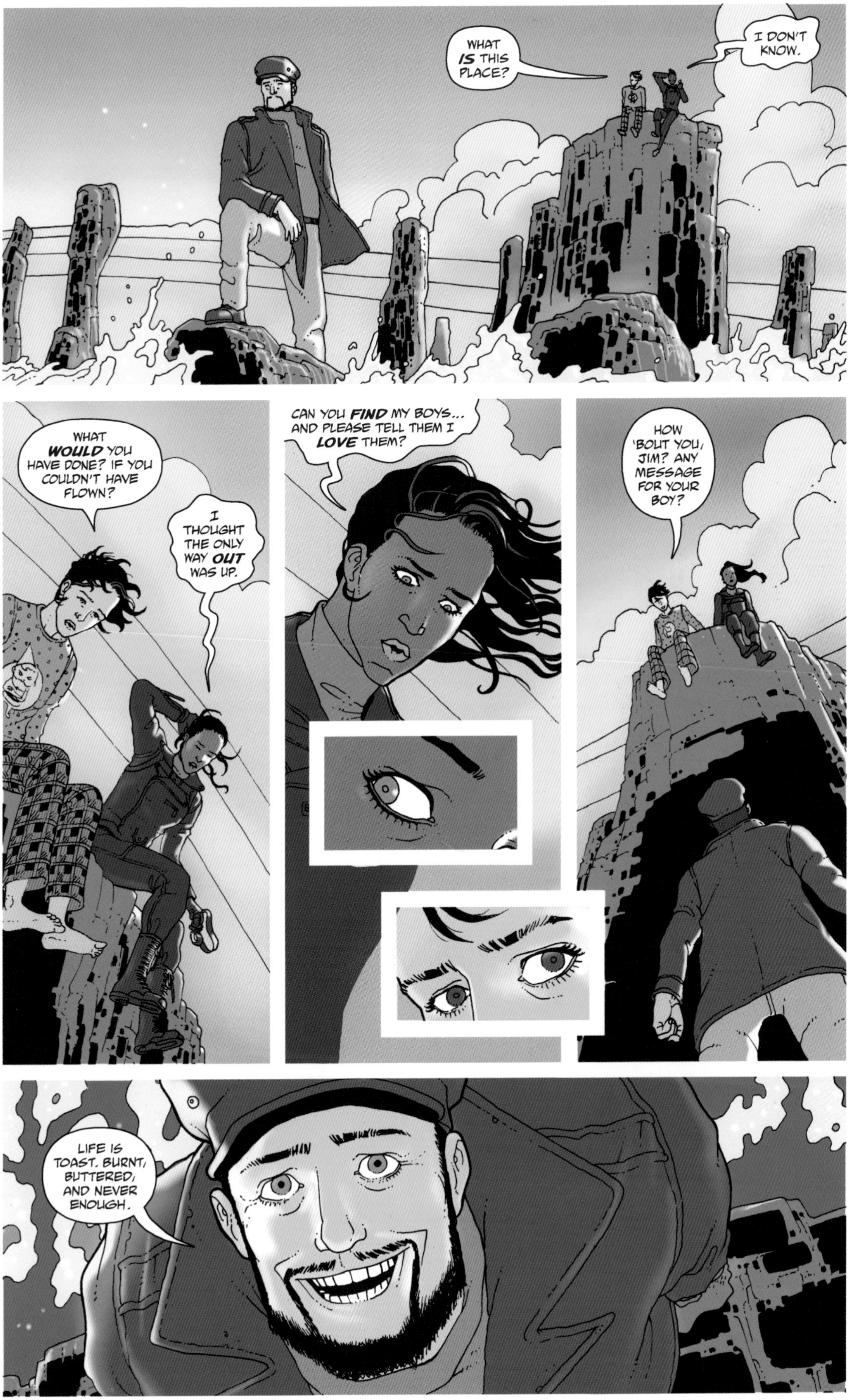
WHAT IS THIS PLACE?
I DON'T KNOW.
WHAT WOULD YOU HAVE DONE? IF YOU COULDN'T HAVE FLOWN?
I THOUGHT THE ONLY WAY OUT WAS UP.
CAN YOU FIND MY BOYS... AND PLEASE TELL THEM I LOVE THEM?
HOW 'BOUT YOU, JIM? ANY MESSAGE FOR YOUR BOY?
LIFE IS TOAST. BURNT, BUTTERED, AND NEVER ENOUGH.

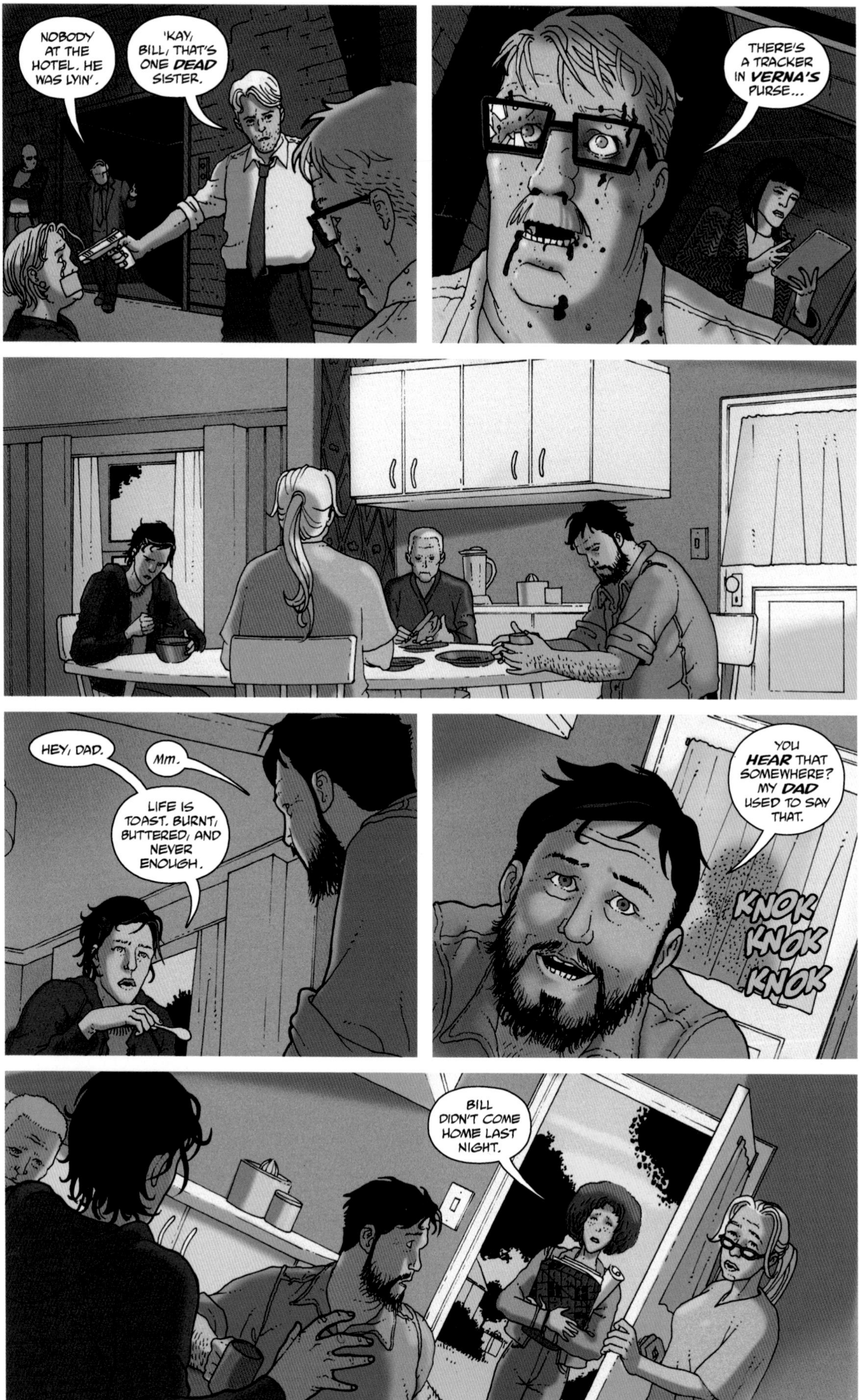
NOBODY AT THE HOTEL. HE WAS LYIN'.
'KAY, BILL, THAT'S ONE DEAD SISTER.
THERE'S A TRACKER IN VERNA'S PURSE...
HEY, DAD.
Mm.
LIFE IS TOAST. BURNT, BUTTERED, AND NEVER ENOUGH.
YOU HEAR THAT SOMEWHERE? MY DAD USED TO SAY THAT.
KNOK KNOK KNOK
BILL DIDN'T COME HOME LAST NIGHT.

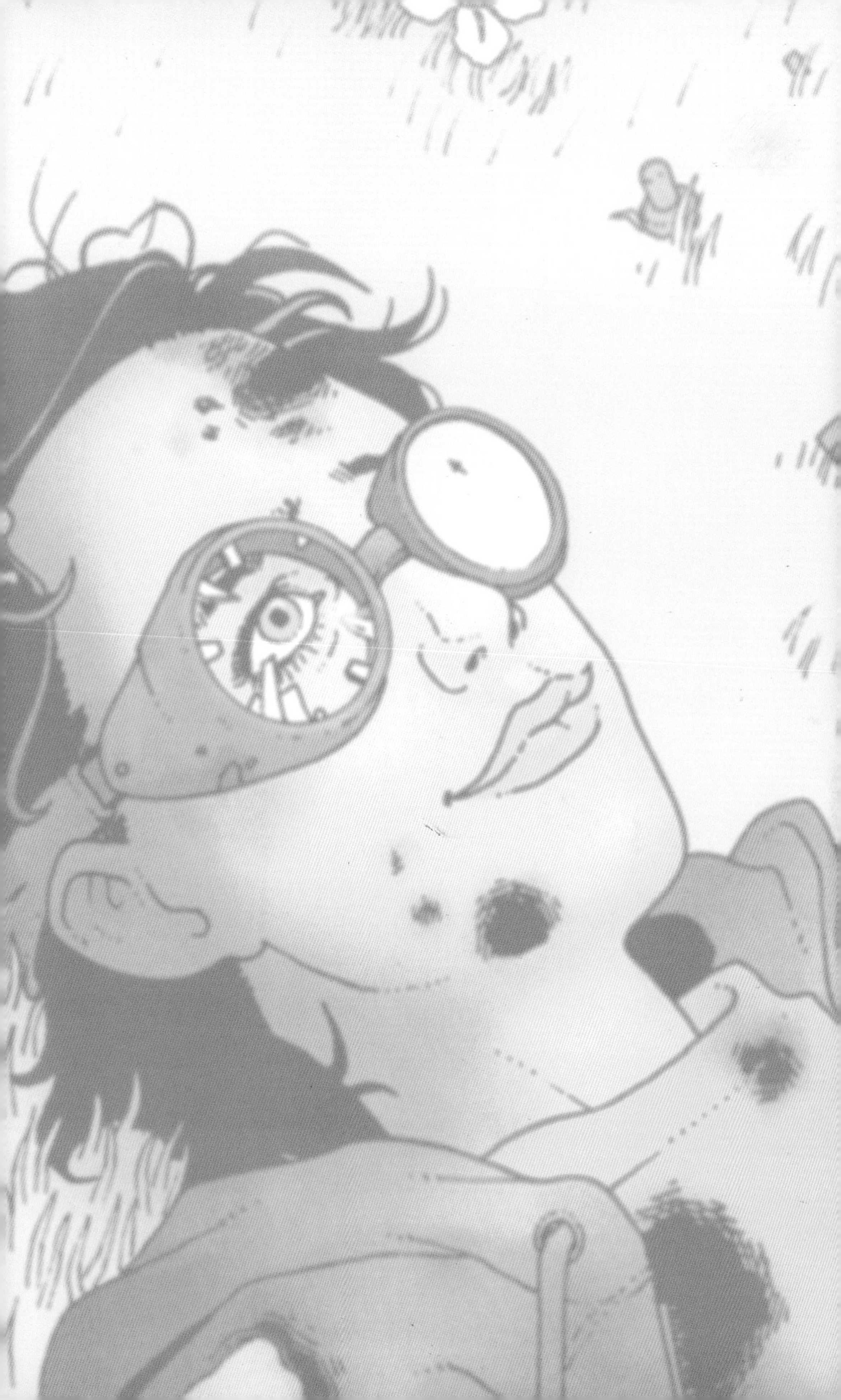

CHAPTER IV
"For she was a Boojum, you see"

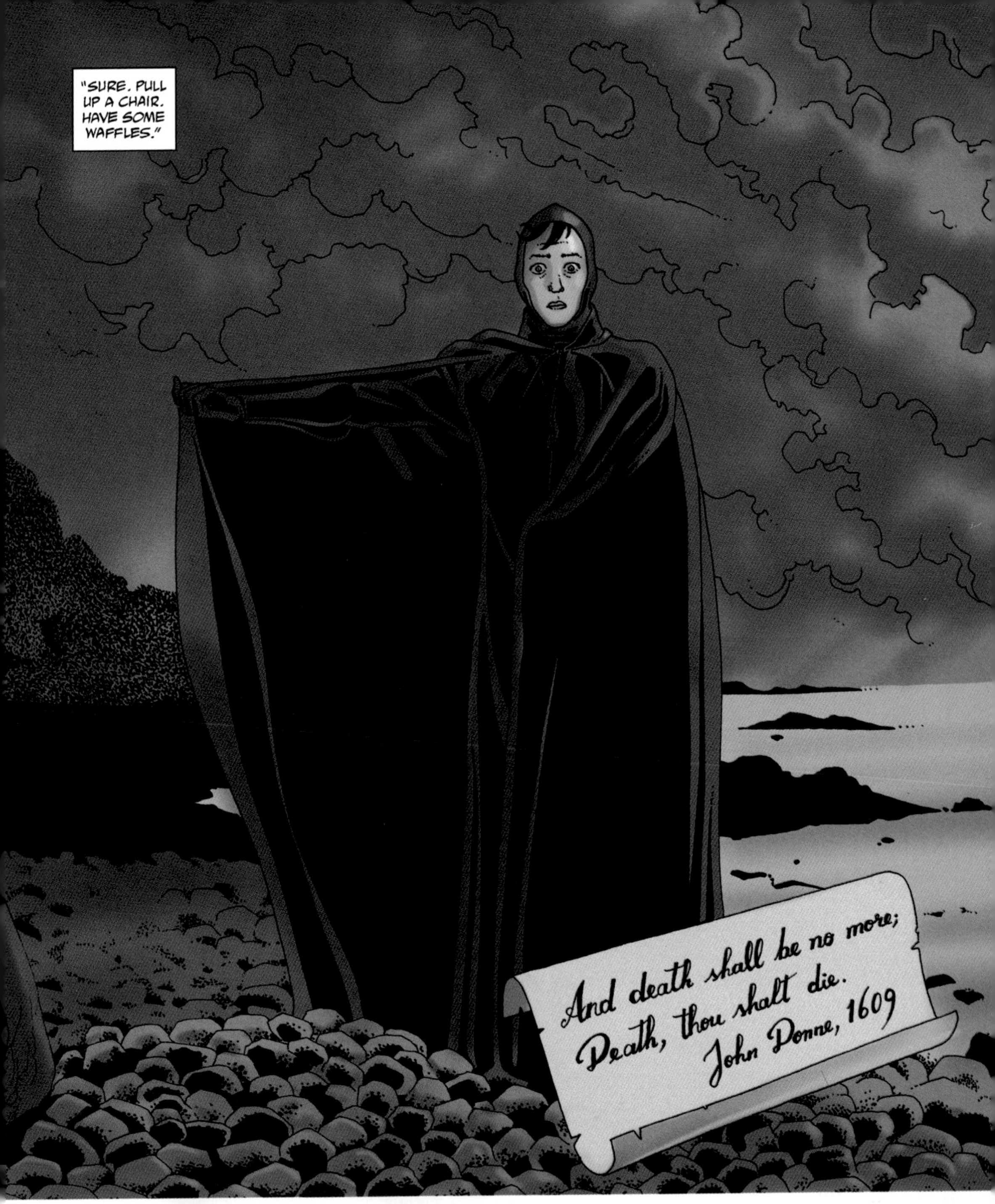
"SURE. PULL UP A CHAIR. HAVE SOME WAFFLES."
And death shall be no more;
Death, thou shalt die.
John Donne, 1609

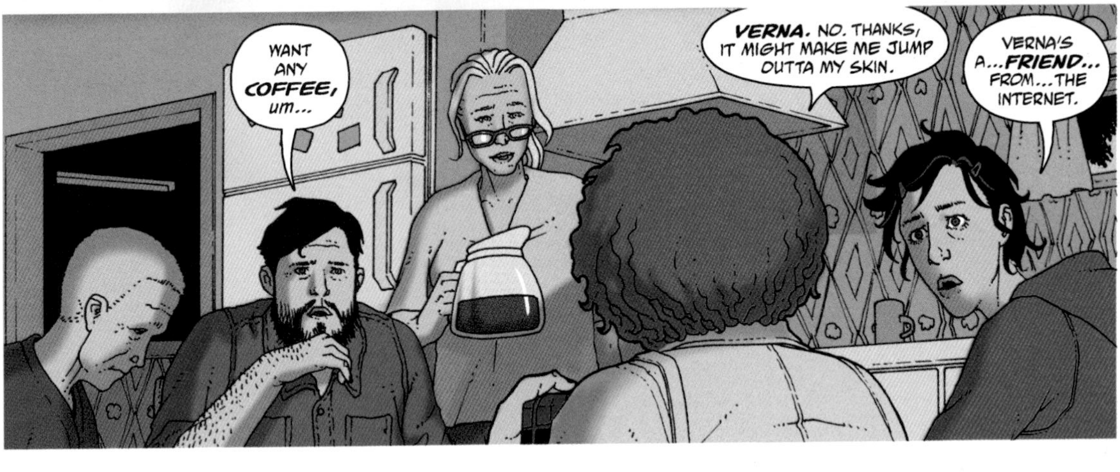
WANT ANY COFFEE, UM...
VERNA. NO. THANKS, IT MIGHT MAKE ME JUMP OUTTA MY SKIN.
VERNA'S A...FRIEND... FROM...THE INTERNET.

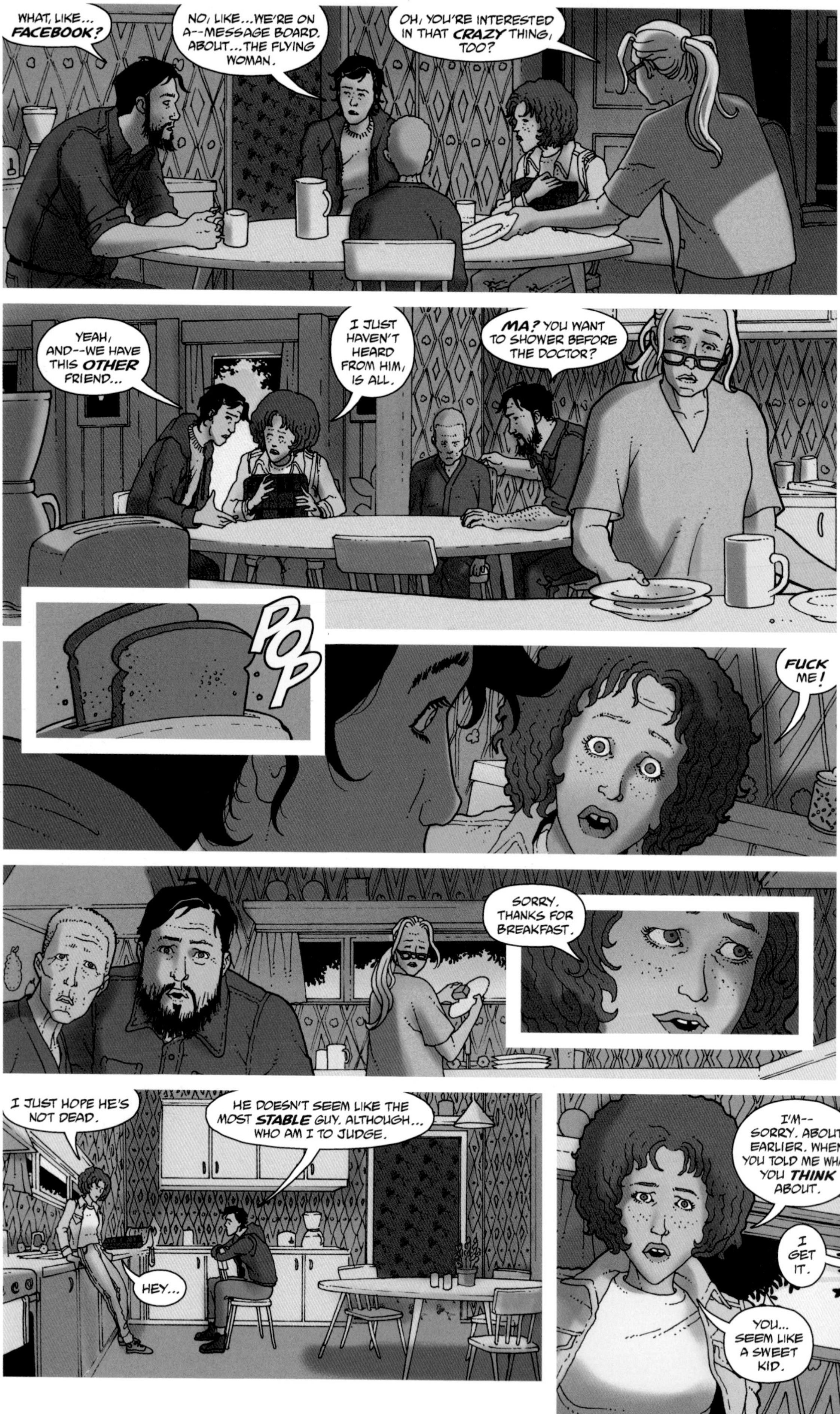
WHAT, LIKE... FACEBOOK?
NO, LIKE...WE'RE ON A--MESSAGE BOARD. ABOUT...THE FLYING WOMAN.
OH, YOU'RE INTERESTED IN THAT CRAZY THING, TOO?
YEAH, AND--WE HAVE THIS OTHER FRIEND...
I JUST HAVEN'T HEARD FROM HIM, IS ALL.
MA? YOU WANT TO SHOWER BEFORE THE DOCTOR?
POP
FUCK ME!
SORRY. THANKS FOR BREAKFAST.
I JUST HOPE HE'S NOT DEAD.
HE DOESN'T SEEM LIKE THE MOST STABLE GUY. ALTHOUGH... WHO AM I TO JUDGE.
HEY...
I'M-- SORRY. ABOUT EARLIER. WHEN YOU TOLD ME WHAT YOU THINK ABOUT.
I GET IT.
YOU... SEEM LIKE A SWEET KID.

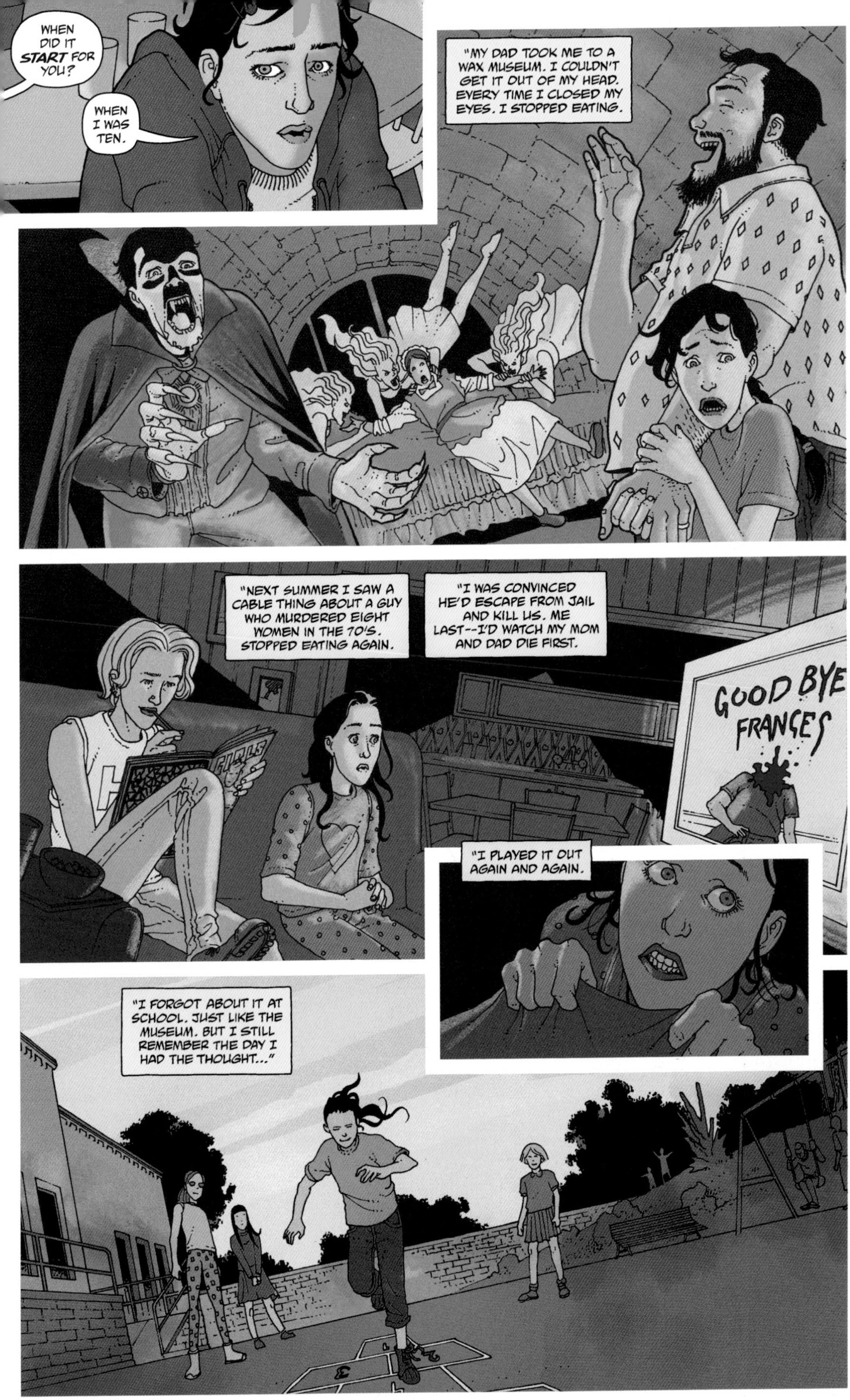
WHEN DID IT START FOR YOU?
WHEN I WAS TEN.
"MY DAD TOOK ME TO A WAX MUSEUM. I COULDN'T GET IT OUT OF MY HEAD. EVERY TIME I CLOSED MY EYES. I STOPPED EATING.
"NEXT SUMMER I SAW A CABLE THING ABOUT A GUY WHO MURDERED EIGHT WOMEN IN THE 70'S. STOPPED EATING AGAIN.
"I WAS CONVINCED HE'D ESCAPE FROM JAIL AND KILL US. ME LAST--I'D WATCH MY MOM AND DAD DIE FIRST.
GOOD BYE FRANCES
"I PLAYED IT OUT AGAIN AND AGAIN.
"I FORGOT ABOUT IT AT SCHOOL. JUST LIKE THE MUSEUM. BUT I STILL REMEMBER THE DAY I HAD THE THOUGHT..."

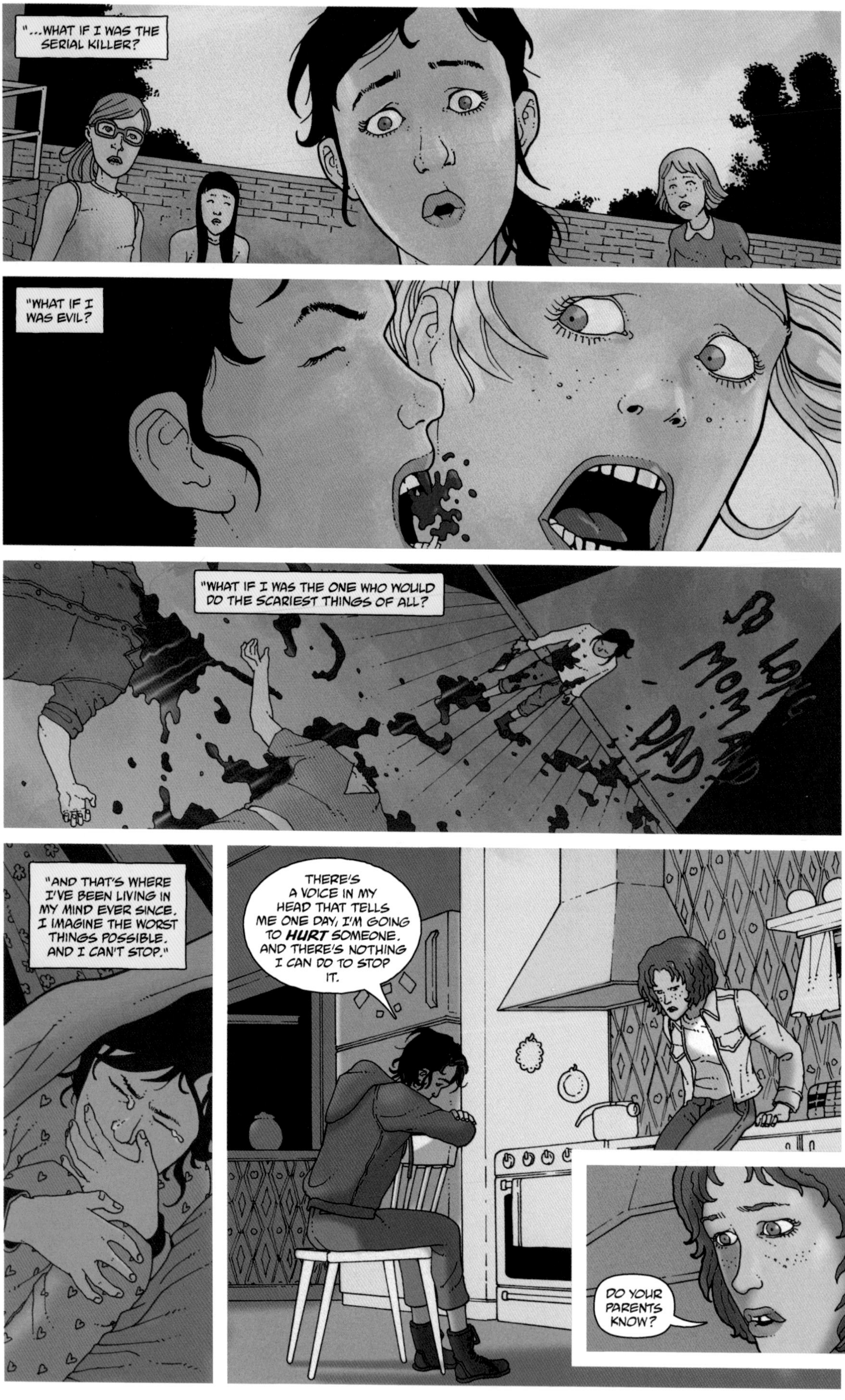
"...WHAT IF I WAS THE SERIAL KILLER?
"WHAT IF I WAS EVIL?
"WHAT IF I WAS THE ONE WHO WOULD DO THE SCARIEST THINGS OF ALL?
"AND THAT'S WHERE I'VE BEEN LIVING IN MY MIND EVER SINCE. I IMAGINE THE WORST THINGS POSSIBLE. AND I CAN'T STOP."
THERE'S A VOICE IN MY HEAD THAT TELLS ME ONE DAY, I'M GOING TO HURT SOMEONE. AND THERE'S NOTHING I CAN DO TO STOP IT.
DO YOUR PARENTS KNOW?

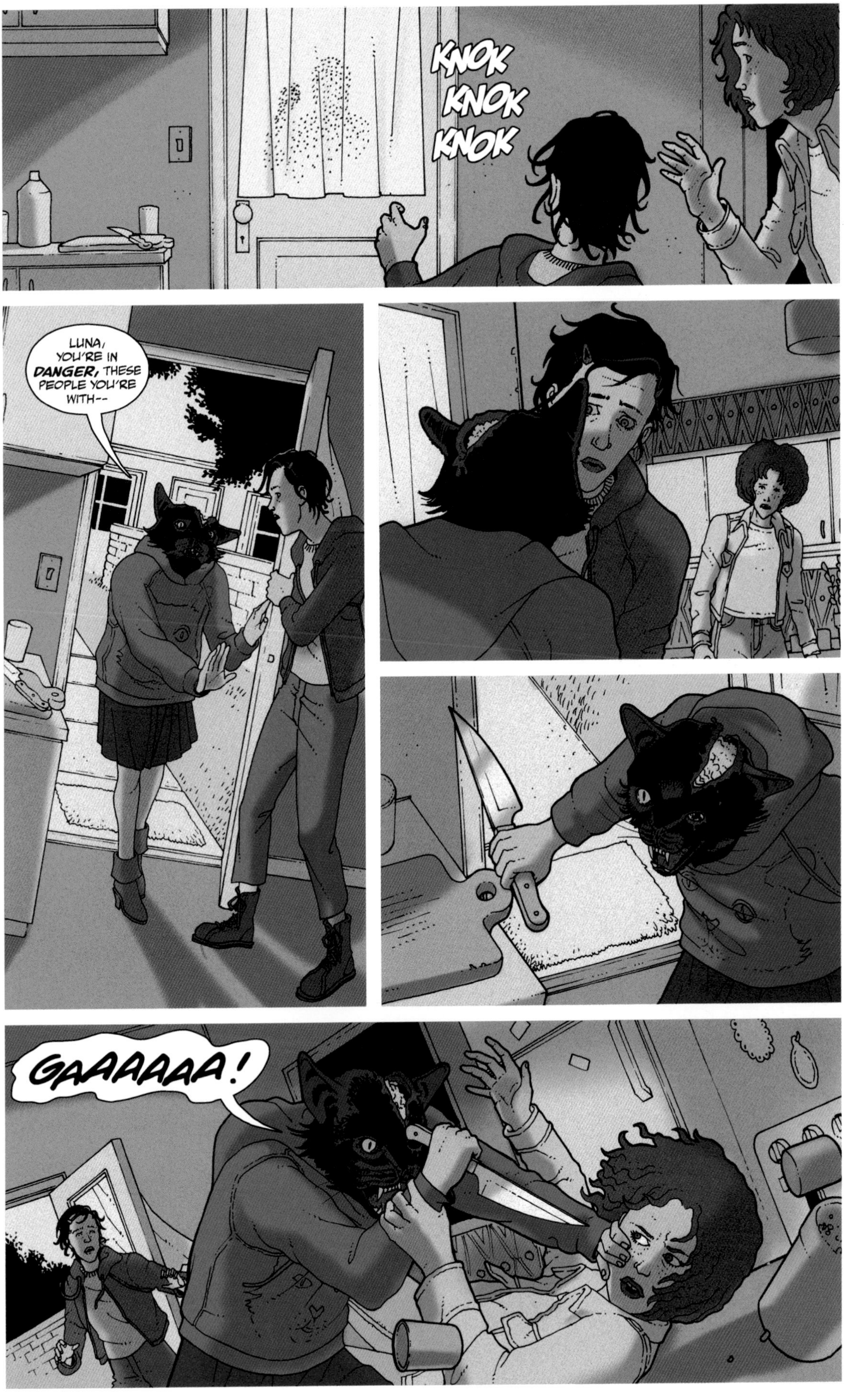
KNOK KNOK KNOK
LUNA, YOU'RE IN DANGER, THESE PEOPLE YOU'RE WITH--
GAAAAAA!

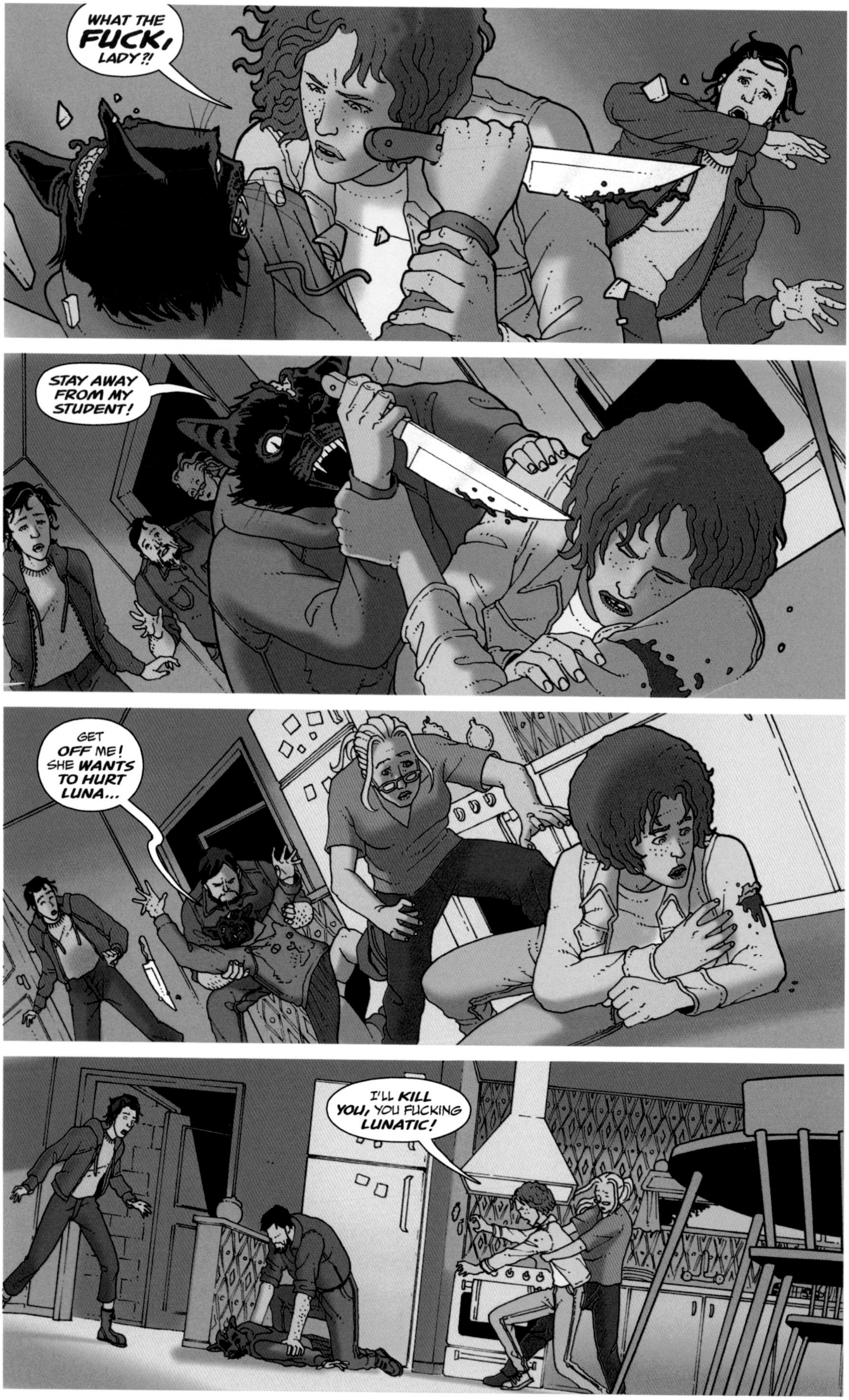
WHAT THE FUCK, LADY?!
STAY AWAY FROM MY STUDENT!
GET OFF ME! SHE WANTS TO HURT LUNA...
I'LL KILL YOU, YOU FUCKING LUNATIC!

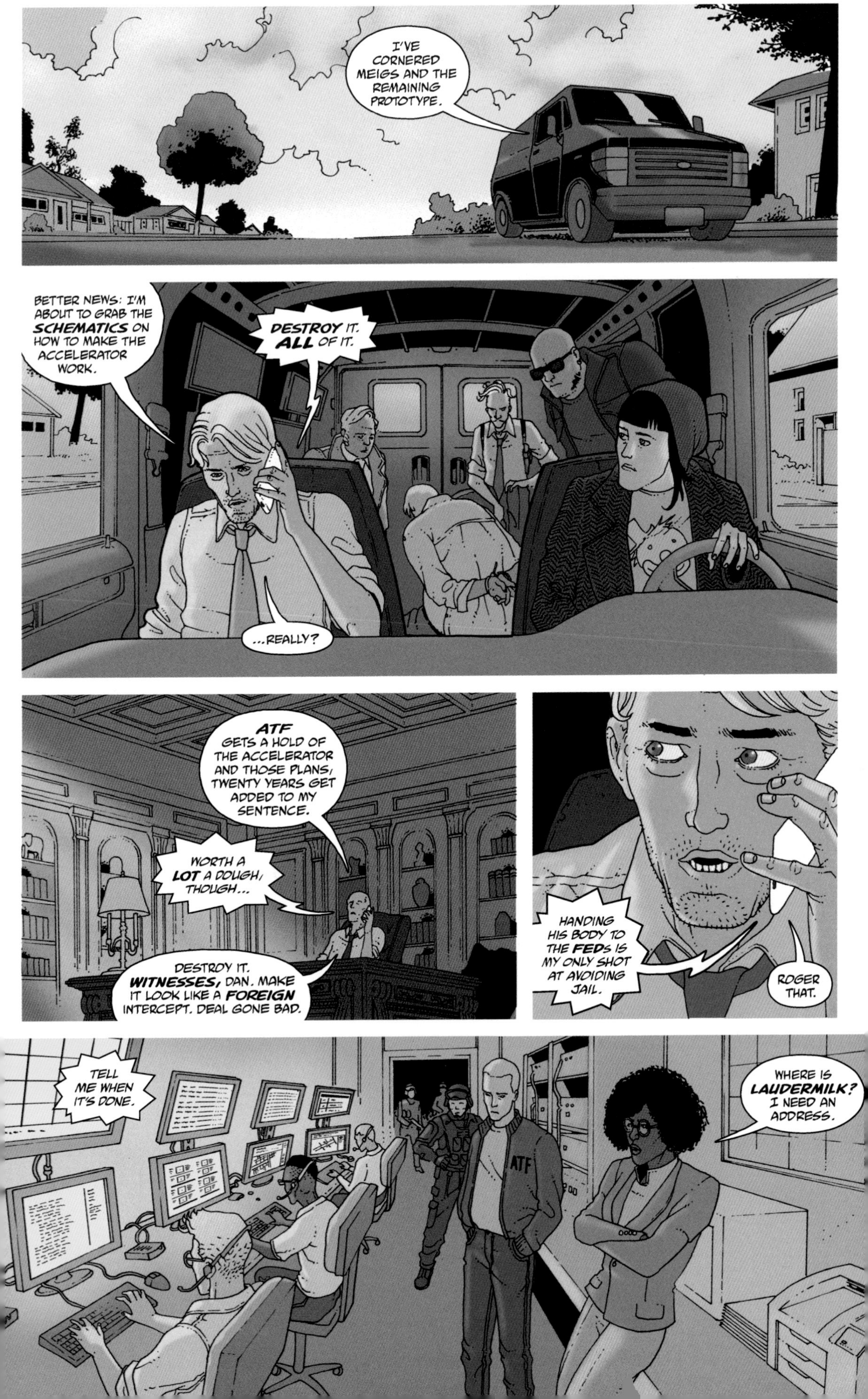
I'VE CORNERED MEIGS AND THE REMAINING PROTOTYPE.
BETTER NEWS: I'M ABOUT TO GRAB THE SCHEMATICS ON HOW TO MAKE THE ACCELERATOR WORK.
DESTROY IT. ALL OF IT.
...REALLY?
ATF GETS A HOLD OF THE ACCELERATOR AND THOSE PLANS, TWENTY YEARS GET ADDED TO MY SENTENCE.
WORTH A LOT A DOUGH, THOUGH...
DESTROY IT. WITNESSES, DAN. MAKE IT LOOK LIKE A FOREIGN INTERCEPT. DEAL GONE BAD.
HANDING HIS BODY TO THE FEDS IS MY ONLY SHOT AT AVOIDING JAIL.
ROGER THAT.
TELL ME WHEN IT'S DONE.
WHERE IS LAUDERMILK? I NEED AN ADDRESS.

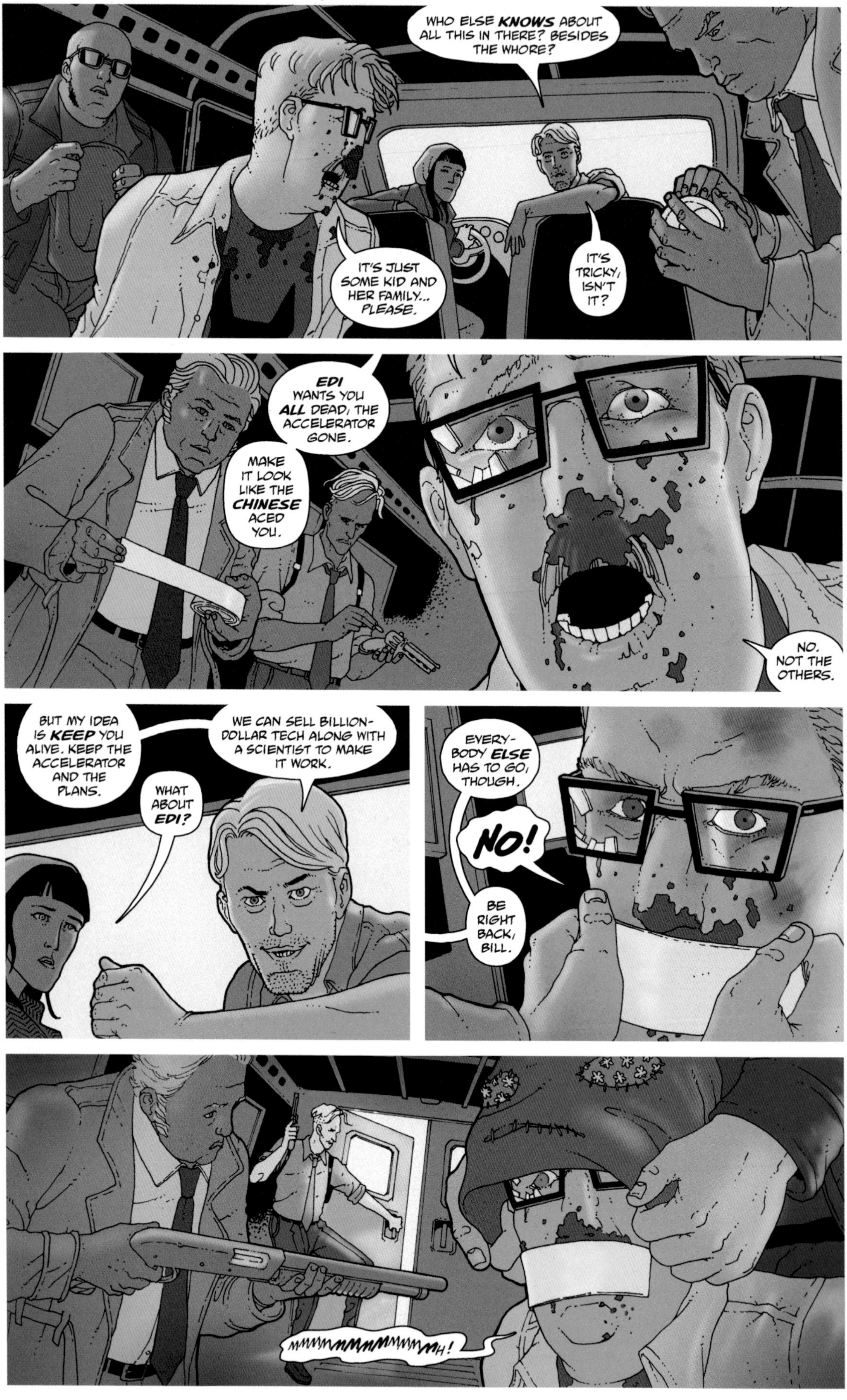
WHO ELSE KNOWS ABOUT ALL THIS IN THERE? BESIDES THE WHORE?
IT'S JUST SOME KID AND HER FAMILY... PLEASE.
IT'S TRICKY, ISN'T IT?
EDI WANTS YOU ALL DEAD, THE ACCELERATOR GONE.
MAKE IT LOOK LIKE THE CHINESE ACED YOU.
NO. NOT THE OTHERS.
BUT MY IDEA IS KEEP YOU ALIVE. KEEP THE ACCELERATOR AND THE PLANS.
WE CAN SELL BILLION-DOLLAR TECH ALONG WITH A SCIENTIST TO MAKE IT WORK.
WHAT ABOUT EDI?
EVERY-BODY ELSE HAS TO GO, THOUGH.
NO!
BE RIGHT BACK, BILL.
MMMMMMMMMMMMMMH!

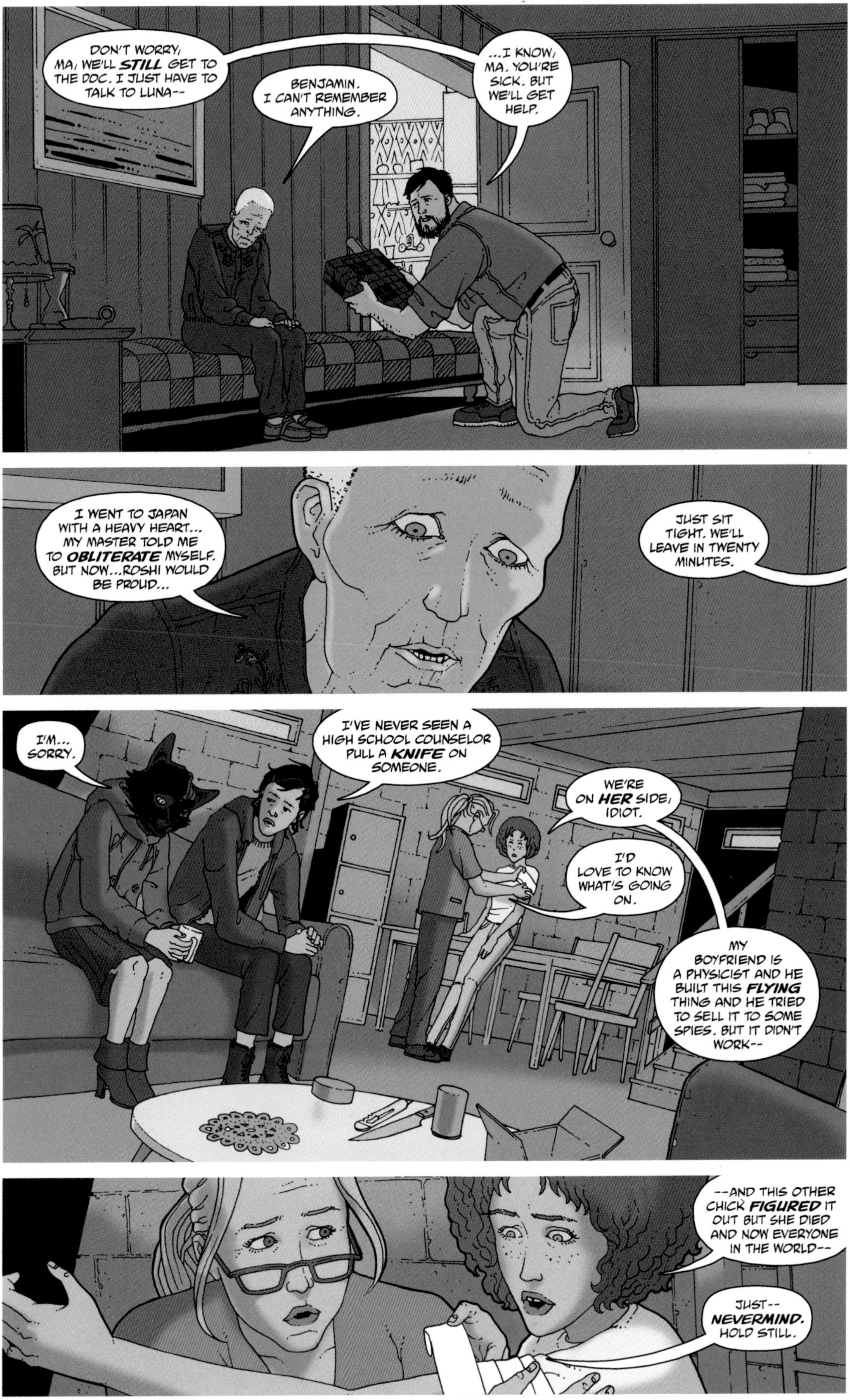
DON'T WORRY, MA, WE'LL STILL GET TO THE DOC. I JUST HAVE TO TALK TO LUNA--
BENJAMIN. I CAN'T REMEMBER ANYTHING.
...I KNOW, MA. YOU'RE SICK. BUT WE'LL GET HELP.
I WENT TO JAPAN WITH A HEAVY HEART... MY MASTER TOLD ME TO OBLITERATE MYSELF. BUT NOW...ROSHI WOULD BE PROUD...
JUST SIT TIGHT. WE'LL LEAVE IN TWENTY MINUTES.
I'M... SORRY.
I'VE NEVER SEEN A HIGH SCHOOL COUNSELOR PULL A KNIFE ON SOMEONE.
WE'RE ON HER SIDE, IDIOT.
I'D LOVE TO KNOW WHAT'S GOING ON.
MY BOYFRIEND IS A PHYSICIST AND HE BUILT THIS FLYING THING AND HE TRIED TO SELL IT TO SOME SPIES. BUT IT DIDN'T WORK--
--AND THIS OTHER CHICK FIGURED IT OUT BUT SHE DIED AND NOW EVERYONE IN THE WORLD--
JUST-- NEVERMIND. HOLD STILL.

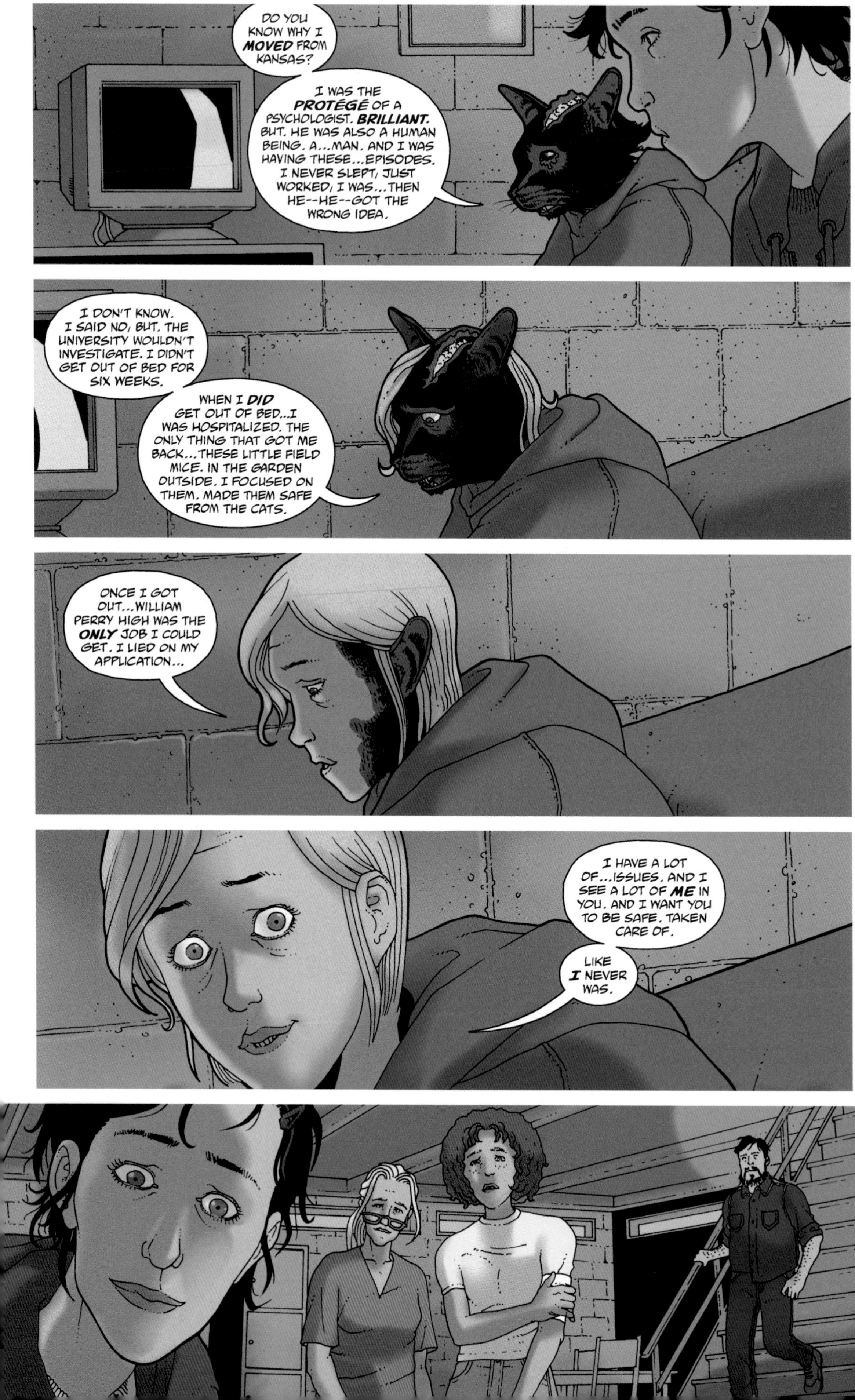
DO YOU KNOW WHY I MOVED FROM KANSAS?
I WAS THE PROTÉGÉ OF A PSYCHOLOGIST. BRILLIANT. BUT. HE WAS ALSO A HUMAN BEING. A...MAN. AND I WAS HAVING THESE...EPISODES. I NEVER SLEPT; JUST WORKED; I WAS...THEN HE--HE--GOT THE WRONG IDEA.
I DON'T KNOW. I SAID NO; BUT. THE UNIVERSITY WOULDN'T INVESTIGATE. I DIDN'T GET OUT OF BED FOR SIX WEEKS.
WHEN I DID GET OUT OF BED...I WAS HOSPITALIZED. THE ONLY THING THAT GOT ME BACK...THESE LITTLE FIELD MICE. IN THE GARDEN OUTSIDE. I FOCUSED ON THEM. MADE THEM SAFE FROM THE CATS.
ONCE I GOT OUT...WILLIAM PERRY HIGH WAS THE ONLY JOB I COULD GET. I LIED ON MY APPLICATION...
I HAVE A LOT OF...ISSUES. AND I SEE A LOT OF ME IN YOU. AND I WANT YOU TO BE SAFE. TAKEN CARE OF.
LIKE I NEVER WAS.

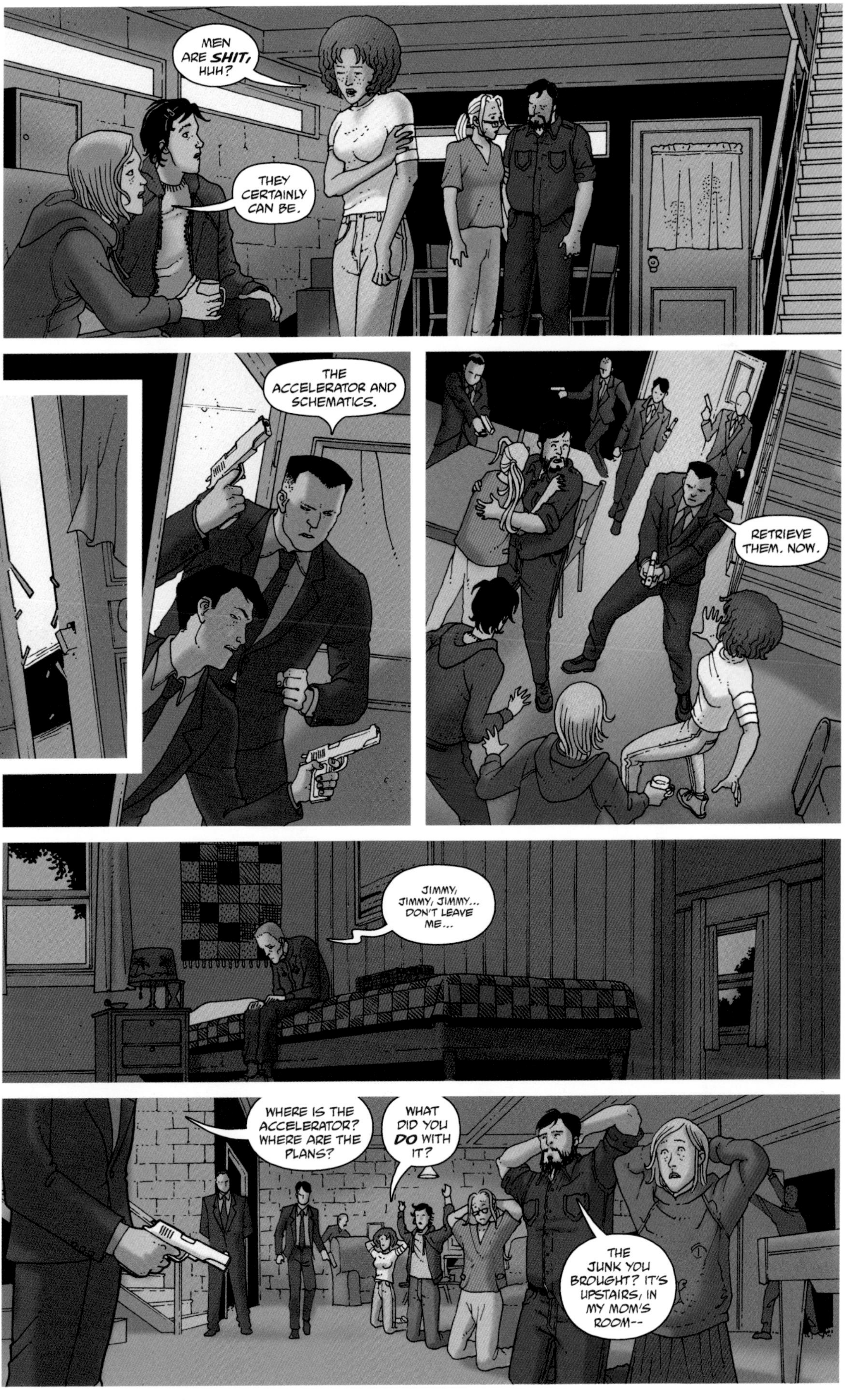
MEN ARE SHIT, HUH?
THEY CERTAINLY CAN BE.
THE ACCELERATOR AND SCHEMATICS.
RETRIEVE THEM. NOW.
JIMMY, JIMMY, JIMMY... DON'T LEAVE ME...
WHERE IS THE ACCELERATOR? WHERE ARE THE PLANS?
WHAT DID YOU DO WITH IT?
THE JUNK YOU BROUGHT? IT'S UPSTAIRS, IN MY MOM'S ROOM--

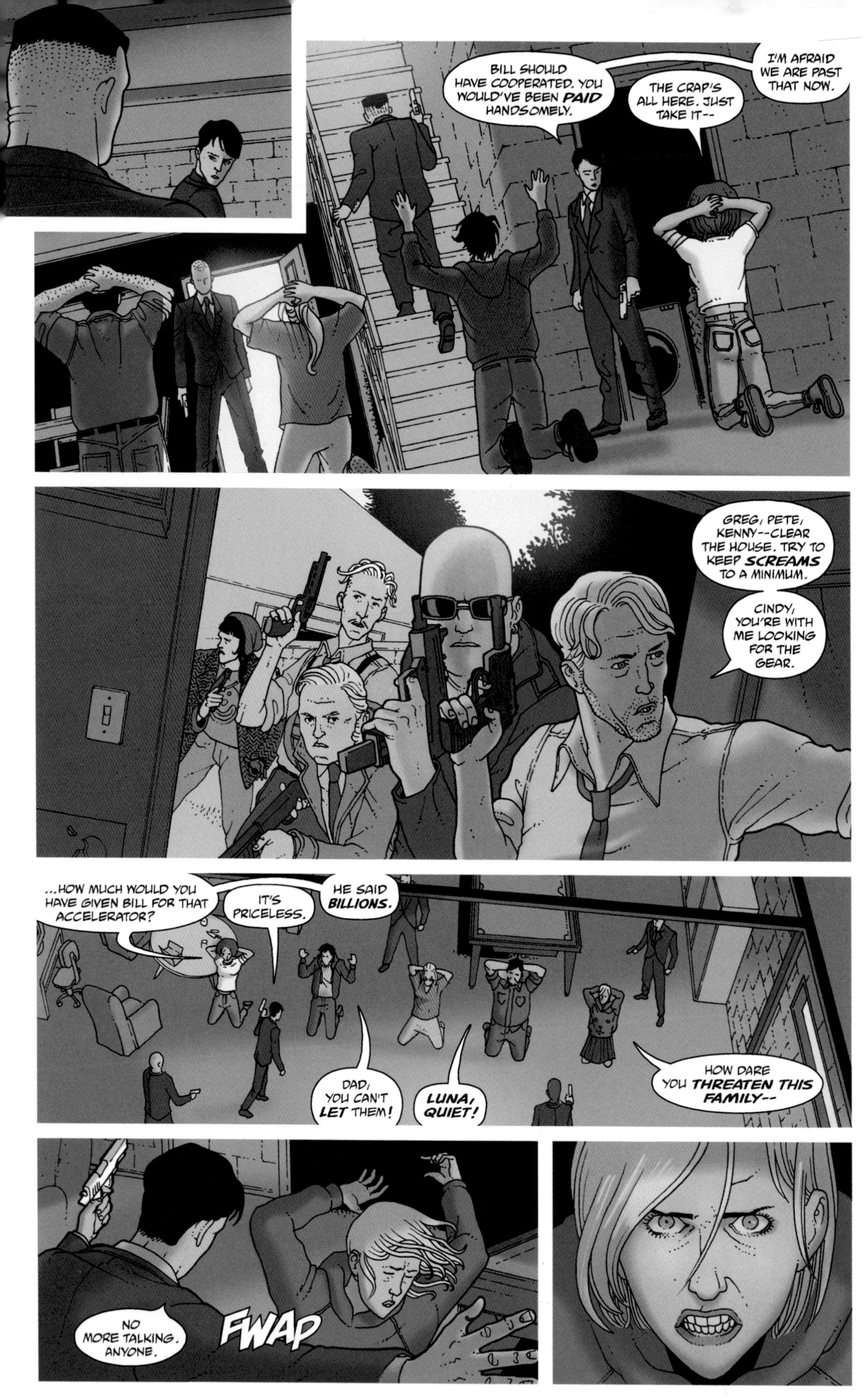
BILL SHOULD HAVE COOPERATED. YOU WOULD'VE BEEN PAID HANDSOMELY.
THE CRAP'S ALL HERE. JUST TAKE IT--
I'M AFRAID WE ARE PAST THAT NOW.
GREG, PETE, KENNY--CLEAR THE HOUSE. TRY TO KEEP SCREAMS TO A MINIMUM.
CINDY, YOU'RE WITH ME LOOKING FOR THE GEAR.
...HOW MUCH WOULD YOU HAVE GIVEN BILL FOR THAT ACCELERATOR?
IT'S PRICELESS.
HE SAID BILLIONS.
DAD, YOU CAN'T LET THEM!
LUNA, QUIET!
HOW DARE YOU THREATEN THIS FAMILY--
NO MORE TALKING. ANYONE.
FWAP

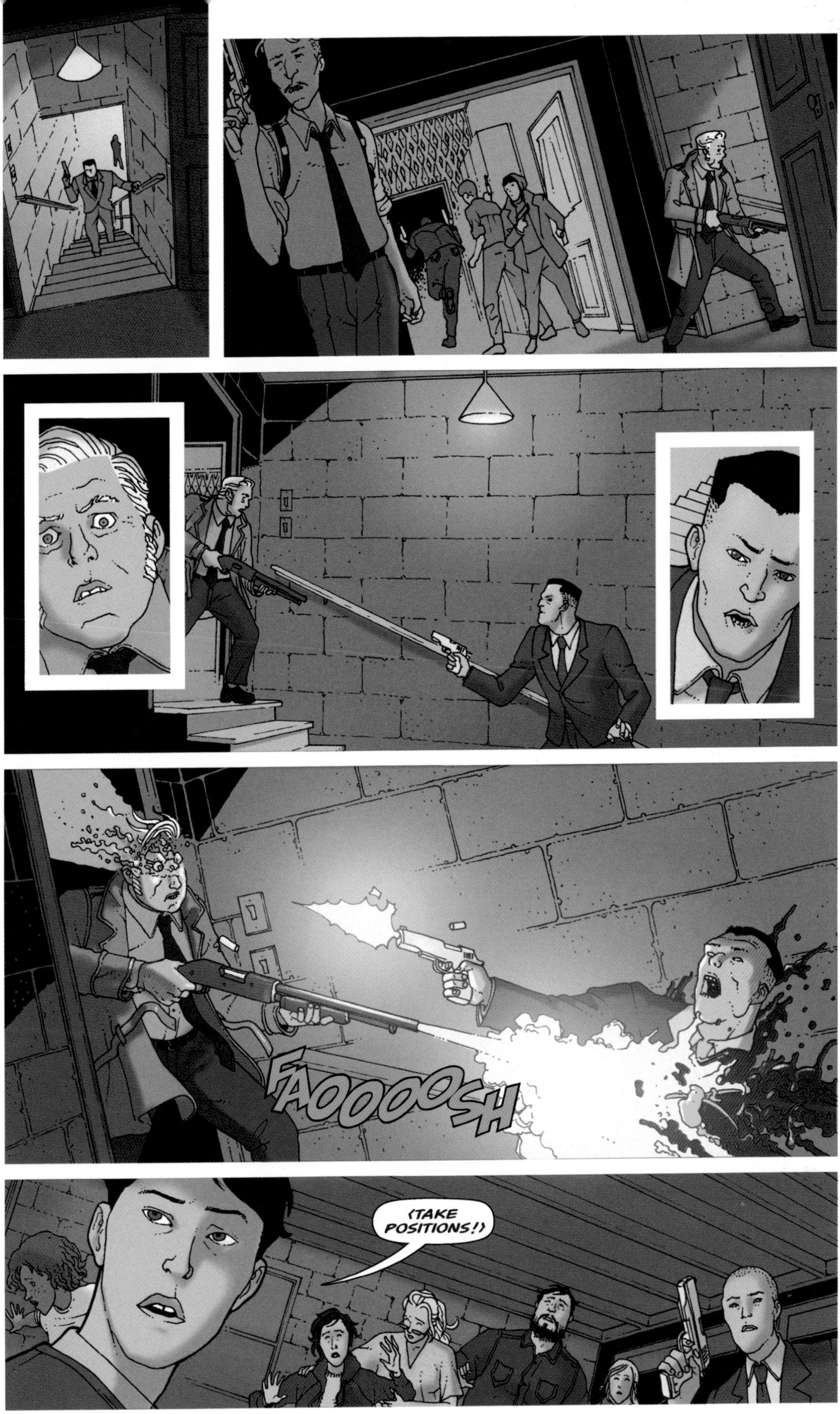
FAOOOOSH
‹TAKE POSITIONS!›

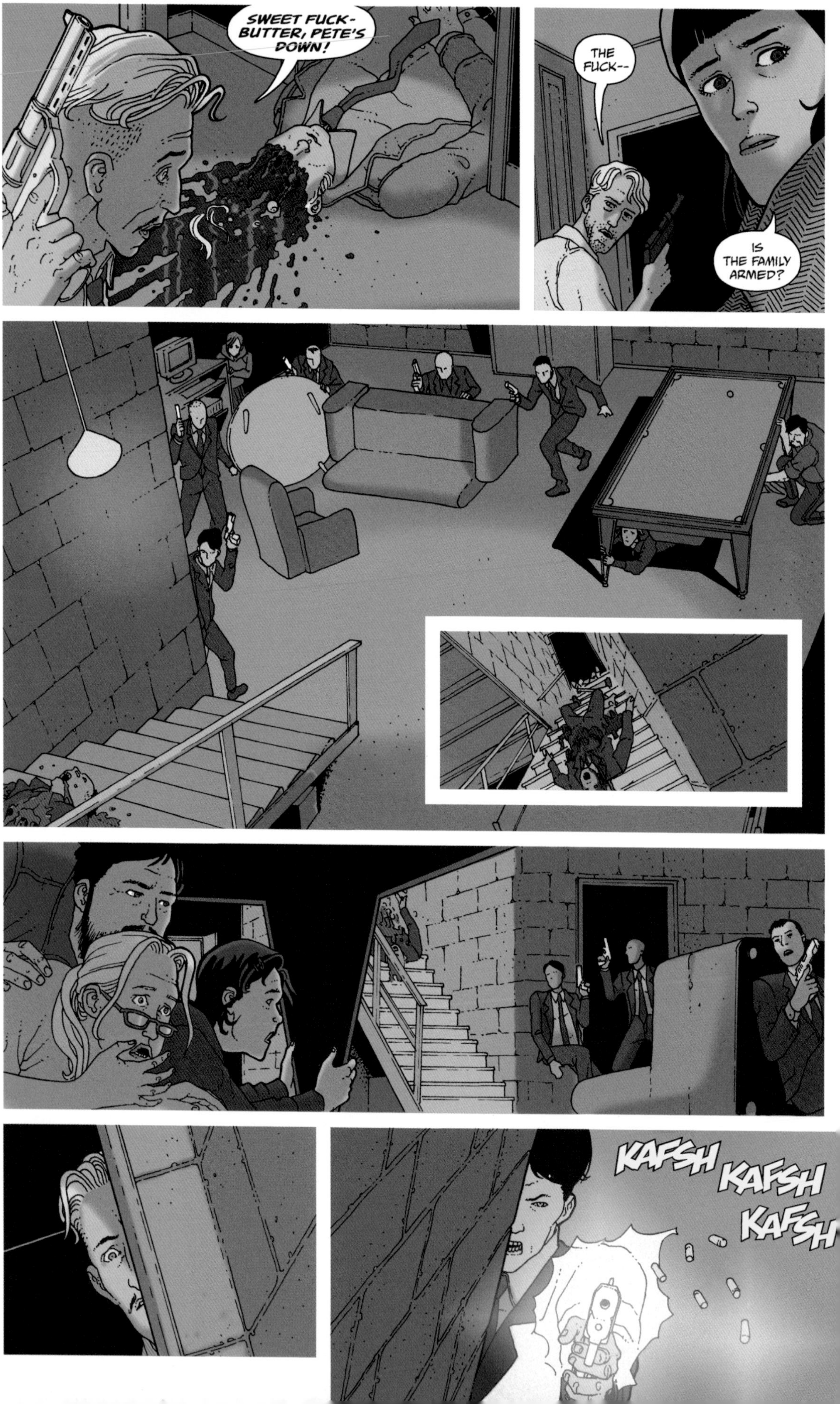
SWEET FUCK-BUTTER, PETE'S DOWN!
THE FUCK--
IS THE FAMILY ARMED?
KAFSH
KAFSH
KAFSH

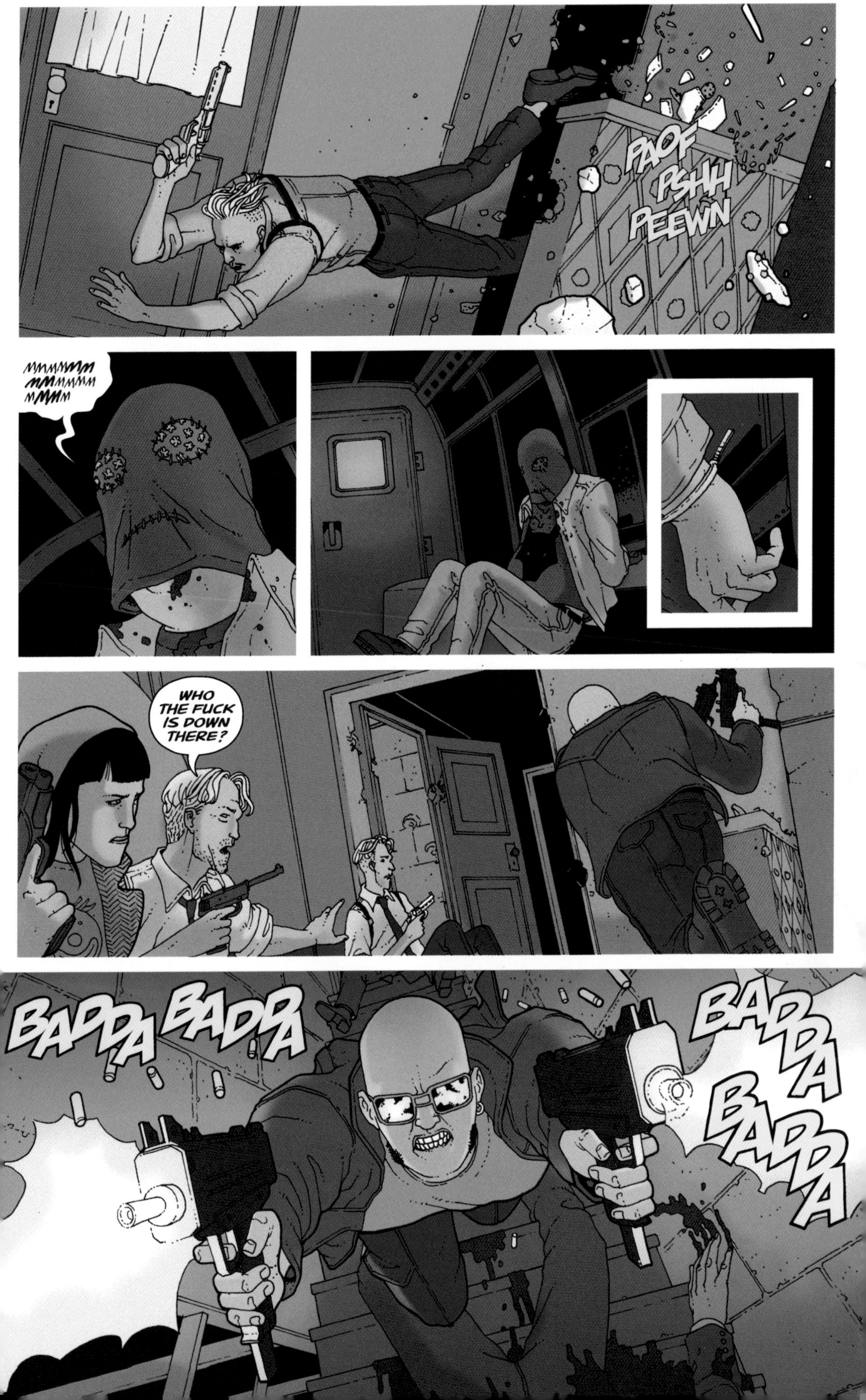
PAOF
PSHH
PEEWN
MMMMMM MMMMMM MMM
WHO THE FUCK IS DOWN THERE?
BADDA BADDA
BADDA
BADDA

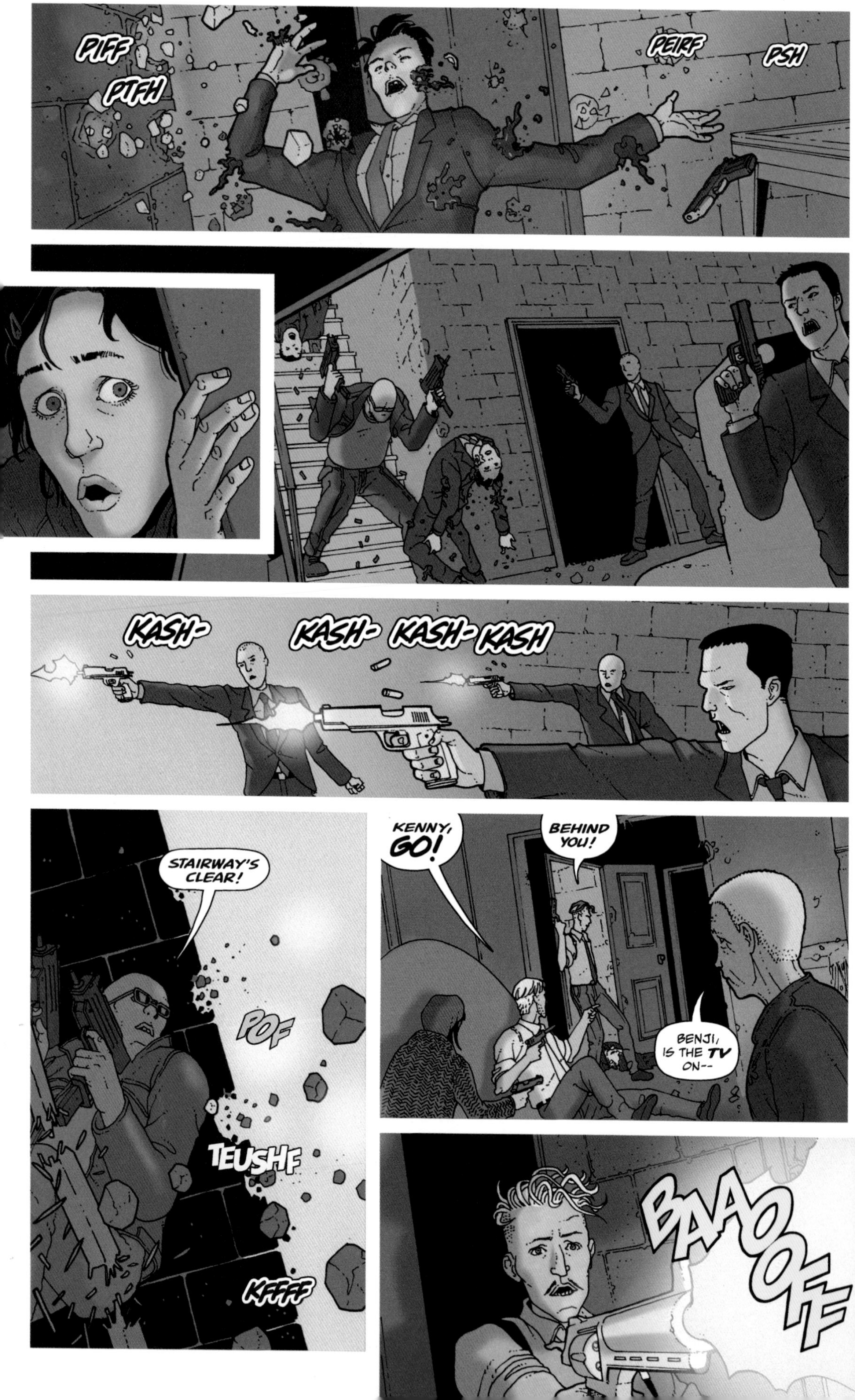
PIFF
PTFH
PEIRF
PSH
KASH-
KASH- KASH- KASH
STAIRWAY'S CLEAR!
POF
TEUSHF
KFFFF
KENNY, GO!
BEHIND YOU!
BENJI, IS THE TV ON--
BAAOOFF

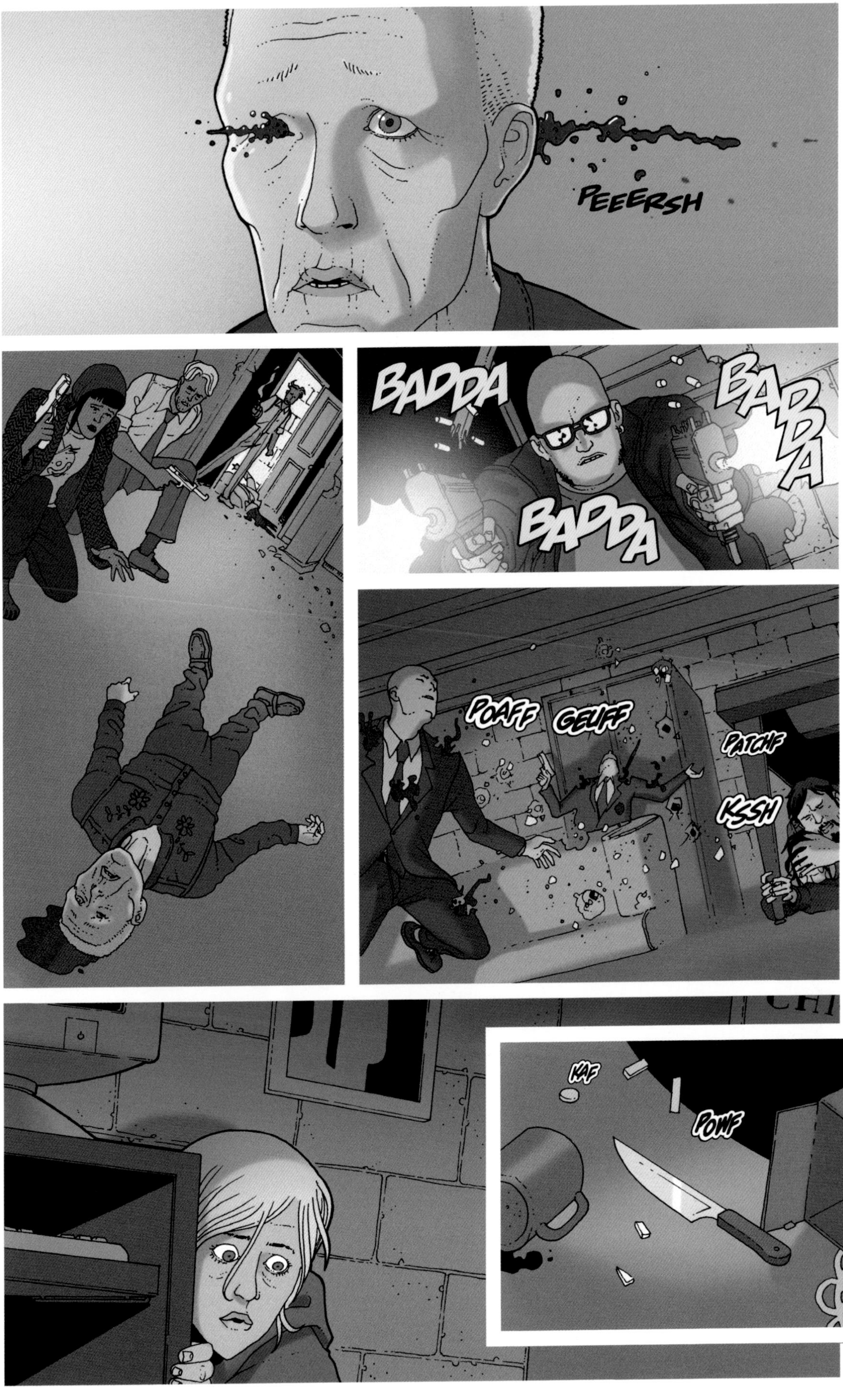
PEEERSH
BADDA
BADA
BADDA
POAFF
GEUFF
PATCHF
KSSH
KAF
POWF

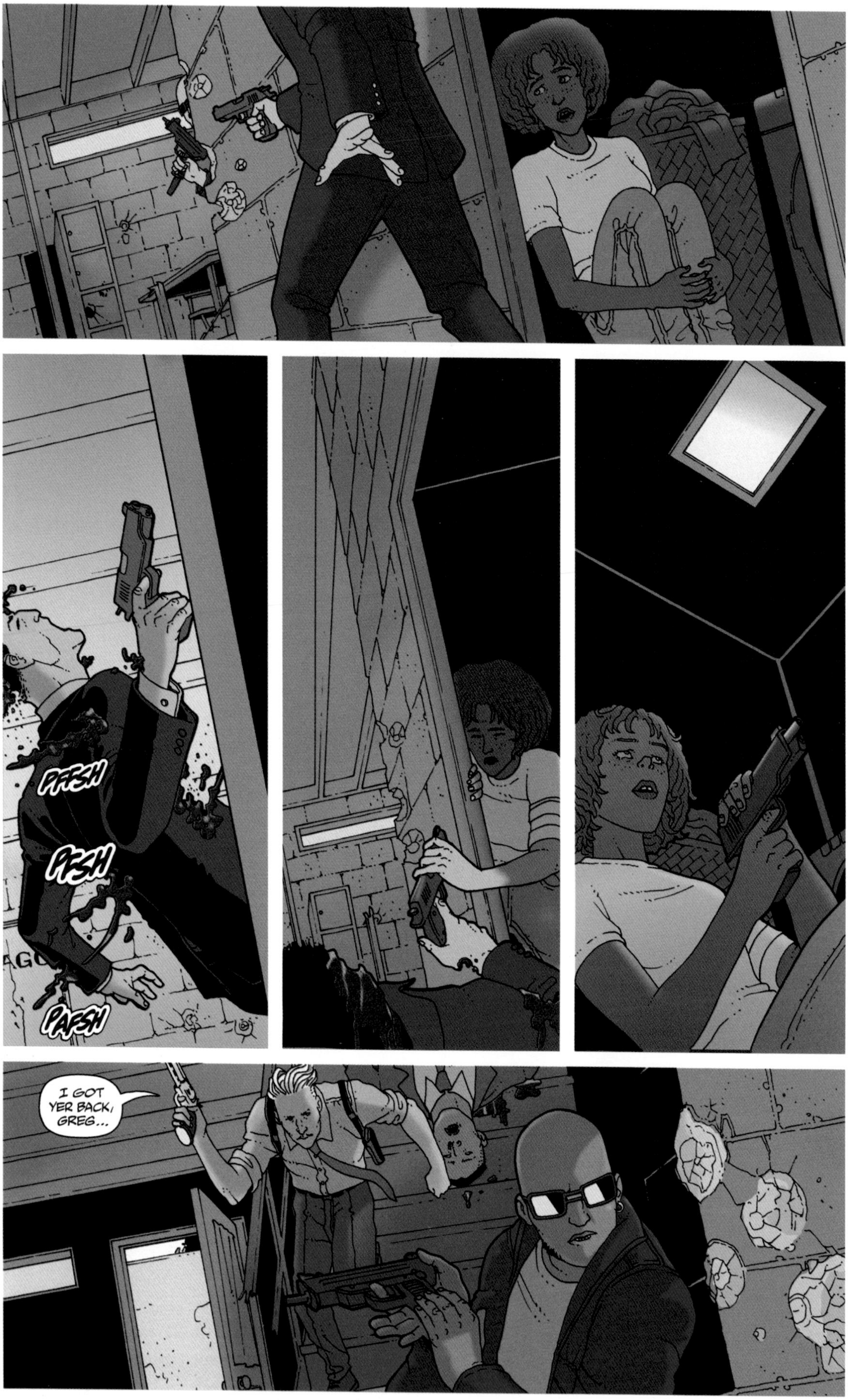
PFFSH
PFFSH
PAFSH
I GOT YER BACK, GREG...

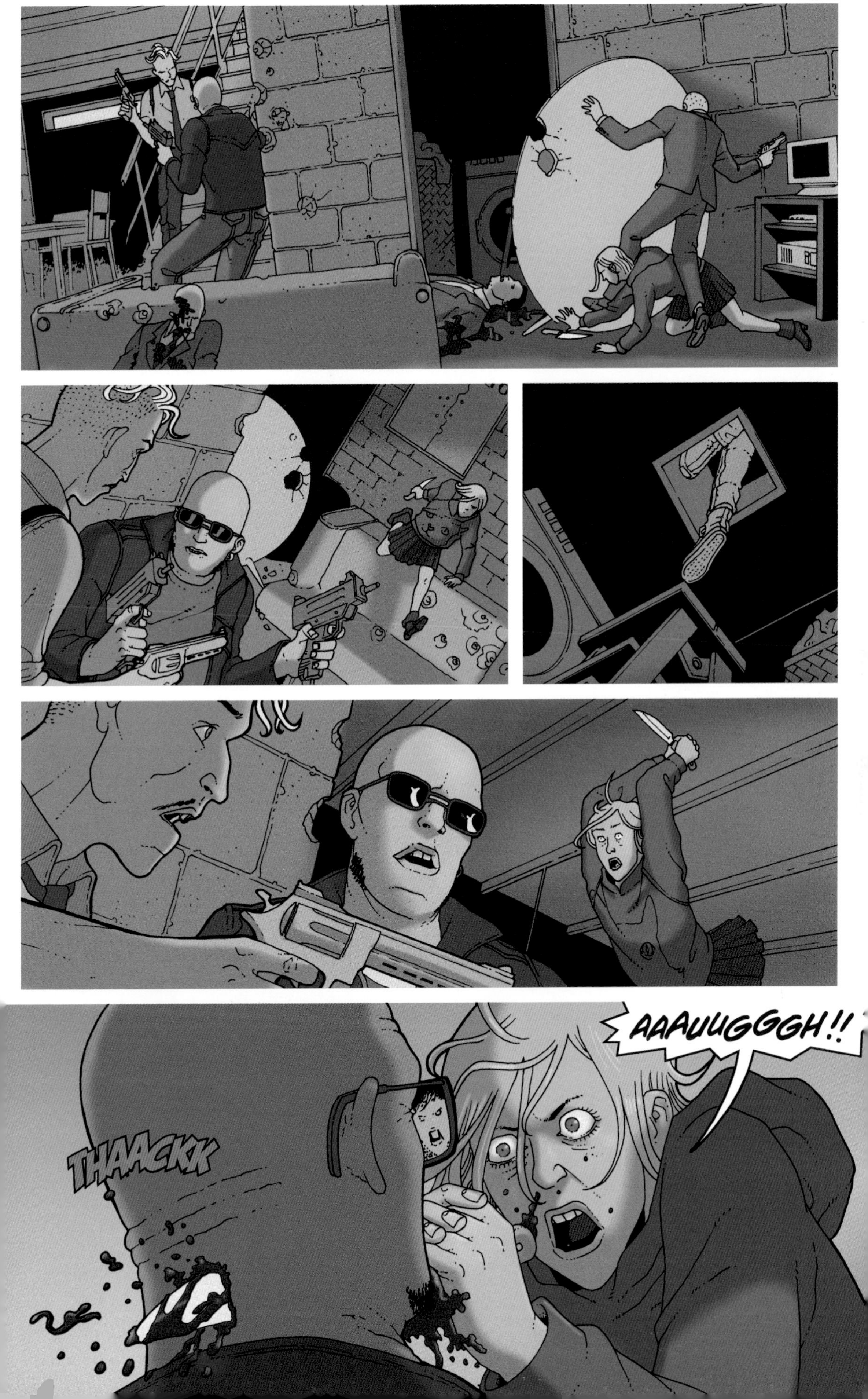
AAAUUGGGH!!
THAACKK

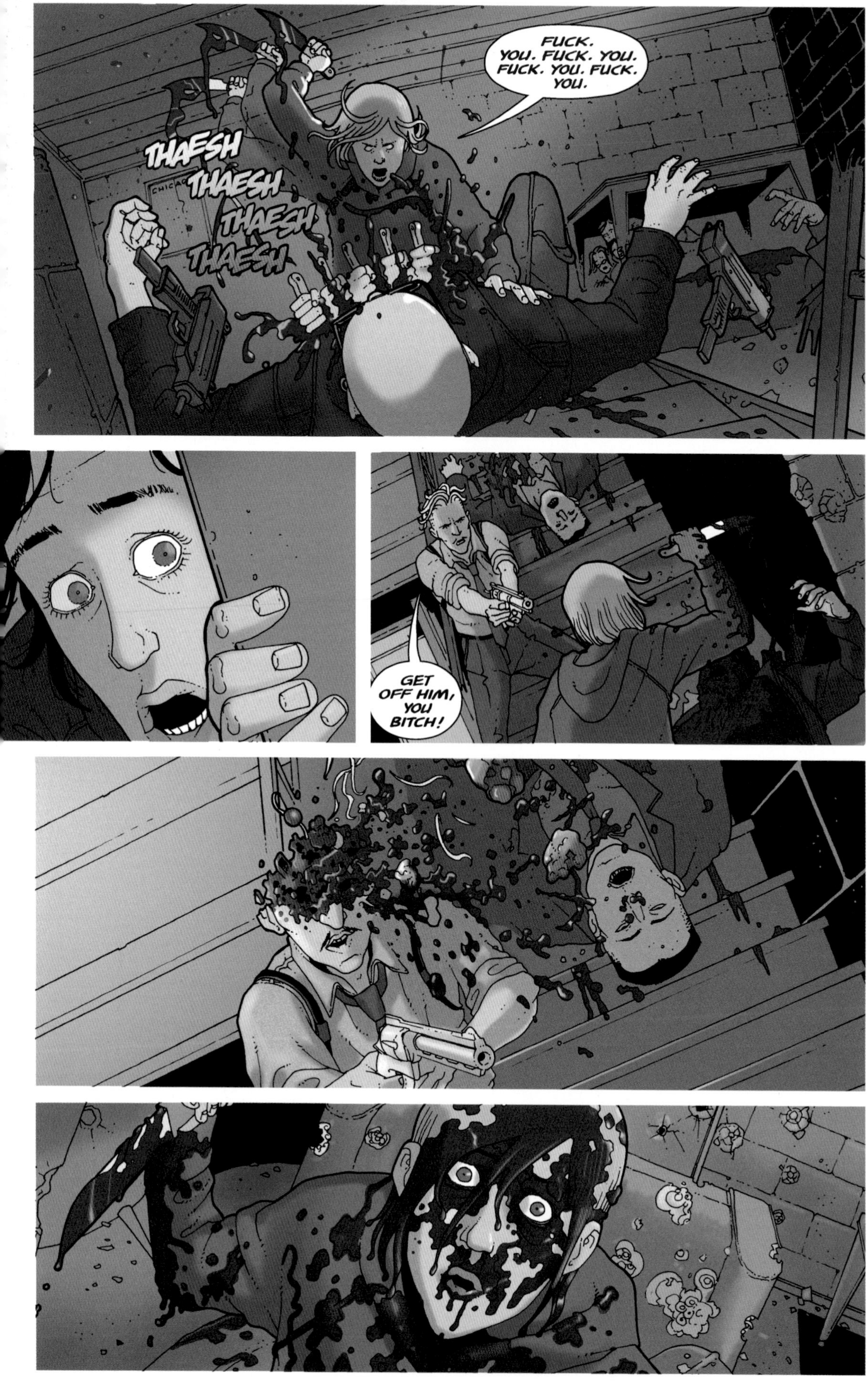
FUCK. YOU. FUCK. YOU. FUCK. YOU. FUCK. YOU.
THAESH
THAESH
THAESH
THAESH
GET OFF HIM, YOU BITCH!

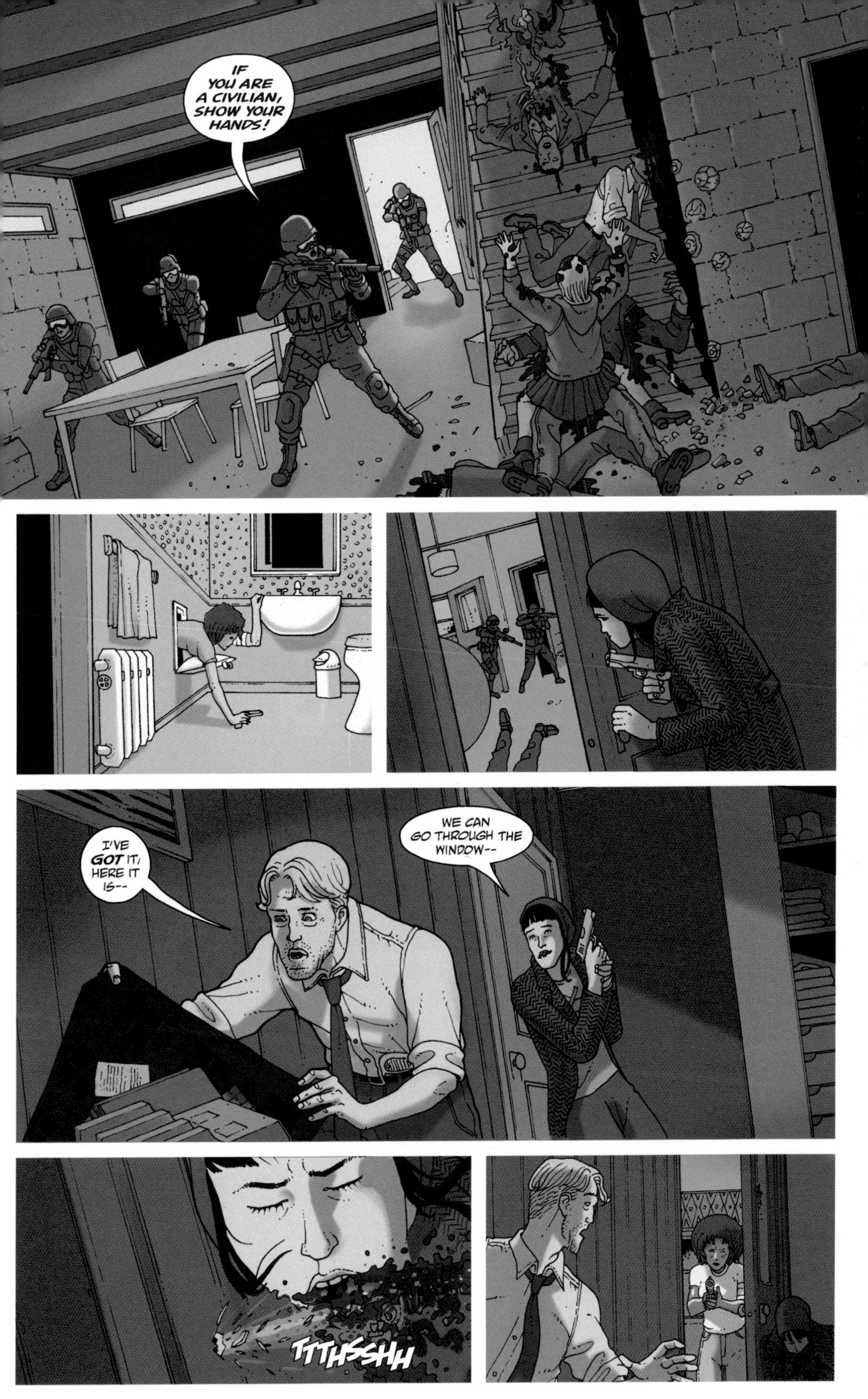
IF YOU ARE A CIVILIAN, SHOW YOUR HANDS!
I'VE GOT IT, HERE IT IS--
WE CAN GO THROUGH THE WINDOW--
TTTHSSHH

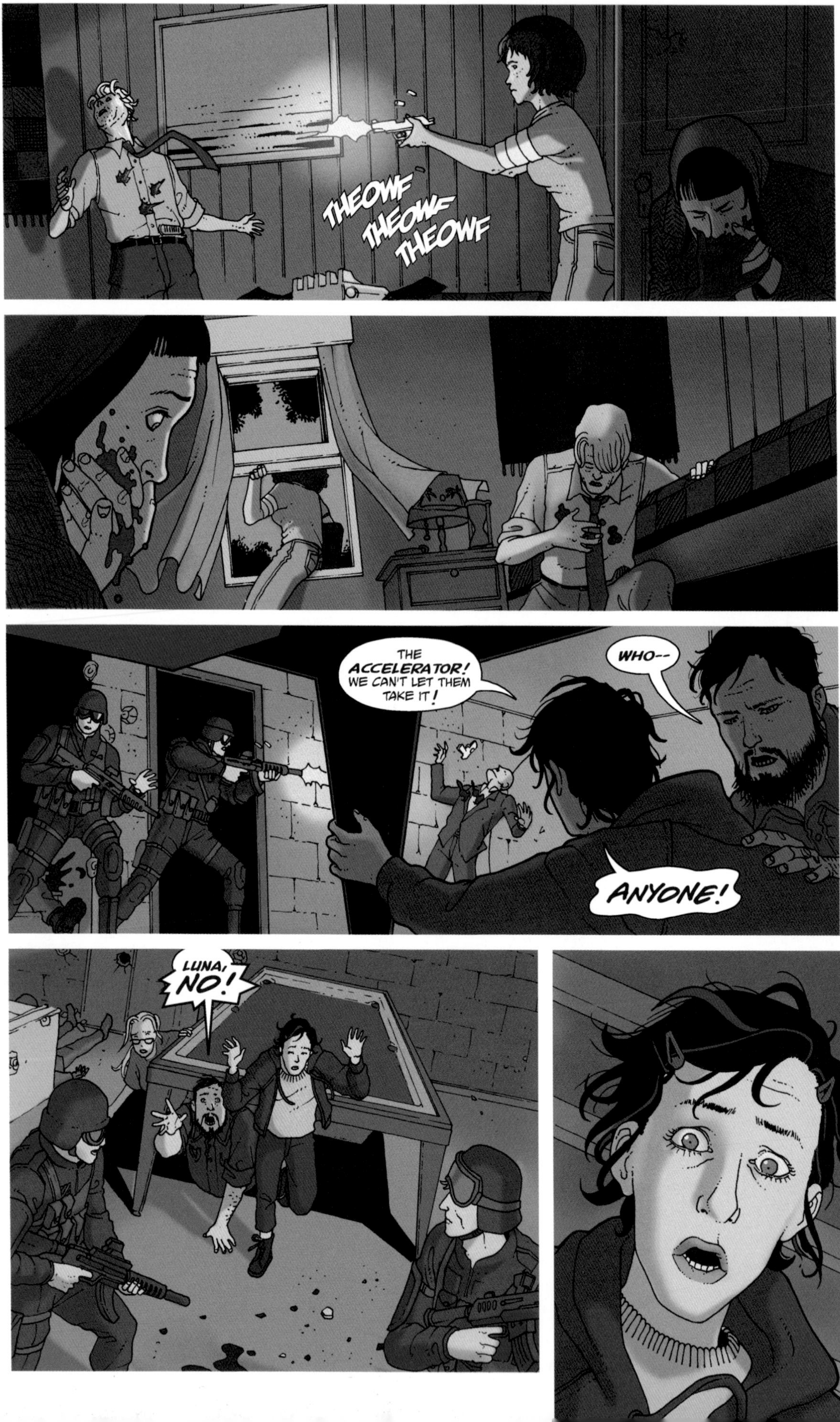
THEOWF THEOWF THEOWF
THE ACCELERATOR! WE CAN'T LET THEM TAKE IT!
WHO--
ANYONE!
LUNA, NO!

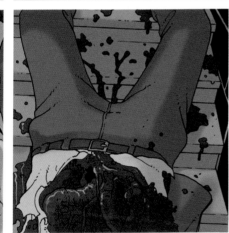

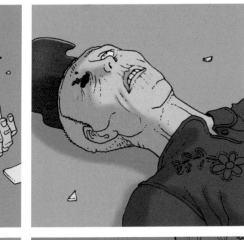

GAMMA.

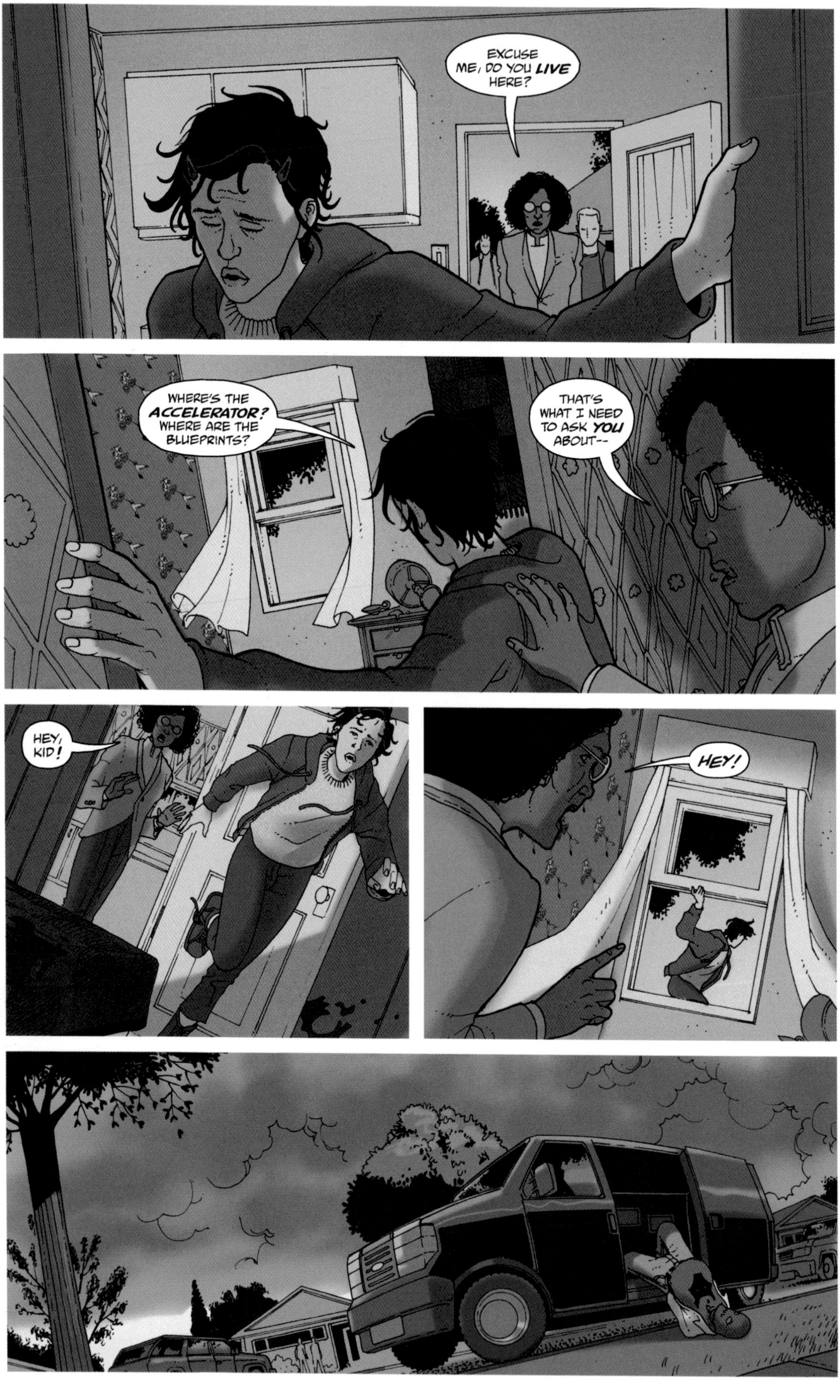
EXCUSE ME, DO YOU LIVE HERE?
WHERE'S THE ACCELERATOR? WHERE ARE THE BLUEPRINTS?
THAT'S WHAT I NEED TO ASK YOU ABOUT--
HEY, KID!
HEY!

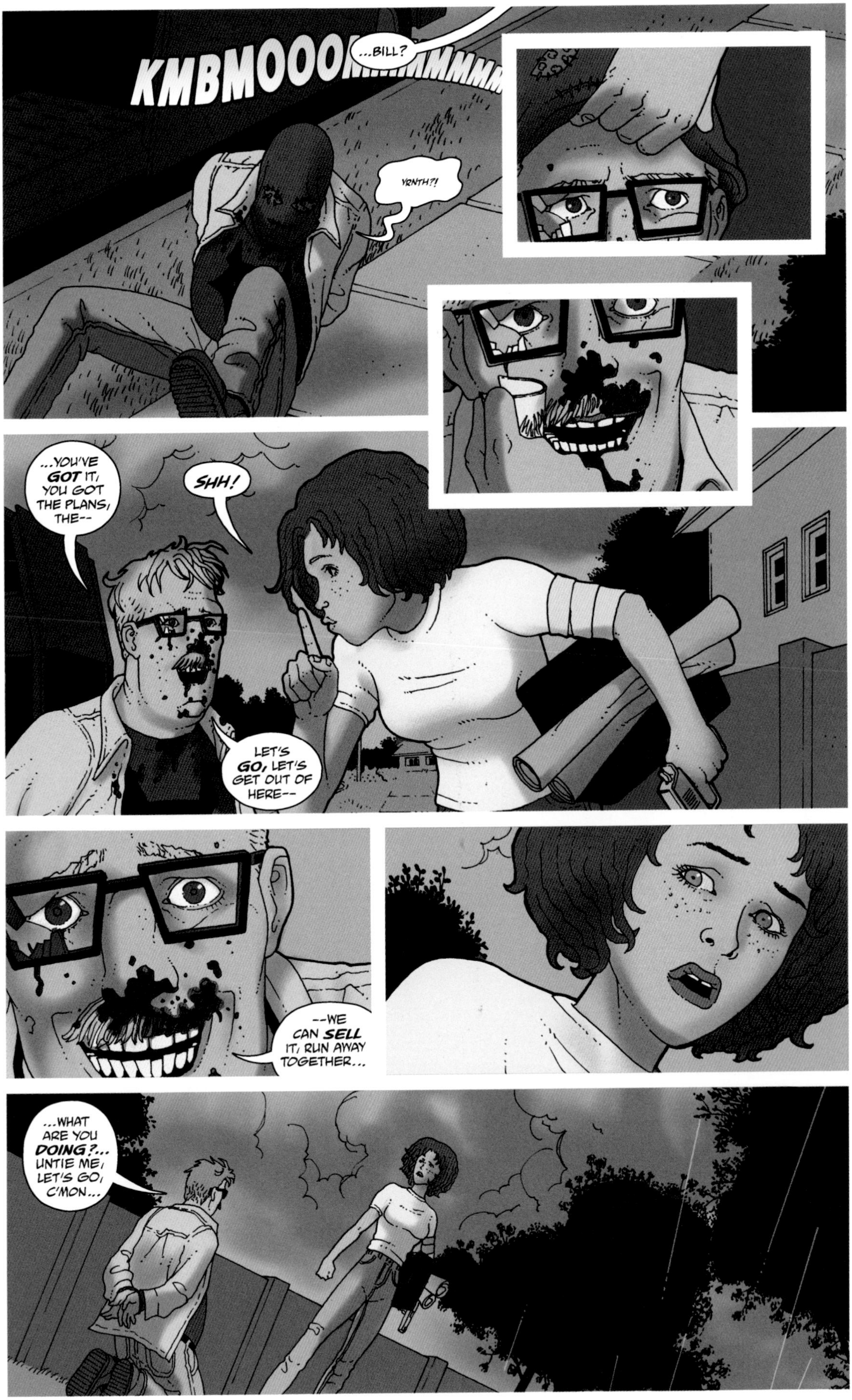
KMBMOOOMMMMMMM
...BILL?
YRNTH?!
...YOU'VE GOT IT, YOU GOT THE PLANS, THE--
SHH!
LET'S GO, LET'S GET OUT OF HERE--
--WE CAN SELL IT, RUN AWAY TOGETHER...
...WHAT ARE YOU DOING?... UNTIE ME, LET'S GO, C'MON...

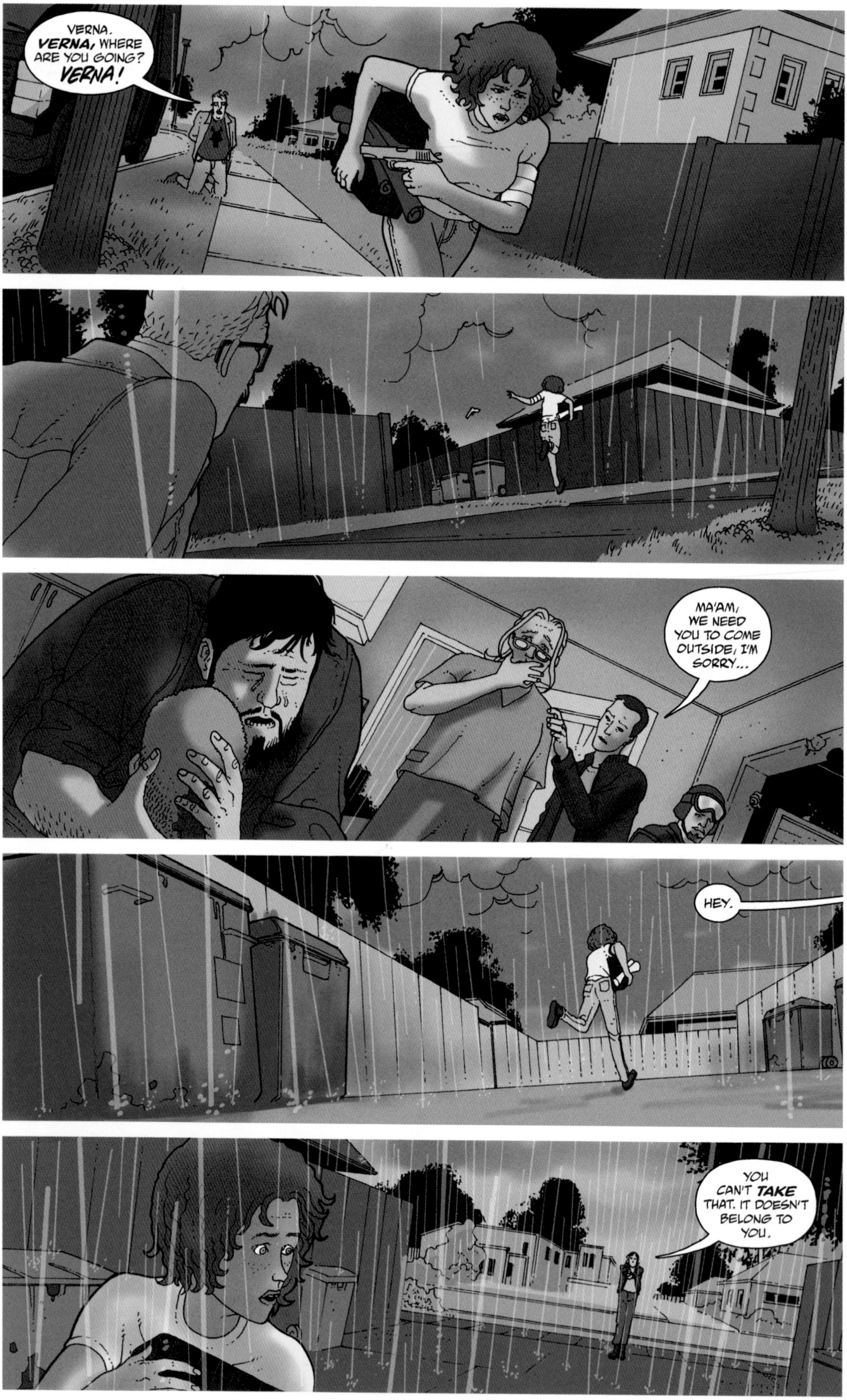
VERNA. VERNA, WHERE ARE YOU GOING? VERNA!
MA'AM, WE NEED YOU TO COME OUTSIDE, I'M SORRY...
HEY.
YOU CAN'T TAKE THAT. IT DOESN'T BELONG TO YOU.

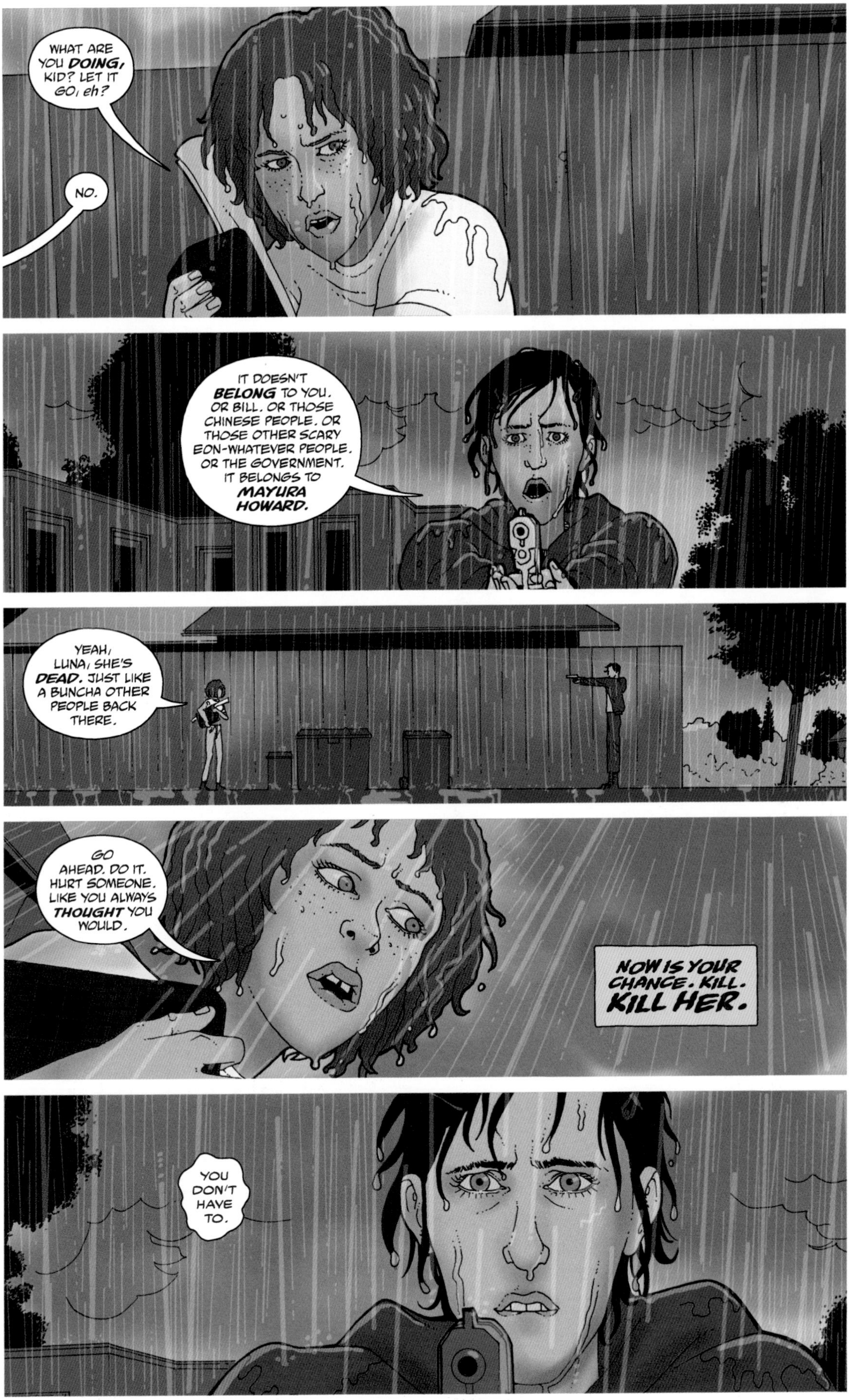
WHAT ARE YOU DOING, KID? LET IT GO, eh?
NO.
IT DOESN'T BELONG TO YOU. OR BILL. OR THOSE CHINESE PEOPLE. OR THOSE OTHER SCARY EON-WHATEVER PEOPLE. OR THE GOVERNMENT. IT BELONGS TO MAYURA HOWARD.
YEAH, LUNA, SHE'S DEAD. JUST LIKE A BUNCHA OTHER PEOPLE BACK THERE.
GO AHEAD. DO IT. HURT SOMEONE. LIKE YOU ALWAYS THOUGHT YOU WOULD.
NOW IS YOUR CHANCE. KILL. KILL HER.
YOU DON'T HAVE TO.

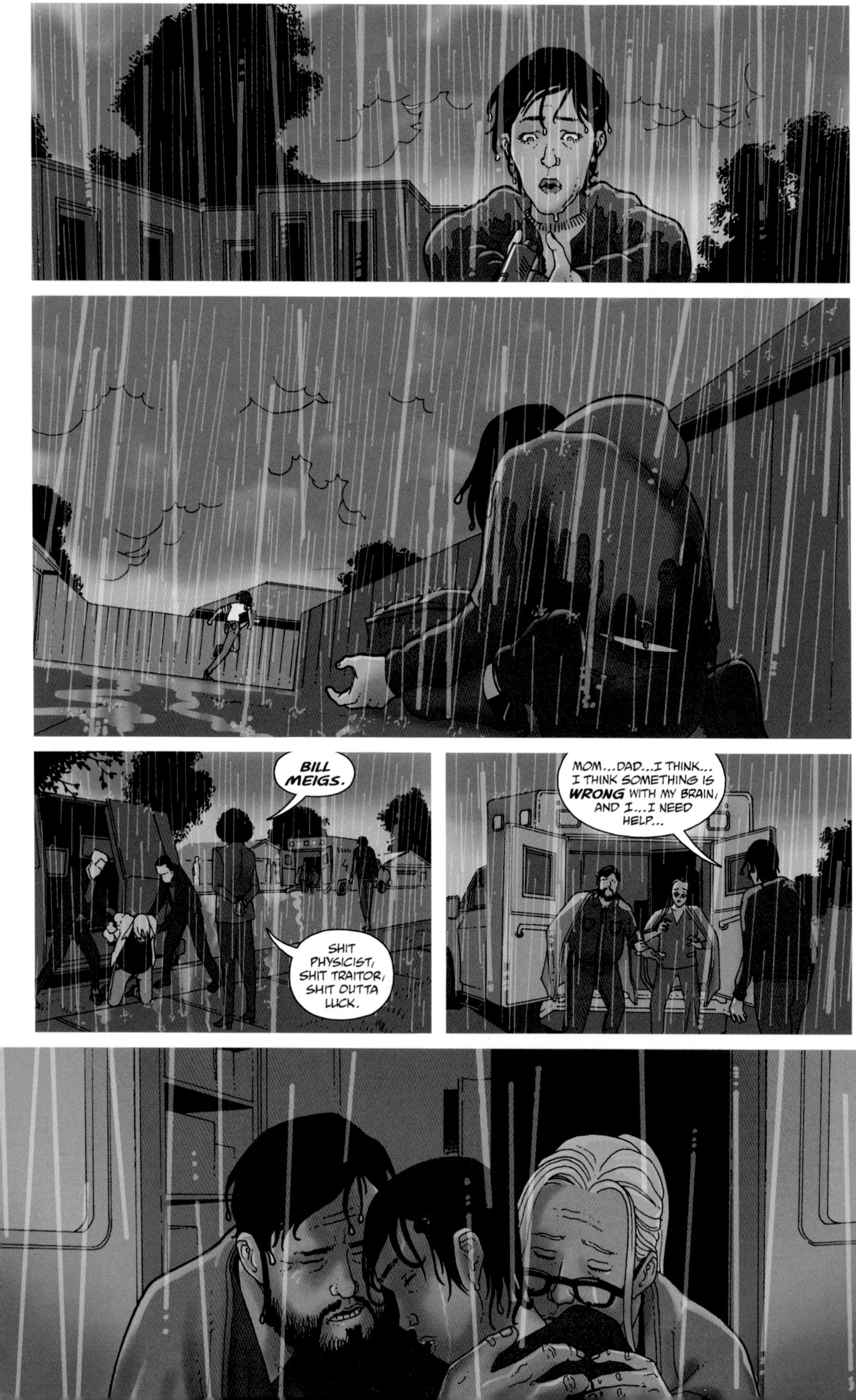
BILL MEIGS.
SHIT PHYSICIST, SHIT TRAITOR, SHIT OUTTA LUCK.
MOM...DAD...I THINK... I THINK SOMETHING IS WRONG WITH MY BRAIN, AND I...I NEED HELP...

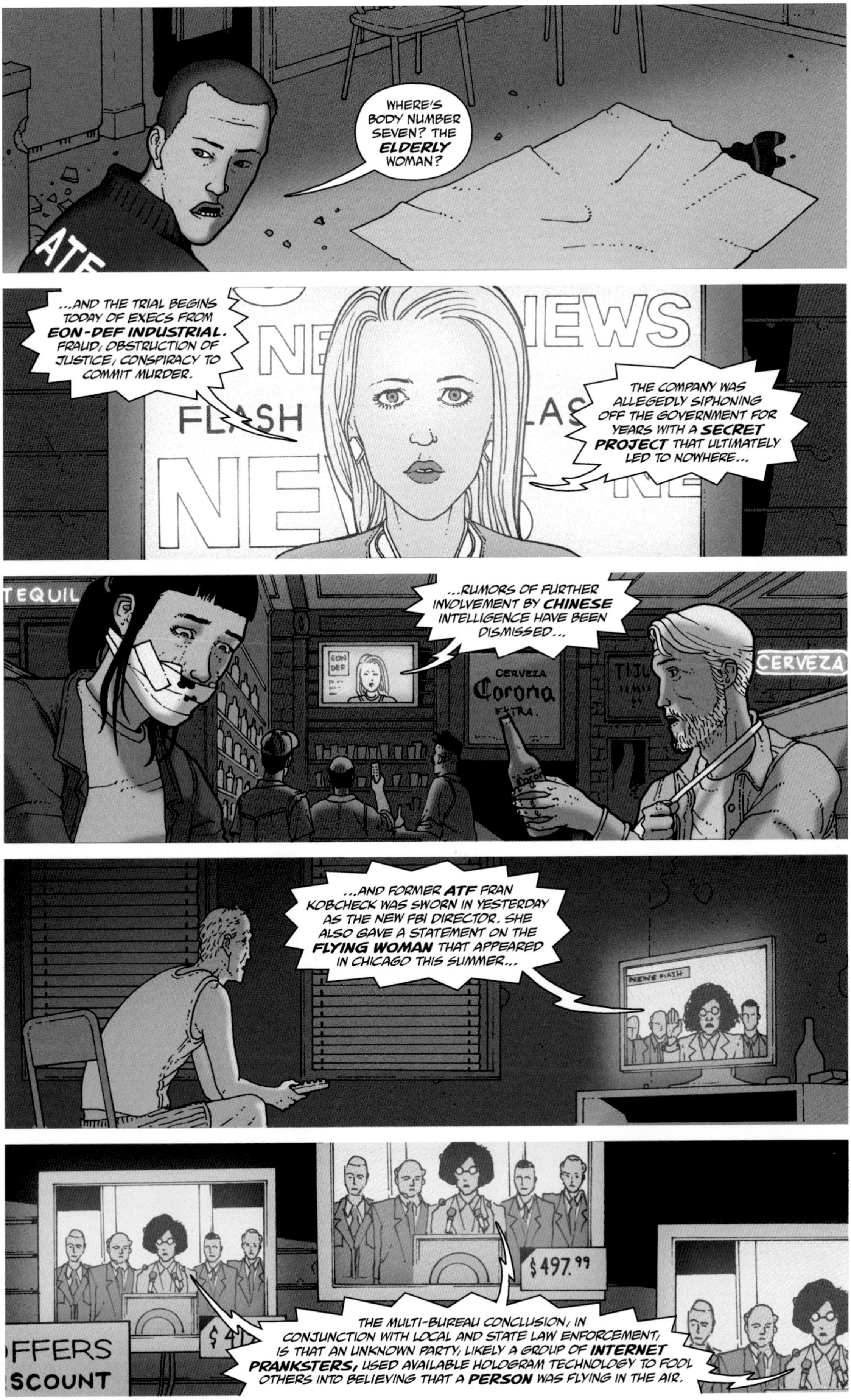

WHERE'S BODY NUMBER SEVEN? THE **ELDERLY** WOMAN?
...AND THE TRIAL BEGINS TODAY OF EXECS FROM **EON-DEF INDUSTRIAL.** FRAUD, OBSTRUCTION OF JUSTICE, CONSPIRACY TO COMMIT MURDER.
THE COMPANY WAS ALLEGEDLY SIPHONING OFF THE GOVERNMENT FOR YEARS WITH A **SECRET PROJECT** THAT ULTIMATELY LED TO NOWHERE...
...RUMORS OF FURTHER INVOLVEMENT BY **CHINESE** INTELLIGENCE HAVE BEEN DISMISSED...
CERVEZA
Corona
EXTRA
CERVEZA
...AND FORMER **ATF** FRAN KOBCHECK WAS SWORN IN YESTERDAY AS THE NEW FBI DIRECTOR. SHE ALSO GAVE A STATEMENT ON THE **FLYING WOMAN** THAT APPEARED IN CHICAGO THIS SUMMER...
$497.99
THE MULTI-BUREAU CONCLUSION, IN CONJUNCTION WITH LOCAL AND STATE LAW ENFORCEMENT, IS THAT AN UNKNOWN PARTY, LIKELY A GROUP OF **INTERNET PRANKSTERS,** USED AVAILABLE HOLOGRAM TECHNOLOGY TO FOOL OTHERS INTO BELIEVING THAT A **PERSON** WAS FLYING IN THE AIR.

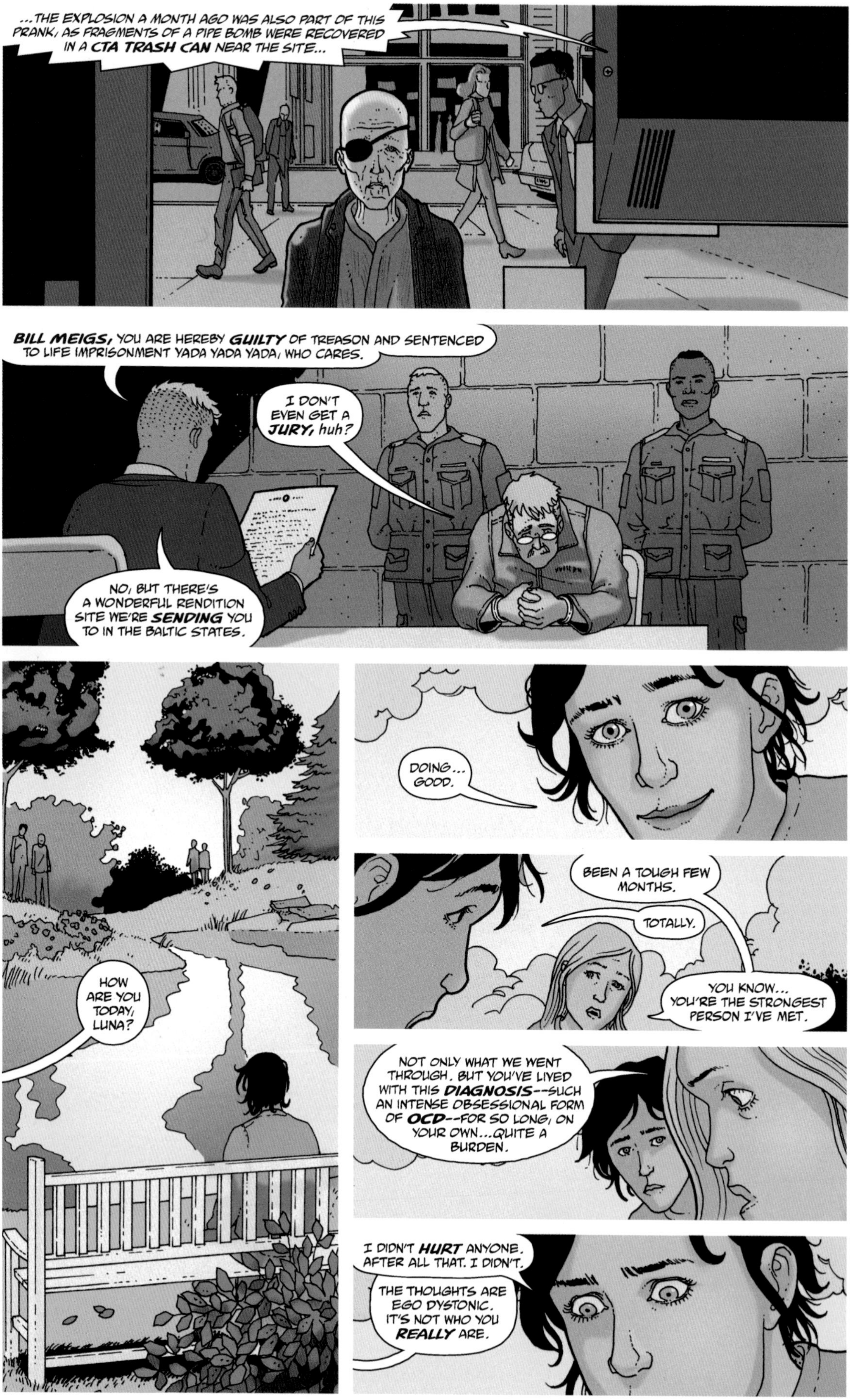
...THE EXPLOSION A MONTH AGO WAS ALSO PART OF THIS PRANK, AS FRAGMENTS OF A PIPE BOMB WERE RECOVERED IN A CTA TRASH CAN NEAR THE SITE...
BILL MEIGS, YOU ARE HEREBY GUILTY OF TREASON AND SENTENCED TO LIFE IMPRISONMENT YADA YADA YADA, WHO CARES.
I DON'T EVEN GET A JURY, huh?
NO, BUT THERE'S A WONDERFUL RENDITION SITE WE'RE SENDING YOU TO IN THE BALTIC STATES.
HOW ARE YOU TODAY, LUNA?
DOING... GOOD.
BEEN A TOUGH FEW MONTHS.
TOTALLY.
YOU KNOW... YOU'RE THE STRONGEST PERSON I'VE MET.
NOT ONLY WHAT WE WENT THROUGH, BUT YOU'VE LIVED WITH THIS DIAGNOSIS--SUCH AN INTENSE OBSESSIONAL FORM OF OCD--FOR SO LONG, ON YOUR OWN...QUITE A BURDEN.
I DIDN'T HURT ANYONE. AFTER ALL THAT. I DIDN'T.
THE THOUGHTS ARE EGO DYSTONIC. IT'S NOT WHO YOU REALLY ARE.

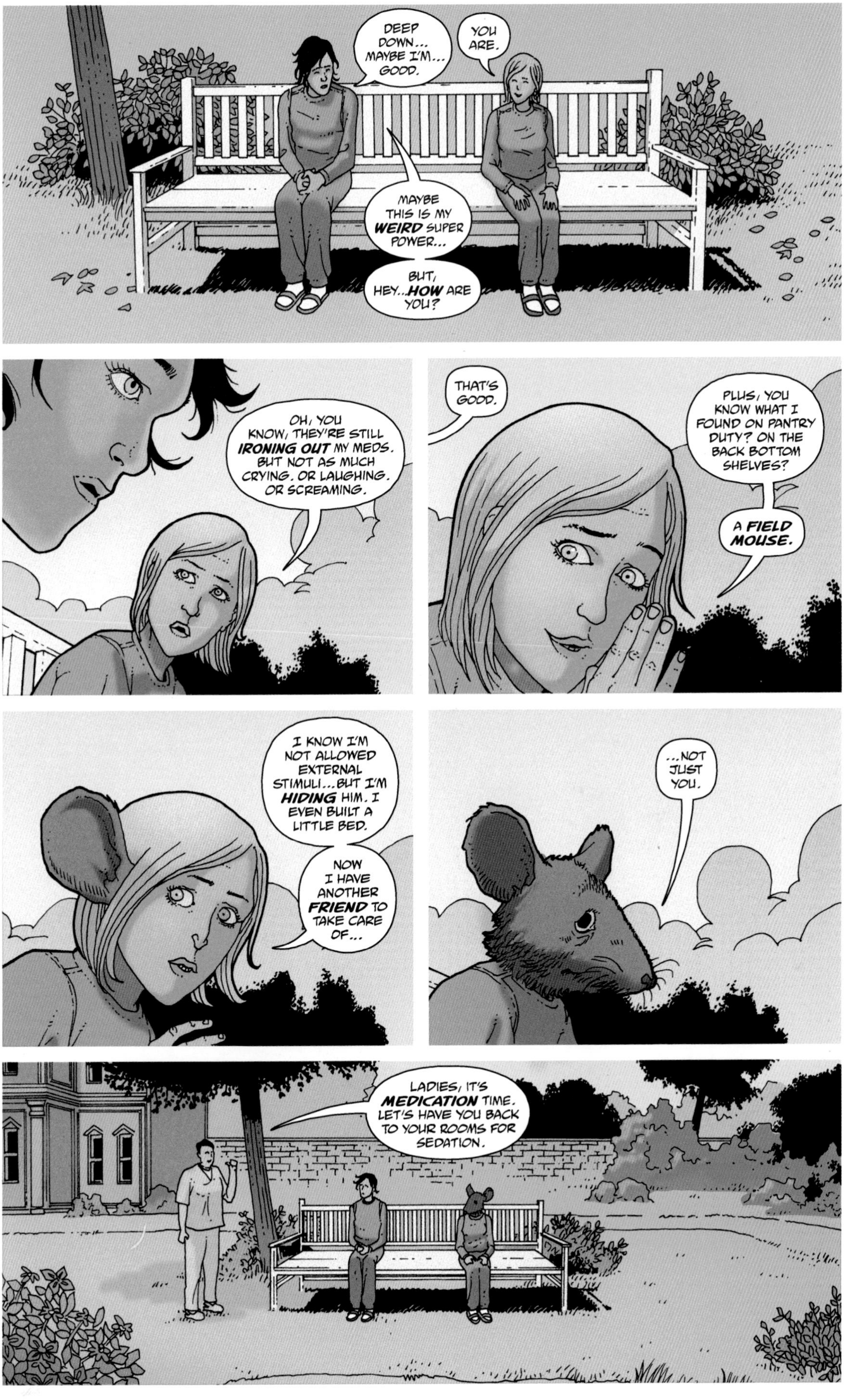
DEEP DOWN... MAYBE I'M... GOOD.
YOU ARE.
MAYBE THIS IS MY WEIRD SUPER POWER...
BUT, HEY...HOW ARE YOU?
OH, YOU KNOW, THEY'RE STILL IRONING OUT MY MEDS. BUT NOT AS MUCH CRYING. OR LAUGHING. OR SCREAMING.
THAT'S GOOD.
PLUS, YOU KNOW WHAT I FOUND ON PANTRY DUTY? ON THE BACK BOTTOM SHELVES?
A FIELD MOUSE.
I KNOW I'M NOT ALLOWED EXTERNAL STIMULI...BUT I'M HIDING HIM. I EVEN BUILT A LITTLE BED.
NOW I HAVE ANOTHER FRIEND TO TAKE CARE OF...
...NOT JUST YOU.
LADIES, IT'S MEDICATION TIME. LET'S HAVE YOU BACK TO YOUR ROOMS FOR SEDATION.

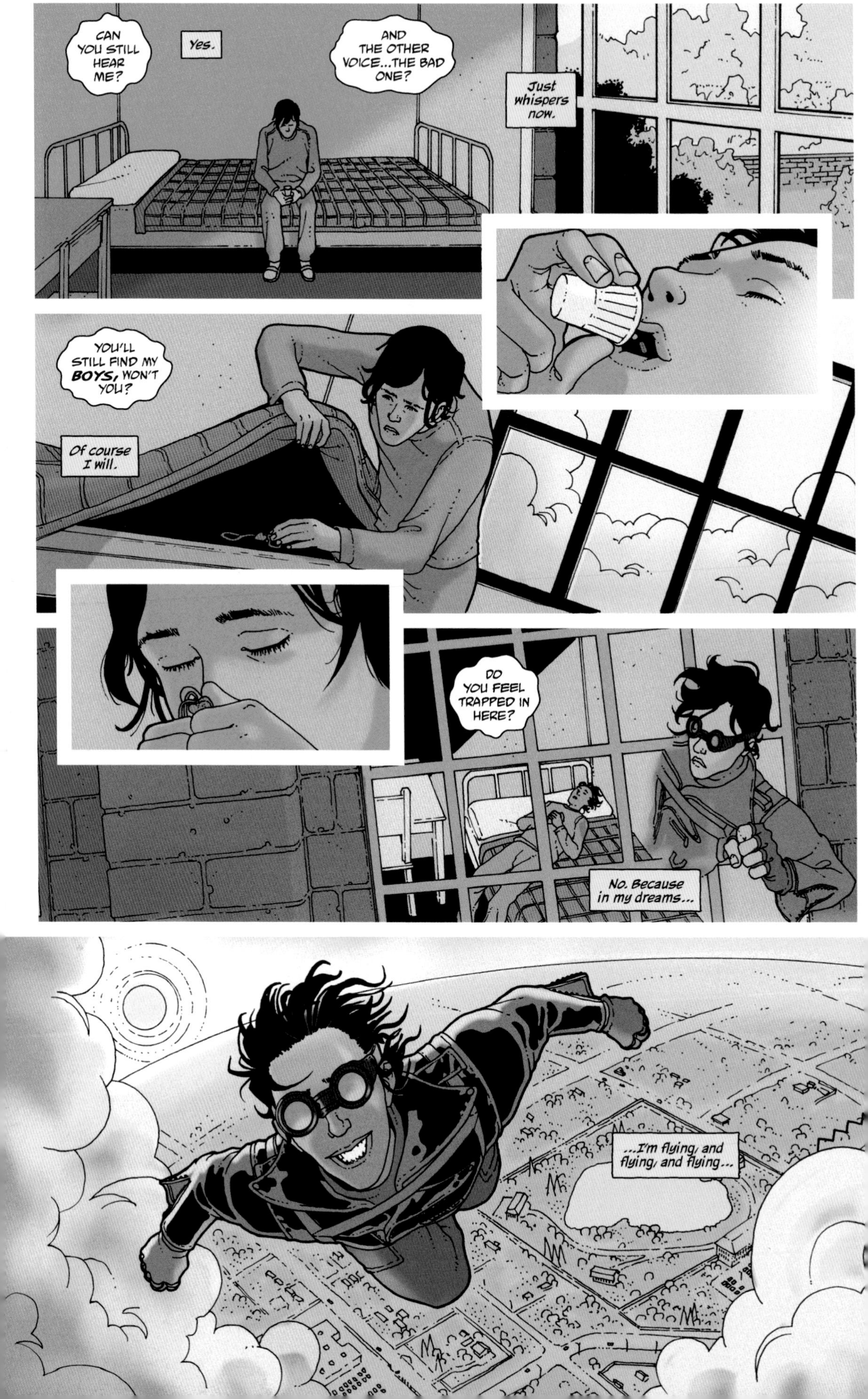
CAN YOU STILL HEAR ME?
Yes.
AND THE OTHER VOICE...THE BAD ONE?
Just whispers now.
YOU'LL STILL FIND MY BOYS, WON'T YOU?
Of course I will.
DO YOU FEEL TRAPPED IN HERE?
No. Because in my dreams...
...I'm flying, and flying, and flying...

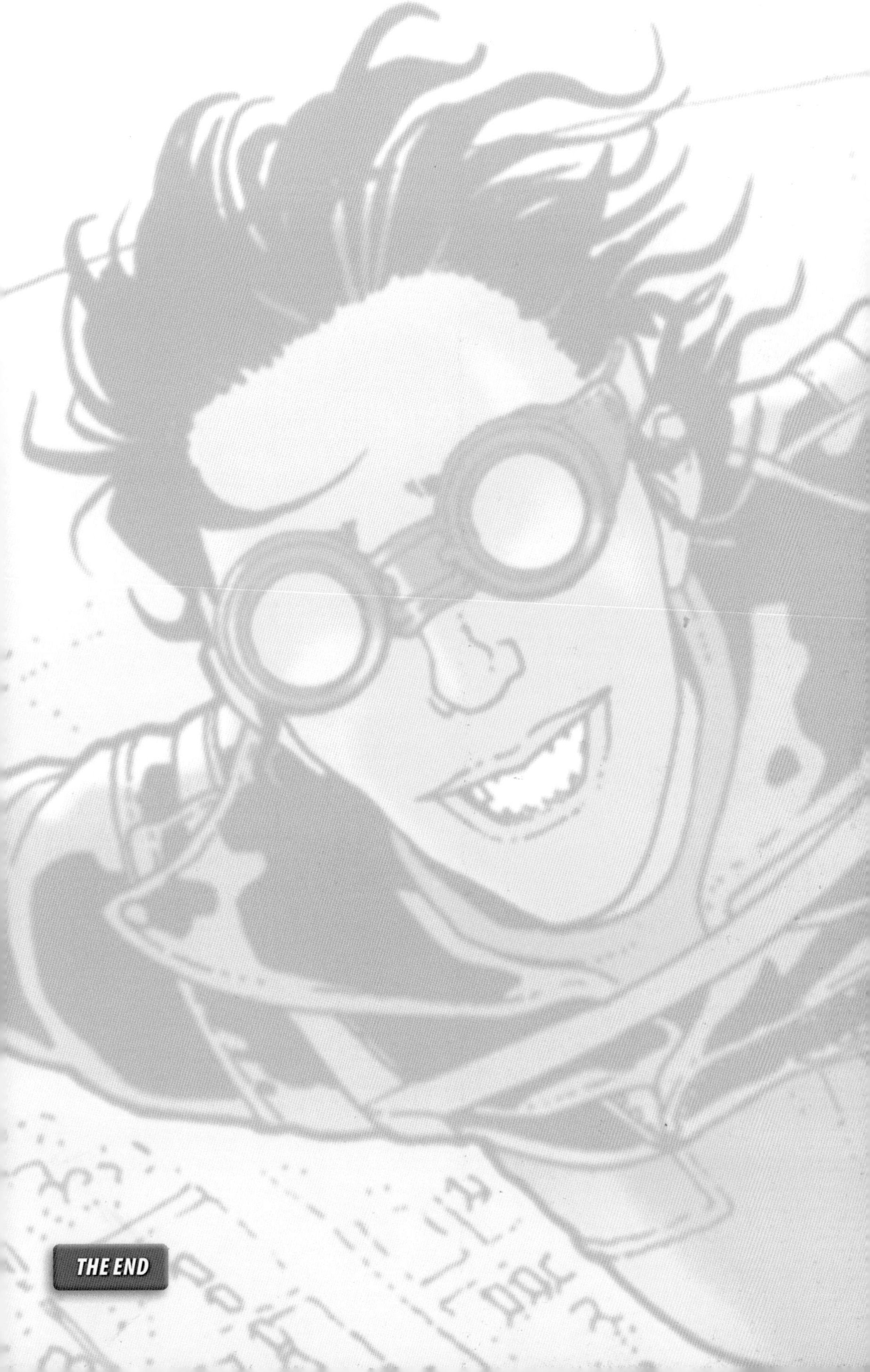
THE END

Someone recently asked me:

Well... first off, we're working in the comic book medium, and flight seems to be one of its most iconic devices. Exploring that idea from the POV of an observer always seemed fascinating to me. What if you were at Starbucks and someone seemingly ROARED by several feet off the ground, and when you ran outside they turned upward and rocketed over the Chrysler Building? Would you ever recover? Would you tell that story over and over for the rest of your life? Or would it fade, would you go back to your phone, to Snapchat, Facebook, et al? I don't know the answer. I wanted the world of this story to be THAT world (which, maybe sadly, feels like OUR world). Some will move on; others can't.

Luna can't.

I find that young kids around my son's age (five and change) often think Batman can fly, and have to be reminded that he can't. This usually makes Batman seem cooler, because he pulls off everything he does "even though he CAN'T fly" (make sure you read that in a snotty kid voice). Flying is so prevalent in the comic medium that a big twist on a popular character is that he actually can't get off the ground without some mechanical help.

But more than comics, the concept of flight has always been deeply embedded in the human psyche as something "more than," something "beyond" our basic abilities, from biblical portrayals of angels to the ways poets seek to capture birds with verse. Flight never leaves the human imagination—it always possesses an alluring otherworldliness that we're forever drawn to, perhaps because flying is something we simply can't do on our own.

If you can fly, you have somehow liberated yourself from all earthly chains—worldly concerns, mundane problems, human conflicts, labels and identities—you're literally "above it all." There's a beautiful freedom in this dream when we pursue it. It's the stuff of our gods, our ancient stories: Jesus hung out for a while, but eventually ascended. Elijah rode off in a flaming chariot. Icarus tried to join the party, but he was punished for attempting to be more than the flesh and blood that he was. Even the terrible Flying Head drove Native American tribes from the Hudson Valley just for fun.

When we DO fly, we, too, become spectral, our stories also become mythological, we elevate ourselves to the stuff of gods: Chuck Yeager breaks the sound barrier, the Wrights soar from Kitty Hawk, the Tuskegee Airmen spit fire, female Russian pilots in WWII become Night Witches, Malaysia 370 vanishes into thin air, a tiny plane with four people in it crashes and transforms into the Day the Music Died.

I remember going to an air show in Texas with my dad once... I was probably Luna's age. It was raining, but we saw a few F16's streak across the sky, and later, they were parked on this little airstrip and you could go talk to the pilots. We did, even though I was in an INCREDIBLY awkward adolescent phase. My dad chatted with one fighter pilot, a woman, who just seemed amazingly, preternaturally connected to her jet. She let me climb up on the wing and walk on it, peer into the cockpit. It was a powerful feeling. I remember some rain later ran off the fuselage and accidentally dripped into my mouth, and afterward I felt as if I had absorbed the plane into my bloodstream.

"Why flying?"

. . . .

I got it in my head that I should go to the Air Force Academy in Colorado. My dad loved that idea, because it meant college would be free. But then I found out my vision wasn't so good—not bad enough to never fly, but bad enough where I could never fly the cool things. I think I qualified for the big cargo planes. No offense to those pilots, but it wasn't what I wanted. It felt like lugging other people's shit around the globe, still tethered to the Earth. I wanted to be in an F16—just me, going faster than sound.

At some point later my dad almost got his pilot's license. After college, I worked for a rather melancholic commercial producer who collected planes. My baby son always stops whatever he's doing in order to point to a jet in the sky or the distant sound of a propeller. There is a persistent feeling of wonder and marvel that I believe will never leave us when it comes to flight.

Of course, you can experience quite the opposite with flight, too—absolute and immense terror. Anything that goes wrong that high in the air REALLY goes wrong. Plane crashes, hot air balloon accidents, even a lower-casualty disaster like the Hindenburg—things like this stick in our mental craws for decades and decades. We can't shake them loose. I was in New York City recently and it still chills me in a primal way when I see someone else on the street pause and look up at the shadow or sound of a close plane.

Keep in mind that Luna Brewster is a kid, and she sees something beautiful and breathtaking explode in front of her eyes. Her already troubled psyche is changed from that point forward. I remember the Challenger disintegrating on live TV when I was four. I remember the Punky Brewster episode where they tried to help the kids process it. But I just don't know if you can with something like that, because it's a complete inversion of everything the dream of flight promises. It's a brutal reminder of our own frailty and failings, and a seeming admonishment of our dare to be more than we are.

But still, we continue to look up.

There's a small airstrip by my house in California that's been there since the 30's. I sometimes drive my two sons over to it, park, and sit with them right on the edge of the tarmac, and watch the planes take off and land. It's mostly little Cessnas, a couple souped-up rich guy hobby planes, maybe one or two old-school aluminum fuselage mail carriers.

The place and the aircraft ain't much to look at, but the boys love it. We sit enraptured, because every few minutes, we watch a tiny human just like us do the impossible—catapult themselves into the wild blue yonder, and circle the mountains and sun.

We watch them grow to a tiny speck, then wait, hoping to see them come back safe, and softly touch the ground again.

— **Christopher Cantwell**

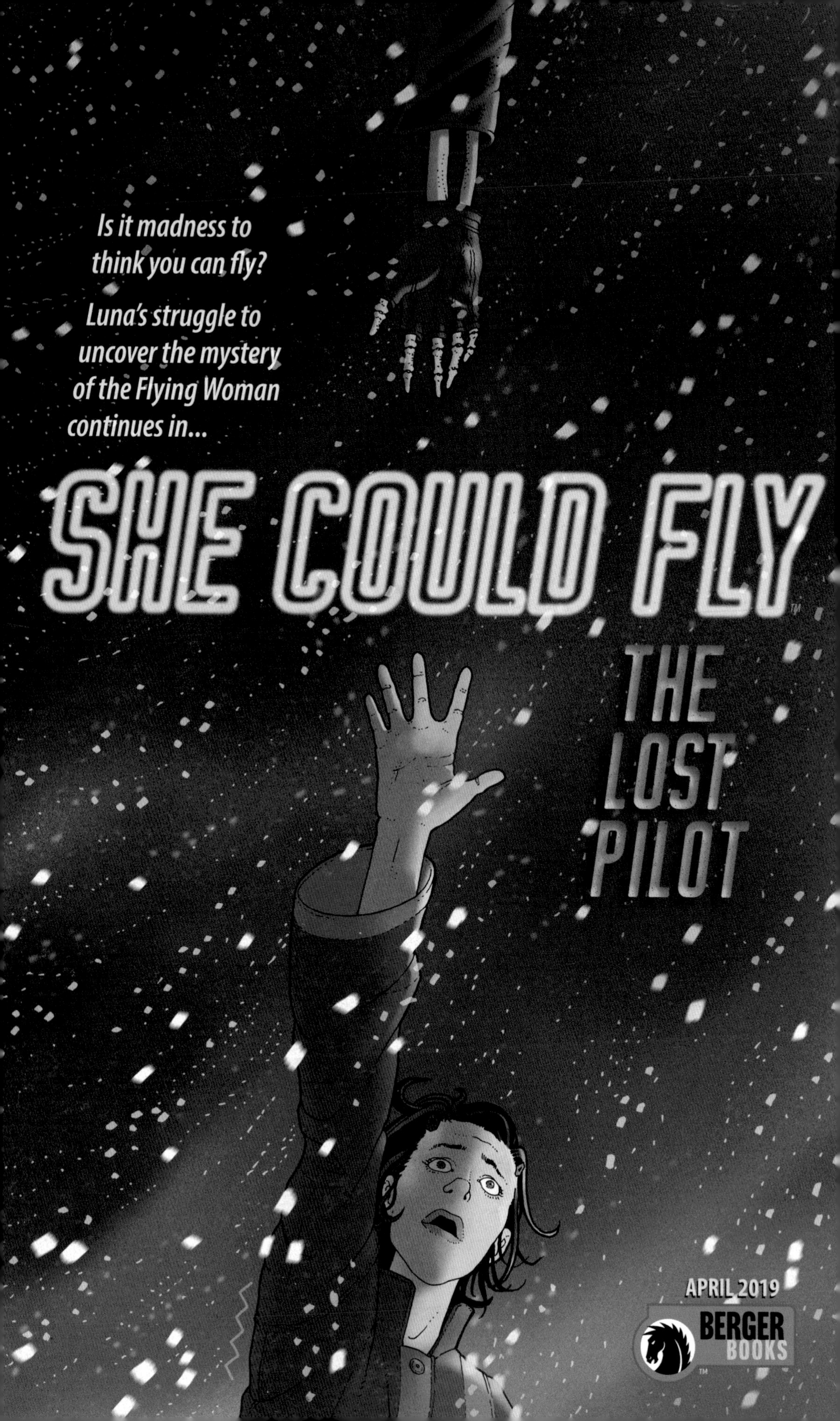
Is it madness to think you can fly?
Luna's struggle to uncover the mystery of the Flying Woman continues in...
SHE COULD FLY™
THE LOST PILOT
APRIL 2019
BERGER BOOKS™